SHEFFIELD HALLAM UNIVERSITY
LEARNING CENTRE
ADSETTS CENTRE, POND STREET,
SHEFFIELD, S1 1WB.

D1423131

£48

ONE WEEK LOAN

2 2 JAN 2002

1 2 APR 2002

- 7 MAY 2002

2 6 FEB 2003

29/09/03

01/10/03

1 6 JAN 2007

2 6 FEB 2007

3 1 JAN 2008

16/3/09

- 8 JUN 2011

SHEFFIELD HALLAM UNIVERSITY
LEARNING CENTRE
WITHDRAWN FROM STOCK

EXPLORING SUSTAINABLE CONSUMPTION

ENVIRONMENTAL POLICY AND THE SOCIAL SCIENCES

EXPLORING SUSTAINABLE CONSUMPTION

ENVIRONMENTAL POLICY AND THE SOCIAL SCIENCES

EDITED BY

MAURIE J. COHEN

New Jersey Institute of Technology, New Jersey, USA

JOSEPH MURPHY

Mansfield College, Oxford, UK

2001

Pergamon
An Imprint of Elsevier Science

Amsterdam – London – New York – Oxford – Paris – Shannon – Tokyo

ELSEVIER SCIENCE Ltd
The Boulevard, Langford Lane
Kidlington, Oxford OX5 1GB, UK

© 2001 Elsevier Science Ltd. All rights reserved.

This work is protected under copyright by Elsevier Science, and the following terms and conditions apply to its use:

Photocopying
Single photocopies of single chapters may be made for personal use as allowed by national copyright laws. Permission of the Publisher and payment of a fee is required for all other photocopying, including multiple or systematic copying, copying for advertising or promotional purposes, resale, and all forms of document delivery. Special rates are available for educational institutions that wish to make photocopies for non-profit educational classroom use.

Permissions may be sought directly from Elsevier Science Global Rights Department, PO Box 800, Oxford OX5 1DX, UK; phone: (+44) 1865 843830, fax: (+44) 1865 853333, e-mail: permissions@elsevier.co.uk. You may also contact Global Rights directly through Elsevier's home page (http://www.elsevier.nl), by selecting 'Obtaining Permissions'.

In the USA, users may clear permissions and make payments through the Copyright Clearance Center, Inc., 222 Rosewood Drive, Danvers, MA 01923, USA; phone: (+1) (978) 7508400, fax: (+1) (978) 7504744, and in the UK through the Copyright Licensing Agency Rapid Clearance Service (CLARCS), 90 Tottenham Court Road, London W1P 0LP, UK; phone: (+44) 207 631 5555; fax: (+44) 207 631 5500. Other countries may have a local reprographic rights agency for payments.

Derivative Works
Tables of contents may be reproduced for internal circulation, but permission of Elsevier Science is required for external resale or distribution of such material.
Permission of the Publisher is required for all other derivative works, including compilations and translations.

Electronic Storage or Usage
Permission of the Publisher is required to store or use electronically any material contained in this work, including any chapter or part of a chapter.

Except as outlined above, no part of this work may be reproduced, stored in a retrieval system or transmitted in any form or by any means, electronic, mechanical, photocopying, recording or otherwise, without prior written permission of the Publisher.
Address permissions requests to: Elsevier Science Global Rights Department, at the mail, fax and e-mail addresses noted above.

Notice
No responsibility is assumed by the Publisher for any injury and/or damage to persons or property as a matter of products liability, negligence or otherwise, or from any use or operation of any methods, products, instructions or ideas contained in the material herein. Because of rapid advances in themedical sciences, in particular, independent verification of diagnoses and drug dosages should be made.

First edition 2001

Library of Congress Cataloging in Publication Data
A catalog record from the Library of Congress has been applied for.

British Library Cataloguing in Publication Data
A catalog record from the Library of Congress has been applied for.

ISBN 0-08-043920-9

♾The paper used in this publication meets the requirements of ANSI/NISO Z39.48-1992 (Permanence of Paper).
Printed in The Netherlands.

Contents

List of Figures

List of Tables

Contributors

Heather Chappells is a PhD student in the Department of Sociology, Cartmel College, University of Lancaster, UK.

Maurie J. Cohen is assistant professor at the New Jersey Institute of Technology, USA.

Emma Dewberry is a lecturer in the Department of Design, Goldsmith's College, University of London, UK.

Kate Fletcher is a lecturer in the Department of Design, Goldsmith's College, University of London, UK.

Phillip Goggin is a lecturer in the Department of Design, Goldsmith's College, University of London, UK.

David Goodman is professor in the Department of Environmental Studies, University of California at Santa Cruz, USA.

Michael Goodman is a PhD student in the Department of Environmental Studies, University of California at Santa Cruz, USA.

Josiah McC. Heyman is professor in the Department of Social Sciences, Michigan Technological University, USA.

Kersty Hobson is a postdoctoral fellow with the Research School of Social Sciences, Australian National University, Australia.

Joseph Murphy is a research fellow in the Oxford Centre for the Environment, Ethics & Society, Mansfield College, University of Oxford, UK.

Markku Oksanen is a research fellow with the Academy of Finland based in the Philosophy Department, University of Turku, Finland.

Jouni Paavola is a research fellow with the Oxford Centre for the Environment, Ethics & Society, Mansfield College, University of Oxford, UK.

Michael Redclift is professor in the Geography Department, King's College, University of London, UK.

Jan Selby is a lecturer in the Department of Politics and International Relations, Cartmel College, University of Lancaster, UK.

Elizabeth Shove is a senior lecturer in the Department of Sociology, Cartmel College, University of Lancaster, UK.

Stephen Zavestoski is assistant professor in the Department of Sociology, Providence College, USA.

Preface

This book began its life in a series of four seminars sponsored by the UK's Economic and Social Research Council (ESRC) under the title "Sustainable Consumption and Lifestyles: Integrating Environmental and Social Science Perspectives". The Oxford Centre for the Environment, Ethics and Society (OCEES) at Mansfield College and the Department of Environmental Social Sciences at Keele University served jointly as the convenors of these discussions between 1998 and 2000. The seminars brought together two loose groupings of researchers. On one hand, we invited environmental social scientists concerned about the physical impacts of consumption, the use of natural resources and the capacity of the earth to absorb an ever-increasing volume of wastes. On the other hand, the meetings included scholars from the fields of sociology, anthropology, and cultural studies who focused their attention on the role of consumption in identity formation and communication, but had little interest in the environmental impacts of these activities.

As one might suspect, this was, from the start, an ambitious endeavour. Within the realm of environmental studies, as in many other areas of intellectual inquiry, there has recently been a great outpouring of rhetorical support for the pursuit of interdisciplinarity. However, few guides outlining how to achieve this noble goal exist. We therefore viewed the series of ESRC seminars not only as a chance to formulate some potentially valuable insights regarding the social and environmental implications of modern lifestyles, but also as an opportunity to promote interdisciplinarity and meaningful communication across several academic disciplines.

Assembling a group of scholars able to embark on such a project was more difficult than initially anticipated. The main problem proved to be the monumental divide between realist and constructivist approaches — one that runs deep within the social sciences. The environmental scholars tended to take the negative physical impacts of consumption as their point of departure whereas the consumption scholars were more interested in how people use material goods to socially construct their own realities. From the outset it proved quite difficult to find ways to talk effectively across this gap.

Another problem was the tendency for the two groups to adopt different positions with respect to analysis and prescription. The environmental scholars were typically interested in practical actions and were quicker to adopt a critical stance toward the consumption practices common in rich countries today. In contrast, the consumption scholars were antagonistic to the idea of adopting normative positions with respect to consumption. Moreover, they were often openly hostile to the idea of engaging in discussions aimed at encouraging the transformation of existing consumption patterns in order to reduce their environmental impacts. Because of these dilemmas some participants withdrew from the project and others replaced them. Through this iterative process we eventually identified a core group of researchers who were prepared to straddle the realist-constructivist divide and to contribute meaningfully to the pursuit of an interdisciplinary dialogue on the connections between consumption and the environment. They were also willing to adopt normative positions with respect to consumption, environment and development issues.

In April 1999 the study of sustainable consumption at OCEES and the preparation of this book received extra momentum from the establishment of the Oxford Commission on Sustainable Consumption. Based at Mansfield College, the Commission was formed to act as a catalyst for the action needed from citizens, governments, business, media organisations and others to pursue sustainable consumption. In particular, this endeavour involves identifying and promoting best practice and the Commission will submit a report on consumption to the Earth Summit+10 meeting of the United Nations in 2002. This volume represents a significant contribution to the ongoing work of the Commission.

We would like to express our appreciation to our colleagues at OCEES and the Fellows of Mansfield College for numerous enlightening discussions on the subject of consumption and the environment. In particular, we would like to thank Caroline Bastable, Michael Freedan, Antonia Layard, Anne Maclachlan, Laurie Michaelis, John Muddiman, Jouni Paavola, Neil Summerton and Bhaskar Vira. For their support we are especially indebted to David Marquand, the current Principal of Mansfield College, and his immediate predecessor, Dennis Trevelyan.

Clearly this project would not have been possible without generous financial assistance from several sponsoring organisations. We are grateful to the ESRC for financing the initial seminar series and to the Ove Arup Foundation and to UK Waste Ltd for funding the Research Fellowships at OCEES (the latter through the Landfill Tax Credit Scheme). Obviously a book is unlikely to see the light of day unless it is supported by a publisher and for his enthusiastic response to our initial proposal and for escorting the manuscript through to publication we are grateful to David Clark of Elsevier. Lastly, we would also like to thank all the authors who contributed to this volume.

Maurie J. Cohen and Joseph Murphy
Oxford, February 2001

Part I

Introduction

Chapter 1

Consumption, Environment and Public Policy

Joseph Murphy and Maurie J. Cohen

1. Introduction

During the years since the 1992 Earth Summit in Río de Janeiro consumption has emerged as a significant environmental policy issue. Agenda 21, the conference's framework for sustainable development, devoted an entire chapter to consumption.[1] In it the satisfaction of a seemingly endless stream of consumer desires was identified as a major cause of global environmental problems. With hardly a pause, the newly minted United Nations Commission for Sustainable Development initiated a research programme to examine more rigorously the challenges associated with any attempt to achieve more sustainable consumption. Elsewhere within the networks of environmental high politics the Organisation for Economic Co-operation and Development, the Paris-based association that serves as a diplomatic club for the world's most affluent nations, quickly mustered some of its own resources for a parallel investigation (see for example OECD 1996; OECD 1997; OECD 1998).[2]

With bewildering speed a long list of learned societies, national governments and non-governmental organisations also rushed to articulate positions concerning the environmental effects of contemporary consumption practices. For instance, the Councils of the Royal Society of London and the United States National Academy of Sciences issued a joint statement in 1997 calling for a "better understanding of human consumption and related behaviours and technologies". This unusual collaboration went on to suggest that modifications in consumption practices were needed to assist in "the transition to a sustainable, desirable life for the world's people in the coming century." (IOCU 1993:xx) Some national governments, the most prominent perhaps being the Netherlands, have initiated multi-year research and policy programmes designed to reduce the environmental impacts of consumption in their countries and abroad (Aarts *et al.*, 1995; Noorman and

---

[1] A number of commentators have discussed the highly negotiated and contingent nature of Chapter 4 of Agenda 21, the section of the report explicitly concerned with consumption. Indeed, representatives at the pre-conference sessions encountered great difficulty coming to agreement on both substantive themes and technical details concerning the role of consumption as a contributing factor to global environmental deterioration. Numerous passages in the final document were 'bracketed' meaning that the intent was to revisit these issues in the period following the Earth Summit.

[2] The Copenhagen-based Nordic Council of Ministers is another secondary policymaking institution that has played an important role in advancing sustainable consumption as an agenda item in international deliberations.

Exploring Sustainable Consumption: Environmental Policy and the Social Sciences, Volume 1, pages 3–17.
Copyright © 2001 by Elsevier Science Ltd.
All rights of reproduction in any form reserved.
ISBN: 0-08-043920-9

Uiterkamp 1993; Spaargaren 1997). Traditionally concerned only with promoting consumer protection and increasing the range of choices available to consumers, advocates such as the International Organisation of Consumer Unions have also begun to press for less environmentally damaging forms of consumption.

Taken as a whole, these developments mark an unmistakable watershed in the understanding of environmental problems for purposes of public policymaking. For the past two centuries, and particularly during the last thirty years, solving environmental problems has been construed as a producer responsibility and consumers have been placed at a distance from the assignment of culpability. Such an allocation of blame has given rise to familiar forms of regulation in the world's wealthiest countries aimed at modifying production techniques and technologies. For instance, policymakers have typically viewed acid deposition in productionist terms, an interpretation that has resulted in legislation requiring operators of large combustion plants to install flue-gas desulphurisation equipment designed to cleanse emission streams. Also present, but much less prominent in this respect, have been proposals to shift electricity production away from coal toward less environmentally damaging fuel sources such as natural gas, wind and solar. Pollution problems generally have been targets for a variety of techno-fix solutions aimed at modifying the means of production. Even the design of more energy-efficient household appliances represents an obligation that has been placed squarely on the shoulders of producers. There has been little serious thought or effort devoted to regulating consumption itself in order to address environmental problems.[3]

Policymakers and consumers have therefore been quick to blame industry for environmental problems. Meanwhile, a growing array of global environmental problems, ranging from climate change to ozone depletion to declining biodiversity, has been blamed by some on high population growth rates in many of the world's poorest countries. Such an interpretation has suggested that if the world is serious about dealing with the environmental crisis, the first imperative is to address the demographic "disaster" in the Third World. Accordingly, international assistance programs, often disregarding the protests of target-country governments, have aggressively sought to disseminate modern forms of family planning to defuse the population "timebomb".

What this discussion suggests is that over the past four or five decades consumers in the richest nations have largely avoided being identified as responsible for the environmentally damaging effects of their consumption practices in part because other targets and explanations have been offered. This distancing has been encouraged by elected officials in the richest countries who have been reluctant to question consumer decision making, aspirations and sovereignty. This approach has been reinforced recently by the neo-liberal

---

[3]The main area where this needs to be qualified is energy. From the 1970s onward there have been some attempts to encourage consumers to use less energy. However, these have not been entirely successful. The US shifted responsibility for demand side management to producers partly because it became clear that government efforts to encourage frugality were the object of derision. Jimmy Carter's famous address to the nation in which he encouraged citizens to turn down the thermostat and put on an extra sweater is still widely remembered as the classic failure to launch a consumption debate, although the environment was not the primary concern. Nevertheless, most European governments have maintained programmes to encourage energy conservation in the home and private car use.

orthodoxy, which asserts that any political interference with consumer autonomy violates rights, and, more practically, is a recipe for economic and electoral disaster. One of the most notable effects of the 1992 Earth Summit has been to begin to call this interpretation into question and to initiate a process in which consumption is now coming to be viewed as a legitimate domain for environmental policymaking.

Despite this new interest in consumption, efforts to create a dialogue on how to link consumption with the environment have often been quite confused due to difficulties faced in pinning down core concepts and drawing boundaries around the discussion. Much of this difficulty stems from the fact that consumption is, on one hand, a very real material activity involving physical units of oil, wood, steel, and so forth. On the other hand, the acquisition of goods is undeniably tightly bound up with cultural practices aimed at achieving numerous social objectives including the production or reproduction of values, a cohesive society and individual identity. Consideration of the environmental impacts of consumption has traditionally privileged the material perspective and this has given rise to familiar moral appeals to consumers cautioning them, for example, to avoid artificial fibres in their clothing, to use public transportation, to purchase energy-efficient refrigerators and to adopt vegetarian diets. It is perhaps no surprise that these campaigns have been relatively unsuccessful in eliciting desired behavioural changes and, even in cases of apparently favourable adjustment people can find it difficult to act in a way that is consistent with what they believe.

To move the debate forward, this book folds into the customary materialistic view of consumption a series of more complex and nuanced perspectives on consumption and the environment drawn from the social sciences. During the past decade several branches of the social sciences — most prominently the disciplines of sociology, anthropology, history and cultural studies — have experienced an explosion of interest in the study of consumption as a set of social and cultural activities (key contributions include Miller 1995; Campbell 1987; Fine and Leopold 1993; Warde 1997). Consumption is seen by scholars working in these fields as a window of critical importance on modern/post-modern societies. Many contend that consumption has replaced production as the pivotal realm of social activity in an increasingly fragmented world. In this world, material objects as symbols serve as essential tools of communication. Curiously though they have been largely silent on matters of ecological impact. We hope that this volume will succeed in integrating the conventional view of consumption as the material throughput of resources (often with pronounced environmental consequences) with an understanding of the political, social and cultural significance of these practices. We believe it is only through such a synthesis that it will be possible to provide a theoretically sound and empirically rigorous basis for environmental policy that aims to move affluent nations toward more sustainable consumption patterns.

2. Boundaries and Definitions in Environment-Consumption Debates

Policy dialogue on sustainable consumption has to date been poorly focused and muddled, largely because of the ambiguous nature of core concepts and the problem of how to draw boundaries around the discussion. Political theorist Thomas Princen has considered the problem of defining consumption in a way that is useful for analysing environmental problems and his work provides a useful starting point (Princen 1999). Princen argues that for a variety of reasons the clarity and value of efforts to conceptually link consumption and the environment are often limited. One common problem is defining consumption in a way that is too broad to be useful. Princen contends that a good example of this is the influential perspective advanced by biologist Norman Myers who defines consumption as "human transformations of material and energy" (Myers 1997; see also the accompanying rejoinder by J. Vincent and T. Panayotou). Arguably, such an expansive definition fails to establish consumption as a useful focus for public policy or the social sciences.[4] Associated discussions are condemned to remain hopelessly mired within the poorly defined realm of study that has come to be known as the human dimensions of global environmental change.

In many respects we encounter the opposite problem when we approach consumption from a narrowly disciplinary perspective, overly influenced by the assumptions and prejudices of a particular academic point of view. This dilemma is perhaps most concretely illustrated by the discussions that customarily take place among economists, although they are by no means the only offenders. Economists tend to define consumption simply as the exchange of goods in a market. The risks of adopting such an approach are considerable, mainly because there are plenty of consumption practices that do not involve financial exchange in markets. A gender bias, for example, becomes clear when we recognise that men are commonly the consumers of meals prepared by women. In a conventional domestic setting no money changes hands, though it would if the same service were to be provided in a restaurant. More generally substantial quantities of resources are used around the world outside the formal economy. Another problem is that by emphasising financial exchange economists are inevitably and prematurely drawn toward market-based public policy recommendations.

More generally, as Princen explains, there has been a tendency simply to conflate the emerging interest in consumption with a variety of existing debates. The most obvious ones are critiques of materialism, inequity between North and South, and population growth. Materialism, for example, has been roundly condemned for decades because of its supposedly alienating and ultimately dissatisfying nature (see various contributions in Crocker and Linden 1998.) Such critiques often have religious origins and stem from deep-seated misgivings about the social consequences of self-indulgent and immodest lifestyles. There has been a trend, with the rise of environmental problems, simply to graft the environmental critique of consumption onto critiques of this kind. In the area of the global distribution of wealth and opportunity a similar thing has happened. As Princen (1999, p. 352) says

> If the problem is one of inequity, no analytic advantage is gained by calling
> it consumption. Adding the environment and calling the problem consump-
> tion only muddles the long-standing debates of North and South, haves and

---

[4]Indeed, it is such thinking that has largely been responsible for relegating the study of consumption within the social sciences to a decidedly second class status, one best pursued by individuals with backgrounds in marketing and related disciplines. For a thorough discussion of the stigmatised position of consumption as a focus for serious intellectual inquiry refer to Douglas and Isherwood (1979).

have-nots, rich and poor, powerful and powerless, to include environmental inequities. These problems are real and serious, but, a priori, there is no reason why consumption per se should be identified as the problem.

In many ways the issue of population growth is similar. It is related, but analytically separate, from consumption and there is nothing gained by simply conflating them.

The task that Princen sets himself, therefore, is how to approach consumption in a way that acknowledges its complex character, establishes it as a discrete and useful conceptual category, and, at the same time, links it to the environment. His solution is to endorse a definition that emphasises material impacts. This acknowledges that consumption is a natural act, necessary for organisms to survive. Over-consumption occurs when consumption undermines the life-support system of a species. As he states:

> the human behaviour that intersects with the biophysical realm can be termed *material provisioning*, that is the appropriation of material and energy for survival and reproduction ... In sum, an ecologically grounded definition of consumption takes as a starting point human material provisioning and the draw on ecosystem services (Princen 1999 p. 355–356).

Such a 'using-up-of-resources' approach transcends the common production-consumption dichotomy.

Although this approach certainly satisfies what Princen sets out to achieve — namely the linking of consumption to environmental impacts — it does so at considerable cost, and a solely physical-systems approach offers an inadequate basis for discussions of sustainable consumption for several reasons. First, it has little or no relevance to consumption itself. People do not consider themselves to be 'materially provisioning.' In emphasising the physical dimensions of consumption, its social aspects are lost completely. This way of proceeding is narrowly disciplinary in much the same way as the economists' approach about which Princen is correctly quite critical. Second, Princen ignores the fact that consumption-environment interactions do not occur only at the material level. The environment is also very much a socially constructed aspect of consumption. Princen and others may argue that this aspect of consumption is not important because it does not involve *real* material impacts, but in practice it will. Also, the social construction of consumption-environment linkages is likely to be central to public policy and an exclusively material view of consumption and the environment risks missing an opportunity. Finally, and more serious still for prospects of developing a workable understanding of sustainable consumption, is the fact that a physical-systems approach to consumption does not allow issues of equity to enter easily into the discussion, within or between countries.

For these reasons, operationalising sustainable consumption within the conventional dichotomy of production and consumption seems appropriate. This allows direct engagement with prevailing approaches to public policy (which invariably continue to focus on production). It also enables easy interaction with academic social science where disciplines have historically tended to emphasise production and production-related explanations of society. However, endorsing a loose production-consumption approach is not the same as sanctioning a supply-demand framework that will tend to lead to discussions of exchange in markets and externalities. That said, because production-consumption is not radically removed it is still possible for those with a supply-demand mind-set to engage with such a discussion.

Against this background we can describe the boundaries around the sustainable consumption debate to which the discussion contained in this book will conform. In the context of the traditional production-consumption dichotomy consumption involves people acquiring (often but not necessarily in markets using money) and using objects, services, and places. This is not to deny that institutions are also consumers, however consumption by institutions does not provide the focus for the discussion that follows.[5] The environment enters in at different levels e.g., the physical and the socially constructed. It is the physical impacts of consumption that are of primary concern from a sustainability point of view, either because of their impacts on other people (often distant both geographically and temporally) or simply because of their implications for ecosystem integrity. However, the social construction of the environment is also very significant because, for example, the idea of 'nature' is often mobilised by producers to promote consumption of particular goods.[6] Also, public policy to achieve sustainable consumption may involve constructing environmental concern among consumers as a prerequisite for changes in their acquisition practices. The social dimensions of sustainable consumption involve primarily questions of distribution and equity. Such considerations may raise issues about the distribution of the negative impacts of consumption or the very distribution of opportunities to consume.

3. Consumption and Environment: A 'Levers, Knobs and Dials' View of Public Policy

We make an explicit attempt in this book to think about public policy and practical actions while making use of the informative capabilities of a broad range of the social sciences. To set the scene for the discussion that follows it is useful to describe, and possibly to caricature slightly for purposes of emphasis, existing approaches to consumption and environment problems. When policymakers engage with a problem it is inevitable that their proposals will be heavily influenced by the assumptions they make about what it is that is being manipulated. These assumptions are linked to the type of knowledge being applied. This is particularly the case with respect to consumption-related environmental problems where arguably it is the world-views of economists and technologists that dominate.

---

[5] It can be argued that consumption by institutions is substantially more important from the perspective of limiting environmental impacts than what takes place at the individual and household levels. We do not disagree with this claim, but choose in the current context to focus our attention on non-institutional consumers.

[6] Even so-called eco-friendly forms of consumption require the non-recoverable utilisation of resources and as such lead to some of the same forms of environmental deterioration as more conventional consumption. For an illuminating treatment of this consumerist mode refer to Price (1995).

Policymakers (public or private sector) typically make a variety of judgements about consumers and markets that have their origin in neo-classical economics. It is also common to hear members of the public voice similar opinions, even though their own actions often reveal them to be false. For example, consumers are generally thought to be autonomous and rational. They are autonomous in the sense that their consumption decisions are not influenced by other consumers and rational in the sense that they are egoistic beings interested only in maximising personal welfare. Another important dimension of the economist's perspective that infiltrates conventional thinking involves the market. The market is where consumers express their preferences by demanding goods. A standard assumption about markets is that to work efficiently prices must be correct and information must be readily available.

On the basis of this model a range of consumption-focused environmental policies immediately offer themselves. Many of them seem obvious. If, for example, a market is not functioning properly two explanations seem probable — either information is not conveniently accessible or the prices are not accurate.[7] Such apparent circumstances often produce a variety of proposals aimed at 'internalising the cost of environmental damage', 'removing perverse subsidies' and dealing with the 'information deficit.' We can refer to this as the eco-taxes and the eco-labelling approach to consumption and environment problems and it has attracted considerable support in recent years.[8]

The purpose of this volume is partly to undermine this atomistic and economistic mode of public policymaking in the area of consumption and the environment and to build a richer and more accurate view of consumption. The papers in this book clearly establish, for example, that consumers are in practice profoundly influenced by what other consumers buy. We also establish beyond doubt that consumers are not rational and egoistic welfare maximisers in the way economists customarily suggest. Consumers may be rational in the sense that they act purposefully to achieve particular goals, but their consumption practices are likely to be informed by a diverse range of ethical beliefs and value positions. In the face of these insights the eco-taxes and eco-labelling approach to policymaking is revealed as unhelpfully simplistic.

The second dominant form of knowledge influencing public policy at the nexus between consumption and the environment derives from the design and engineering professions.[9] The technologist's key assumption is that all consumption-related environmental problems

---

[7]There is also a substantial literature on "barriers" that refers to transaction costs, market entry barriers, imperfect competition and these lead to other policy proposals.

[8]Especially in northern Europe, ecological taxation in the form of carbon taxes and roadway charges has received a strong political embrace, although practical application has been less widespread, in part as a means of encouraging a shift away from taxes on labour toward taxes on environmentally harmful activities. A good review of the status of eco-taxation as a tool of environmental policymaking is offered by Tim O'Riordan (1997). Eco-labeling has become a common device and it is regularly used to identify the environmentally significant components and processes of products ranging from timber to tuna. The expectation is that consumers value such information and that it will aid them in purchasing goods that embody higher levels of environmental responsibility.

[9]Of course the design profession is very diverse. The argument here is built on one approach to design, which focuses on technology and materials. Design also has a "soft" side which is more focused on social relationships. Chapter 12 of this volume emerges from the design tradition and shows that not all approaches in that tradition can be criticised along the lines that follow.

can ultimately be solved through technical inventiveness. This assumption is grounded in a view that sees society as a machine whose purpose is to meet human needs. As such, the key constitutive social relationships involve resource and material flows, energy inputs and outputs. The ultimate goal is to make the system as efficient as possible in its use of resources and energy. Technological innovation is central to this project.[10] The economist simplifies the individual by assuming a limited number of universal characteristics; the technologist loses sight of the individual and society, except as the recipient of final goods and services or as a source of problems to be solved.

The policy proposals that emerge from the technologist's worldview commonly emphasise supply-side initiatives, not surprisingly because it is manufacturers and entrepreneurs who can mobilise the forces of innovation to solve society's problems. At its most limited scale this involves redesigning products to reduce their impact on the environment, particularly in the use phase. Such an approach has, for example, been regularly utilised to increase the fuel efficiency of automobiles. More recently, life-cycle assessment has become a frequently used tool to conduct these kinds of analyses and to aid in the ranking of various alternatives. Occasionally, the technologist may endorse more radical redesigns of products that have the potential to transform society and to ameliorate the environmental impacts of consumption. Tele-working to reduce commuting problems is an instance of this kind of 'outside the box' thinking. Take-back obligations requiring manufacturers to recover their products at the end of their useful lives and various product design and performance standards are policy options linked to this perspective.

While technological innovations, particularly those of a more visionary nature, no doubt have considerable potential to reduce the environmental impact of contemporary lifestyles, a technology-focused approach to sustainable consumption is extremely problematic for a number of reasons.[11] Firstly, underpinning the technological worldview is often an uncritical technological optimism. Arguably this is at least partly responsible for many of the environmental problems that we currently face. Second, in pushing society to the periphery technologists operate with little or no understanding of human agency and commonly fail to consider how people may change their behaviour to avoid realising the designed 'solution.' Finally, this perspective typically gives inadequate thought to the social costs of technology such as second order effects and impacts on marginalised groups.

In practice, therefore, despite their dominant positions in the policymaking process, the economist's and technologist's approaches to sustainable consumption are inadequate. But with these problems in mind it is worth reflecting on why, paradoxically, they are apparently so appealing to policymakers. We can identify a number of factors. First, the division of labour associated with the creation of discrete academic disciplines and perspectives is surely a necessary condition for the emergence of partial perspectives which come to dominate policy making. In the absence of somewhat arbitrary and reductionist boundaries

---

[10]A celebrated example of this perspective is Julian Simon (1986) *The Ultimate Resource 2*. For an excellent treatment of technocentrism within the history of ideas see Pepper (1996). The more general point being made here is that such thinking is central to essentially all forms of engineering education and practice.

[11]The new fields of industrial ecology and ecological design are largely organised around the reconceptualisation of manufacturing systems and the radical redesign of products (see, for example, von Weizäcker *et al.*, 1997; Zelov and Cousineau 1997).

such incomplete views of consumption (and social affairs more generally) would not be possible (Dickens 1996). Second, because these disciplines grossly understate the complexity of the world they promise relatively easy solutions and are therefore politically attractive if not effective. Third, the economic and technological approaches have much in common with each other and not surprisingly interventions deriving from them often operate in tandem and to some extent dovetail together. Both essentially offer a "levers, knobs and dials" view of the world. In academic circles this perspective might be called instrumentalist and mechanistic, and both are based on an atomistic ontology. Society itself is not really part of the picture at all. Finally, it is also the case that policymaking bodies often have cultures that promote similar perspectives. Bureaucratic organisations tend to employ people with either an economic or a technological worldview and contract research from institutions that are able to use the language and discourse. This does not just mean that alternatives get overlooked because they are outside the line of vision. Analyses of policy networks and discourses suggest that only people able to use the dominant approach will be seen as legitimate contributors to policy discussions (Hajer 1995).

Our aim here is not to disable the prevailing model guiding policymaking and to leave nothing in its place. Most of the contributors to this volume are sympathetic to the claim that contemporary consumption practices are woefully problematic from an environmental standpoint and are in need of modification and that achieving this will require new approaches to policymaking. Our objective in assembling this collection is to offer a more robust and comprehensive way of conceptualising the complex relationship between consumption and the environment and to forge recommendations that are consistent with this interpretation.

In many respects, therefore, this discussion helps to establish the task of this book. Somewhat ambitiously, we seek to draw on a diverse range of the social sciences that have evolved a sophisticated understanding of the relationship between consumption and the environment to outline new approaches to public policy in this area. It is necessary to show that an alternative is possible. At the same time, we should not casually discard the contributions made by economists and technologists. People *are* spurred on to behave in particular ways by concerns for personal welfare and prices do influence consumption practices. The point is that over-reliance on these perspectives leads to a heavily blinkered view. Furthermore, in our quest for acceptable solutions to some extraordinary problems it has become common to interpret this partial picture as constituting the full landscape. In a similar spirit, and to prevent misinterpretations of our intent, it is important to re-emphasise that technology may indeed have a major role to play in addressing a broad range of consumption and the environment problems. However, the role of technological innovation is surely less than is claimed by its most enthusiastic supporters and, if experience is any guide, such ingenuity is likely to throw up any number of unanticipated (and essentially unpredictable) surprises.

4. The Road Ahead

The first section of this book builds on the introduction and examines the new policy debate in more detail. In Chapter 2 Maurie Cohen examines the emergence of sustainable consumption as a distinguishable environmental discourse from an historical perspective. He discusses the most influential policy pronouncements of the past three decades and describes how conventional explanations of global environmental deterioration were initially rooted in concerns about population growth in the developing countries. This discourse's privileged position is explained largely by the ability of the world's wealthiest countries to monopolise the debate within international institutions. By attributing responsibility for global environmental problems to the combination of rampant birth rates and poverty, the affluent nations managed to avoid confronting directly how domestic practices were impinging upon global ecological health. Cohen argues that it was not until publication of the Brundtland Report in 1987 that an alternative interpretation began to offer a challenge. At the same time climate change and other novel trans-boundary issues were beginning to reconfigure international environmental politics and newly created forums gave developing countries new institutional settings in which to challenge the dominant perspective. Countries such as China, India and Brazil contended that the high rates of consumption in affluent nations were responsible for misuse of global resources and waste sinks. Constructive domestic action by rich countries was seen as necessary before attempts were made to constrain the growth prospects of people in the developing world. Particularly important for pressing forward this claim were the preparatory deliberations leading up to the 1992 Earth Summit in Río de Janeiro in which developing countries worked to overturn the prevailing environmental orthodoxy and to develop a new explanation of global environmental problems.

In Chapter 3 Joseph Murphy analyses the European Union's approach to environmental policy and consumption. Various European Union policies, regulations and directives are discussed and the theory of ecological modernisation is introduced and developed to provide a benchmark against which current approaches are assessed. In order to explain the nature of policy outputs a structural-institutional policy analysis model is applied and the analysis is developed further using ideas from discourse analysis. In the area of consumption Murphy argues EU environmental policy is particularly weak. It does little more than encourage the redesign of products and their purchase by better-informed consumers. It appears to be based on simplistic neo-classical economic assumptions about consumers and at the same time is underpinned by an uncritical technological optimism. The final section of this chapter explains why European environmental policy in this area has these shortcomings. Murphy draws attention to the influence of macro-economic pressures on the EU, particularly the overriding goal of being competitive with the United States, and how this makes questioning consumption in any profound way extremely difficult. He also highlights the importance of smaller scale influences such as policy networks dominated by particular assumptions about environmental problems and how they can be solved.

The chapters by Cohen and Murphy establish that there may be an opportunity for the social sciences to contribute to the policy debate in the area of consumption-related environmental problems. Parts III–VI of this book each consider linked disciplinary perspectives on consumption-environment issues as a first step toward this goal. The approaches range from political theory and economics (Part III) to psychology and social psychology (Part VI) with geography, anthropology, sociology and cultural studies covered in the middle sections.

Markku Oksanen discusses 'Liberal neutrality and consumption' in Chapter 4. From the perspective of a philosopher and political theorist Oksanen focuses particularly on how intervention by a public authority into the consumption practices of individuals can be justified in liberal political systems.[12] Oksanen reminds us that in liberalism the state is required to be neutral with regard to the actions of individuals. In the area of consumption this is seen in the idea of consumer sovereignty and this creates a considerable barrier to an active consumption policy. Oksanen pursues his discussion with reference to the consumption of fox furs. This case is challenging because although it is ethically problematic it does not place a significant burden on the environment in a physical sense. Also, it does not result in harm to other people and therefore the accepted justification for government intervention does not apply. Oksanen argues that this case establishes two important points. First, it draws attention to the anthropocentric nature of liberalism. Second, it raises fundamental questions about the idea of state neutrality. Following John O'Neill he distinguishes between two alternative understandings of state neutrality in liberalism. A "dialogic" view involves making laws based on deliberation and compromise and requires us to believe we can resolve differences and find solutions to problems in the public sphere. A "non-dialogic" view involves leaving things unresolved because it is impossible to reach a solution by means of debate. In this case controversial and complex problems associated with consumption will get decided in the market place. Oksanen concludes that government intervention to deal with consumption-related environmental and ethical problems is possible in a liberal political system but it may require a dialogic view of government neutrality.

The fox fur case raises the problem of value pluralism in the area of consumption and how to deal with it. Jouni Paavola builds on this in Chapter 5. In his contribution 'Economics, ethics and green consumerism' Paavola focuses first on the market and not the public sphere. He points out that in the standard model, particularly in economics, the consumer is seen as a rational actor interested only in maximising personal welfare within the constraints of a set budget and with limitless access to information about alternatives. This model of the consumer is built on what Paavola calls "self-centred welfarism". He suggests that the idea of relying on such a consumer to deliver sustainable consumption is not particularly appealing for obvious reasons. However, he goes on to establish that the model is simplistic because consumers regularly make use of ethical positions other than self-centred welfarism. The reality is inter- and intra-value pluralism. A consumer that is rational in a wider sense simply consumes in a way that is consistent with her/his values. Paavola concludes that individual action informed by an ethical concern for the environment is best able to transform the impact of consumption on the environment if agents do not act as self-centred welfarists. This will inevitably increase the protection given to the environment. However, to have an impact such values would have to generally present in society. If they are not collective action to structure the market so that it necessarily delivers particular outcomes may be required.

---

[12]The focus on liberal political systems is appropriate because most of the high consumption societies have such systems.

In Chapter 6 David Goodman and Michael Goodman examine food production-consumption networks and food labelling. Labels are discussed as "discursive resources" which can be used to create new producer-consumer networks and the discussion explores two views of sustainable consumption. The "universalist" viewpoint sees sustainable consumption practices as a sub-set of normal capitalist production and consumption activities. The "progressive" viewpoint suggests sustainable consumption practices are linked to entirely different ethics and organisational forms, which can coexist with capitalist ones and potentially restrict them. Sustainable consumption in this case involves the growth of new producer-consumer networks cemented by shared values and commitments. Evidence of the second version is found in some of the production-consumption networks discussed in the chapter. However, as the authors describe, such networks may struggle to maintain their identity and over time can take on the characteristics of networks commonly linked to the universalist viewpoint. Much of the chapter examines how this convergence and translation takes place. Fair Trade is examined as a challenging and positive example of eco-labelling operating on the margins of the conventional agro-food system. It is antagonistic to neo-liberal logic of commodity production and world trade and links consumers, nature and producer groups. Goodman and Goodman argue it is a political and institutional challenge (not economic at this point) to the conventional agro-food system. This chapter is particularly useful because it draws attention to the relatively limited agenda associated with much eco-labelling.

In contrast, in Chapter 7 Michael Redclift examines the consumption of places in the form of eco-tourism. In his chapter 'Changing nature: the consumption of space and the construction of nature on the Mayan Riviera' a variety of tourist developments are contrasted, each of which uses the idea of nature in some way to attract rich foreign tourists/consumers. The examples vary from resorts with no real environmental controls to an International Biosphere Reserve and World Heritage Site. He examines how ideas of eco-tourism and sustainable tourism are used to advance commercial and environmental objectives. To develop the discussion Redclift makes use of the distinction between "inside" and "outside" meanings. "Inside meanings" are what goods mean to people themselves as a result of institutional and cultural practices. Outside meanings are established by the structural conditions under which behaviour actually takes place — the economic, social and political context of behaviour. He argues that in the case of eco-tourism the structural determinants of environmental change and sustainability are closely linked to the symbolic representation of nature. Redclift concludes that a clear distinction between nature in a tourist eco-park and nature in a government reserve cannot be drawn. It is correspondingly difficult to specify an objectively correct use of the idea of sustainable consumption in the area of eco-tourism when meaning and use is context dependent.

In Chapter 8 Josiah Heyman examines the creation of "new consumers" in the manufacturing cities on Mexico's northern border. He approaches consumption and environment issues as an anthropologist. Based on extensive fieldwork he offers a fascinating explanation of working class family consumption. Heyman begins by arguing that facile assumptions about consumption abound. It is often seen as simply related to "wants" and "desires" that somehow reside in a decision-making unit, usually the individual or the family. In his chapter Heyman offers a much more detailed explanation focussing on what happens when people move from the country to an industrial centre where their lives are fundamentally transformed in ways that necessarily result in different consumption practices. The purchase of domestic appliances and linking to centralised utilities, for example, allows households to cope with the change from being free to allocate farming and household tasks amongst an entire family to a rigid model where males devote time to wage labour and children spend more time at school. It also helps them to deal with other influences such as the greater emphasis on neatness and cleanliness in schools and factories compared to rural life. Heyman argues that any meaningful effort to affect consumption will require popular involvement and commitment and may also depend on consumption becoming a political issue. Policies must work with the needs of people and not against them and they must recognise structural constraints and influences that act on people's lives. He also reminds us not to forget about the social dimension when focussing on environmental issues and suggests that action should give hardworking but poor and highly constrained consumers a wider range of realistic choices.

Heather Chappells, Jan Selby, and Elizabeth Shove in 'Control and flow' (Chapter 9) reconsider the relations between consumption, technology and the environment from a sociological perspective. In particular, this approach provides a useful contrast to the way in which the role of technology is commonly viewed in relation to consumption-environment debates e.g., as a "solution" or way of increasing efficiency. Focussing on the control and flow of water, the authors suggest that a typical public policy approach is to view water as an unproblematically homogenous resource that can be managed through common economic or institutional incentives alone. As an alternative they argue that water is in fact highly malleable and that fundamental questions about what it is and how it is channelled, contained and constituted need to be re-opened if we are to achieve more sustainable consumption. In particular they contend that more attention needs to be paid to the productive role of technologies — which not only control chaotic flows but also play a part in constituting waters and subjects. To illustrate this, the chapter considers the "co-constitutive" effects of three broad genres of technology — barriers, containers and purifiers. Drawing on examples from the UK and Palestine the authors show how technologies reflect the societies that deploy them and influence how consumption practices can be configured and organised.

In Chapter 10 Stephen Zavestoski discusses individual identity and the self. In 'Environmental concern and anti-consumerism in the self-concept' he aims to determine if concern about over-consumption emerges from the same idea of the self as concern over the environment more generally. Various self-selecting groups are examined and qualitative and quantitative data are analysed. The data suggests that the value basis of environmentalism and anti-consumerism may be similar but not the same. Anti-consumerist attitudes appear to emerge out of a narrow and more self-interested/egotistical sense of self whereas environmental concern involves a broader sense of the self and a moral community that has expanded to some extent to include nature. Anti-consumerist sentiment is linked to lack of fulfilment, excessive stress, agitation, malaise and so on. The search for a simple lifestyle is therefore selfishly motivated to some extent. Environmentalist attitudes are often more altruistic. The conclusion is that the apparent growing dissatisfaction with consumerism in some social groups is not necessarily linked to concern for the environment although reduced consumption is likely to be beneficial for it.

In Chapter 11 'Sustainable lifestyles: rethinking barriers and behaviour change' Kersty Hobson examines environmental communication strategies and how people react to them. Based on her study of the UK's Action at Home programme she criticises the model of the individual that is built into public policy in this area and then develops an alternative based on an argumentative understanding of the individual and identity formation. Drawing on the psychologist Billig she argues that thought is a constantly constructive and destructive act. Argumentative aspects of social life are essential and people need to enter into debates about lifestyles, with themselves and others, in order to understand themselves and their situation. Essentially environmental communication programmes are an opportunity to do this. This understanding moves the debate away from one where attitudes are understood simply as verbalisations of inner beliefs. It also undermines assumptions about willing participants suffering from an information deficit. The chapter suggests that communication programmes that create opportunities for debate may be more successful at changing behaviour than those that involve information flowing in one direction. Debate is more likely to result in everyday actions moving from "practical consciousness" to "discursive consciousness". However, ultimately, because the home is an important location for the creation of identity it is unlikely that large numbers of people will voluntarily make radical changes to their lifestyles over the short to medium term even if they could.

The diversity of approaches and insights into consumption practices and environmental problems in Parts III–VI clearly establish that the social sciences have an important contribution to make to policy debates in this area. The final section of the book — Part VII — begins to establish what this contribution might be. In Chapter 12 'Sustainable consumption by design' Kate Fletcher, Emma Dewberry and Phillip Goggin explore different strategies for sustainable consumption and the role of design in promoting these. The strategies they explore are *redesigning* that which is consumed (product focus/consuming greener); *reorganising* the way consumption takes place (results focus/consuming differently); and *rediscovering* the nature of needs (questioning the need fulfilled by the object, service or system, and how it is achieved). They argue that design for sustainability strategies can be clustered in these three areas and the timescale and potential environmental benefit increase as you pass from one to the other. The greatest factor improvements will occur over a long period of time and will involve reassessing needs. In a sense what this chapter offers is a manifesto for design for sustainability but the authors recognise that this will only be part of a multi-disciplinary effort if this opportunity is going to be grasped. Running through the chapter is the sense of a creative opportunity that is well beyond the vision of technical and supply-side solutions being discussed by policy makers at the moment. In many ways the task of the final chapter is, building on all the previous ones, to establish how the medium to long-term changes and opportunities outlined in Chapter 12 can be realised.

References

Aarts, W., Goudsblom, J., Schmidt, K., & Spier, F. (1995), *Toward a Morality of Moderation: A Report for the Dutch National Research Programme on Global Air Pollution and Climate Change.* Amsterdam: Amsterdam School for Social Science Research.

Campbell, C. (1987), *The Romantic Ethic and the Spirit of Modern Consumerism*. Oxford: Blackwell.

Crocker, D., & Linden, T. (eds) (1998), *Ethics of Consumption: The Good Life, Justice and Global Stewardship*. Lanham, MD: Rowman and Littlefield.

Douglas, M., & Isherwood, B. (1979), *The World of Goods: Towards an Anthropology of Consumption*. London: Routledge.

Dickens, P. (1996), *Reconstructing Nature: Alienation, Emancipation and the Division of Labour*. London: Routledge.

Fine, B., & Leopold, E. (1993), *The World of Consumption*. London: Routledge.

Hajer, M. (1995), *The Politics of Environmental Discourse*. Oxford: Oxford University Press.

IOCU (International Organisation of Consumers' Unions). (1993), *Beyond the Year 2000: The Transition to Sustainable Consumption: A Policy Document on Environmental Issues*. The Hague: IOCU.

Miller, D. (ed.). (1995), *Acknowledging Consumption: A Review of New Studies*. London: Routledge.

Myers, N. (1997), "Consumption: Challenge to sustainable development ... or distraction?" *Science 276*, 53–57.

Noorman, K. J., & Uiterkamp, T. (ed.). (1998), *Green Households: Domestic Consumers, Environment and Sustainability*. London: Earthscan.

OECD (Organisation for Economic Cooperation and Development). (1996), *Sustainable Consumption and Production*. Paris: OECD.

OECD (Organisation for Economic Cooperation and Development). (1997), *Sustainable Consumption and Production: Clarifying the Concepts*. Paris: OECD.

OECD (Organisation for Economic Cooperation and Development). (1998), *Towards Sustainable Consumption Patterns: A Progress Report on Member Country Initiatives*. Paris: OECD.

O'Riordan, T. (ed.). (1997), *Eco-Taxation*. London: Earthscan.

Pepper, D. (1996), *Modern Environmentalism*. London: Routledge.

Price, J. (1995), "Looking for nature at the mall: A field guide to the nature company." In W. Cronan (ed.) *Uncommon Ground: Rethinking the Human Place in Nature* (pp. 186–203). New York: W. W. Norton.

Princen, P. (1999), "Consumption and Environment: Some conceptual issues." *Ecological Economics 31*, 347–363.

Simon, J. (1986), *The Ultimate Resource 2*. Princeton: Princeton University Press.

Spaargaren, G. (1997), *The Ecological Modernization of Production and Consumption: Essays in Environmental Sociology*. Wageningen: Thesis Landbouw.

von Weizäcker, E., Lovins, A., & Lovins, H. (1997), *Factor Four: Doubling Wealth, Halving Resource Use*. London: Earthscan.

Warde, A. (1997), *Consumption, Food, and Taste*. London: Sage.

Zelov, C., & Cousineau, P. (1997), *Design Outlaws on the Ecological Frontier*. Brooklyn, NY: Knossus Publishing.

Part II

The Politics of Sustainable Consumption

Chapter 2

The Emergent Environmental Policy Discourse on Sustainable Consumption

Maurie J. Cohen

1. Introduction

While consumption has been a long-neglected topic in dominant environmental discourse there are indications that it is now moving closer to the centre of contemporary policy-making. With the rise of sustainable development within mainstream circles as the organising framework for conceptualising the "environmental problematique" processes of material acquisition, particularly in the world's most affluent nations, have begun to attract increasing scrutiny. During most of the modern environmental era (i.e., from circa 1970) the political power of (post-)industrial nations was sufficient to maintain a narrow problem definition of the factors responsible for environmental deterioration on the global level. This prevalent framing attributed increasingly more pervasive ecological deterioration not to consumption, but rather to rampant population growth. Accordingly, legions of development specialists were dispatched to the world's developing countries to advise them that they should first and foremost curb their demographic expansion. Once the birth rate was under control these nations could begin to implement policies to encourage export production that would enable them to overcome the debilitating effects of chronic poverty and declining environmental quality. By defining global environmental problems in terms of population growth wealthy nations managed for several decades to successfully sidestep their own complicity.

Despite the long-standing reticence of the developed nations to accept responsibility for the environmental harm caused by high levels of material consumption, the issue continued to crop up from time to time in international forums. However, the North's ability to maintain its commanding agenda-setting influence, combined with the political ineffectualness and fragmentation of the South, worked to preserve the hegemony of the dominant discourse. The ability of the affluent nations to ascribe their own particularistic delineation around the sources of large-scale environmental change began to come under heavy challenge during the diplomatic preparations leading up to the 1992 Earth Summit. Though economically advanced nations sought to preserve the prevailing problem defini-tion, pressure from newly empowered developing countries, and allied non-governmental organisations (NGOs), proved too powerful. In the post-Summit period consumption gained new stature, especially in European nations, as an organizing theme with which to

Exploring Sustainable Consumption: Environmental Policy and the Social Sciences, Volume 1, pages 21–37.
Copyright © 2001 by Elsevier Science Ltd.
All rights of reproduction in any form reserved.
ISBN: 0-08-043920-9

interpret the widening gap in global economic inequality and the environmental impact of consumerist lifestyles.

Changes in the content of the international environmental policy agenda contributed to this transformed problem definition. During the 1970s and 1980s, the affluent nations, by virtually any measure, made considerable progress toward bringing under control their most offensive forms of pollution. The outbreak of fire on Cleveland's Cuyahoga River, the industrial disaster at Seveso, and the methyl-mercury poisoning of the Japanese population of Minamata captured public attention and led to the implementation of sweeping legislation and the creation of new administrative agencies. Soot-filled air and chemical-saturated waters gave way in the face of a host of managerial interventions. At the same time, the classic environmental dilemmas of the developing countries — desertification, food security, and uncontrolled urban sprawl — were pushed out of prominence by a new class of global environmental problems. Novel issues such as global warming, acid rain, ozone depletion, and declining biodiversity, because they transcended national boundaries and raised seemingly irreconcilable scientific uncertainties, reconfigured environmental politics.

We examine in this chapter some of the critical changes that have taken place in dominant environmental discourse over the past three decades and suggest that consumption is now emerging as a central conceptual frame for policymaking. This survey begins its review with the 1972 publication *The Limits to Growth*, a report that was, along with a small handful of other seminal accounts, largely responsible for launching the modern environmental movement. Despite its crude treatment of consumption and a variety of problematic assumptions, this document did much to place the environment on the international policy agenda. We then advance fifteen years and publication of the Brundtland Report. This landmark endeavour introduced formally the concept of "sustainable development" and signalled the onset of a new era in environmental politics. The chapter then describes how this new framing became manifest in more concrete policy terms in both the European Commission's Fifth Environmental Action Plan and the Agenda 21 Report negotiated at the 1992 United Nations Conference on Environment and Development. To bring this review up to date, and to divine likely future directions for the emergent policy discourse on more sustainable forms of consumption, I discuss two more recent documents: (1) a joint statement by the Royal Society of London and the United States National Academy of Sciences and (2) a consultation paper issued by the UK Department of Transport, Environment, and the Regions. The chapter then proceeds to delineate the role that the Organisation for Economic Cooperation and Development has been playing to shape the inchoate understanding of the relationship between consumption and the environment.

2. The Limits to Growth

Prepared by a distinguished group of MIT researchers as a report to the Club of Rome, *The Limits to Growth* remains more than two decades after its original publication one of the most significant pieces of contemporary environmental scholarship (Meadows *et al.*, 1972). Though most of the authors' famous cybernetic forecasts have proved wide of the mark, their ambitious analysis continues to cast a portentous shadow over environmental thinking. Unfortunately, many of the ensuing debates sparked by the report between cornucopian and apocalyptic conjectures typically generate more heat than light. These still-simmering controversies tend to tell us a great deal about the political and cultural commitments of the protagonists, but frightfully little about the state of the natural environment (see, for example, Myers and Simon 1994). Rather than rehash these tired arguments the following discussion attempts to characterise the way in which *Limits* conceptualises consumption with respect to the environment and to point to how this particular framing has influenced more recent efforts.

The report views environmental deterioration largely in terms of the impact that an increasing global population has on the availability of natural resources. In particular, *Limits* sees exponential demographic growth, most prominently in the developing countries, as placing inexorable pressure on the world's productive capacity to generate food and provision other basic needs. The authors' computerised-systems model also predicts that the pervasive spread of modern lifestyles will hasten depletion of non-renewable commodities (e.g., coal, copper, petroleum). The report does not make any attempt to problematicise consumption as a social activity and treats material acquisition as a simple function of increasing population and industrialisation.

Interestingly, *Limits* makes no attempt to get to grips with the way in which individuals and households develop their materialistic aspirations and it does not discuss the role of central features of modernity such as television, fashion, and advertising in shaping desires. Consumers, to the extent that they appear explicitly in the report's analysis, are depicted as a generic, homogenous mass. For example, the authors discuss the depletion of bauxite entirely in terms of production and do not link the ultimate use of the commodity to the manufacture of aluminium, airplanes, and demand for air travel.

Limits observes that "as a population becomes more wealthy, it tends to consume more resources per person per year" (Meadows *et al.*, 1972:113). There is however a brake on this "run-away train". At a certain point, nations reach a "saturation level of material possessions" at which additional increments of income are spent primarily on services that are less resource consuming (118). Globally, the only mechanism available to temper the extraction rate for natural resources is the inevitable increase in prices that will become manifest as shortages become pronounced.

While the forbidding future portrayed by *Limits* enhanced public awareness of certain environmental problems, its understanding of consumption is truncated and fails to comprehend how contemporary provisioning practices contribute to ecological stress. The authors' depiction of material acquisition is one of pushing, to the point of exhaustion, an ever-increasing volume of natural resources through a pipe. More importantly, the policy recommendations that fall from the report are not especially constructive and are likely to offer inspiration to only the most indefatigable environmentalists.

3. *Our Common Future*

Fifteen years later, after the achievement of considerable, though uneven, progress in advanced nations addressing the effects of localised sources of air and water pollution, the World Commission on Environment and Development issued in 1987 *Our Common*

Future detailing the extensive amount of work that still remained to be done on the international level (WCED 1987). This important document, better known as the Brundtland Report, asserted that developing countries were beset by serious environmental problems and these dilemmas were largely attributable to the effects of poverty, population growth, and unequal terms of trade. The Commission also claimed that the global environment was now threatened by a new range of global ecological concerns which, because of their tendency to transcend national frontiers, were likely to pose grave challenges to existing regulatory institutions. While *Our Common Future* describes these conditions in considerable detail, the document is most notable today for placing the concept "sustainable development" on the international policy agenda. Our purpose here is not to interrogate the efficacy of sustainable development; nonetheless, this concept does provide a useful framework with which to examine how the Brundtland Report conceptualises consumption.

As is well known, the Brundtland Report defined sustainable development as 'development that meets the needs of the present without compromising the ability of future generations to meet their own needs' (WCED 1987:43). Though this definition has become increasingly elastic and devoid of substantive meaning, the Commission originally conceived of sustainable development as resting on two elemental principles: limitations and "needs."[1]

First, the notion of constraints on human development is obviously carried over from *Limits* and earlier thinking in the natural sciences (most specifically ecology). Such neo-Malthusianism contends that increasing population and growing per capita demand for natural resources will strip available supplies and lead to famine, scarcity and wrenching conflict. *Our Common Future* addresses this problem specifically for developing countries and describes the intense pressure on these societies to follow in the footsteps of the advanced nations. Ill-equipped technologically and institutionally, they engage in activities that cause serious and pervasive environmental damage. However, at the core of these destructive processes are the consumption patterns of the world's wealthiest members. The lifestyles common in affluent Northern nations (as well as among Southern elites) encourage disenfranchised agriculturists and industrial labourers to engage in economic activities that are ecologically harmful. The Brundtland Report thus marks an important turning point in the mainstream policy discourse and we begin to see, albeit in primitive form, formal recognition of the unequal contribution of affluent lifestyle-types to environmental problems (see Weale 1992). The authors are quite clear on this point and the Commission advises that we evaluate the "[s]hort-sighted way in which we have often pursued prosperity … [s]ustainable global development requires that those who are more affluent adopt lifestyles within the planet's ecological means" (WCED 1987:8–9).

Second, *Our Common Future* makes a provisional effort to distinguish between needs and desires. The document recognises that

---

[1]Sustainable development is an ecological concept with origins that can be traced back to the mid-nineteenth century. "Sustainability" was inherent in German foresters' original formulations of "sustainable yield" used to estimate rates for harvesting trees. We must therefore be sceptical of the application of this term to a wide range of contexts to which environmentalists and others may seek to apply it. For a more complete discussion refer to Worster 1985.

[p]erceived needs are socially and culturally determined, and sustainable development requires the promotion of values that encourage consumption standards that are within the bounds of the ecologically possible and to which we can all reasonably aspire ... Major changes in policies will be needed to cope with the industrial world's current high levels of consumption ... It is part of our moral obligation to other living beings and future generations (WCED 1987:44, 57).

Despite its attempt to grapple substantively with consumption in more nuanced social-scientific terms, we should be careful about reading this statement as a call to downscale material consumption in the advanced nations and to create ecological space to accommodate the aspirations of the developing world. Rather, the Commission places massive emphasis upon the use of technology and improved social organisation "to make way for a new era of economic growth ... The shift to sustainable development must be powered by a continuing flow of wealth from industry" (WCED 1987). The report's enthusiasm for economic expansion as the engine with which to drive global environmental improvement implies that any concerted effort to modify provisioning patterns in affluent nations would impair progress toward this objective. Paradoxically to some minds, *Our Common Future* argues unequivocally that greater consumption (and increasing national products) is a *sine qua non* for sustainable development. As a result, the Commission agilely avoids having to confront squarely the initial questions that it raises regarding the ethical propriety of contemporary lifestyles in the advanced nations.

4. European Commission *Fifth Environmental Action Programme*

In 1992 the European Commission (EC) published its Fifth Environmental Action Programme (FEAP) to articulate and systematise its priorities in this domain (European Commission 1992). The document sequentially addresses particular policy areas (e.g., solid waste, coastal zone management) and strives, within the constraints of this format, to devote considerable attention to material consumption. As such, the report provides some insight into the ways in which policymakers at the European level were beginning to conceptualise the relationship between consumption and the environment during the early 1990s. While the EC has limited unilateral power to implement policy initiatives, its directives guide individual member-states in formulating their own strategies to maintain compliance.

FEAP is clear at the outset that although it is going to engage with the "wasteful consumption of resources," the EC is not prepared to do so in a way that will court economic crisis. Rather, the Programme contends that improved environmental performance needs to be achieved within the "context of sustained economic growth." After conveying this caveat, the report claims to be "new and radical in its emphasis on the need for changes in current patterns of consumption and behaviour." Such action requires "a sharing of responsibility at all levels of society, including governments, regional and local authorities, non-governmental organisations, financial institutions, production and retail enterprises and individual citizens." While FEAP never discloses the concrete activities that will be required by each of these actors to encourage more environmentally-aware consumption, its general understanding sees the situation in terms of two failings: insufficient information and inadequate costing.

First, the Programme states "policies should be developed in a way which will help consumers to make informed choices on the basis of safety, quality, durability, and general environmental implications." FEAP allocates to the "retail sector" especially significant responsibilities and encourages enterprises to develop eco-labelling programmes that will enable consumers to make decisions that take the environment into consideration. On this general point, the Programme elaborates

> The individual, as a consumer, can make fully informed and rational choices only if the product information with which he/she is provided covers all relevant aspects such as performance, reliability, energy efficiency, durability, running cost, etc. and if this information is given in a neutral form, supported by effective and dependable guarantees.

Second, FAEP contends that prevailing forms of consumption are problematic because products are not priced at their "full cost to society … including their environmental costs." In other words, correcting environmental harm requires accounting more comprehensively for the deleterious effects of production on ecosystems and human health. Present pricing conventions enable producers (and indirectly consumers through artificially-low prices) to shift a portion of their costs onto the wider society. The EC report suggests improvement in this regard is a function of "getting the prices right," a process that entails the implementation of a variety of fiscal instruments (e.g., ecological taxation, pollution charges) to encourage firms to internalise the full costs of their activities. The additional increment in price will then be passed along to consumers in accordance with the demand elasticity of particular products.

Specifically in terms of conceptualising consumption FEAP is most noteworthy for its recognition that the amelioration of environmental problems is not exclusively limited to the production sphere and for moving the issue of material provisioning closer to the centre of discussion (for a discussion specifically of the European Union see Chapter 3).

5. Agenda 21

Preliminary negotiations leading up to the 1992 United Nations Conference on Environment and Development (UNCED) in Río were the backdrop for contentious debate regarding the relative contribution of contemporary consumption practices to global environmental problems. Developing countries and non-governmental organisations struggled to shift responsibility onto the resource-intensive lifestyles of the world's wealthiest nations, while the rich countries themselves worked to maintain the narrow, but increasingly implausible, framing that attributed international ecological degradation to rampant population growth. Though Northern delegations (principally the United States) fought mightily to keep disputes contained within their conventional boundaries, this ultimately proved too difficult a battle. Agenda 21, the summit's final report, observes that

[t]he major cause of the continued deterioration of the global environment is the unsustainable pattern of consumption and production, particularly in industrialised countries, which is a matter of grave concern, aggravating poverty and imbalances (UNCED 1992, §4.3).

This statement heralded a new age in international environmental politics. To probe exactly how Agenda 21 views the ecological implications of material acquisition in the advanced nations it is instructive to focus attention specifically on Chapter 4 of the report entitled "Changing Consumption Patterns".

Cast in deliberate and measured diplomatic language, Agenda 21 conveys an acute awareness that consumption practices in the advanced nations are in need of substantial modification if we are to achieve marked environmental improvement. While Northern consumption is clearly problematic, the report tries to balance this indictment by observing that the real danger lies in the efforts of developing countries to emulate the damaging and wasteful lifestyles of the affluent nations.

Agenda 21 is sparse on specific recommendations on how to encourage less environmentally-destructive consumption, focusing only in general terms on the importance of enhancing the quality of product information available to consumers and the use of economic instruments to improve price signals.[2] With respect to consumer information the report contends that

[g]overnments, in cooperation with industry and other relevant groups, should encourage expansion of environmental labelling and other environmentally related product information programmes designed to assist consumers to make informed choices (UNCED 1992, §4.21).

Agenda 21 recognises however that providing consumers with more comprehensive information is not in itself likely to have an appreciable effect. Such initiatives should also entail programmes to elevate the public's environmental consciousness and to educate consumers about the consequences of their product choices. Such a three-pronged approach can "encourage demand for environmentally sound products and use of products" (UNCED 1992, §4.22).

The careful reader invariably comes away with the impression that Agenda 21 is moving in this consumption-oriented direction with great trepidation due to the political and economic conflicts engendered by such a critique. The report also conveys a palpable awareness of the complexity of consumption as an intellectual issue.

[G]rowing recognition of the importance of addressing consumption has also not yet been matched by an understanding of its implications ... [we need to] develop a better understanding of the role of consumption and

---

[2]Interestingly, the Conference Secretariat was of the opinion that — despite the poor knowledge base on which to base policy decisions — significant progress toward more sustainable consumption could be achieved without allocating significant resources to the endeavour (UNCED 1992 §4.14).

how to bring about more sustainable consumption patterns (UNCED 1992, §4.6 and 4.7).

Despite acknowledging the existence of critical knowledge gaps, consumption is still viewed as an economic activity that can be adjusted through the application of top-down modifications in market mechanisms. It is largely our understanding of how consumers respond to different informational campaigns and price adjustments that requires improvement. Noteworthy is the observation that Agenda 21 displays no awareness that consumption practices are shaped by social and cultural influences as much as they are by economic signals.

6. Joint Statement by The Royal Society and the National Academy of Sciences

Let us now turn our attention to the highly unusual June 1997 joint statement by the Councils of the Royal Society of London and the United States National Academy of Sciences entitled *Towards Sustainable Consumption*.[3] Although an announcement from two distinguished academic institutions obviously does not carry the same significance as official statements by international policymaking bodies, it is instructive to draw attention to this document because it points to directions in which this emergent discourse is likely to move during the next few years.

The Royal Society-National Academy of Sciences communication conveys the interest of the scientific community in bringing its skills to bear "to expedite the transition to a sustainable, desirable life for the world's people in the coming century" (RS-NAS 1997). The essential thrust of this statement is on the explicit ways in which scientific and technological knowledge can be employed to improve current understanding of the impacts of human behaviour on ecological systems. Nonetheless, this resolution is notable for its recognition that "consumption patterns of the richer countries may have to change; and for global patterns of consumption to be sustainable, they must change." Furthermore, this statement suggests "societies need to examine their values and consider how goals can be met with the least damaging consumption" (RS-NAS 1997).

To assist this process of adjustment the scientists claim that we need to develop "a better understanding of human consumption and related behaviours and technologies." They write that

> [s]cientists can help to understand the causes and dynamics of consumptive behaviour. They can also develop indicators that track environmental impacts and link them to consumption activities, build understanding of how environmental and social systems respond to stress, and analyse the effectiveness of different strategies for making and implementing policy choices in the presence of uncertainty (RS-NAS 1997).

---

[3]In a related vein, see Stern *et al.*, 1997 and Heap and Kent 2000.

The two scientific societies are taking the lead on behalf of the InterAcademy Panel on International Issues, an informal organisation of the world's national scientific associations that is planning to take up the issue of consumption in earnest in the future.

To appreciate the full significance of this statement it is useful to examine it in the longer historical context that we have thus far been developing in this chapter. The document represents an important shift not only because august scientific bodies are now suggesting that modern societies need to take a reflexive look at their values and how they achieve their aspirations. This resolution is also significant because it represents a change of worldview for the scientific community. Official science, as embodied in professional associations and other expert bodies, has argued for the past 25 years, that global environmental problems stem largely from high rates of population growth. This assessment has led policymakers to place chief responsibility for these dilemmas on the doorstep of developing countries and to impose upon them the burden for adjustment. To defuse this "demographic time-bomb" industrialised countries have promoted a diverse package of interventions predicated upon technology (e.g., contraception) and social programmes. This particular characterisation has been a powerful force in enabling the affluent nations to divert attention from the environmental destructiveness of their own lifestyles.

Despite some decline in the authority of science among members of the lay public, the state continues to derive tremendous legitimacy from this body of knowledge; at the same time, science gains authority from this relationship because of the authority the state confers upon it. If the view depicted in *Towards Sustainable Consumption* is maintained it will become increasingly difficult for the world's most highly developed countries to avoid painful decisions requiring curbs on material consumption.

7. UK Consultation Paper: *Sustainable Development — Opportunities for Change*

To gauge more recent developments taking place at the confluence between consumption and the environment it is instructive to look at the UK government's February 1998 consultation paper entitled *Sustainable Development: Opportunities for Change*. This document enables us to gain some insight into how sustainable consumption has taken root within the political context of a particular country. Most of the note perpetuates what has become conventional thinking in environmental-policy circles around sustainable development. It views progress to promote more sustainable consumption as a challenge for producers in that they should aim to design more energy- and resource-efficient technologies.

This consultation paper however devotes a considerable amount of attention to the role of consumers. The document contains passages stating that

> [t]o promote ... more sustainable production and consumption we need to stimulate and support those influences which encourage producers to provide better goods and services while using resources more efficiently ... Consumers can have a huge impact on sustainable development through their influence as purchasers (DETR 1998).

This statement indicates that the policy discourse that has been promoted in European councils has begun to filter down to the national level. However, as was the case in the EC Programme, the role of consumers is seen as being largely instrumental and one that places pressure on producers to modify their recalcitrant ways.

We can derive from this consultation paper two valuable insights into how the policy discourse around consumption and the environment is likely to develop in the future.

First, the paper provides the first time in our survey that we come across the term "sustainable production and consumption."[4] "Sustainable production" has become familiar enough and is embedded in recent interest in industrial ecology and various environmental-improvement strategies targeted toward business managers (see, for example, Schmidheiny 1992; Welford and Gouldson 1993). Such an emphasis is not surprising given the dominant view that environmental problems arise principally from the production sphere. Moreover, changes in process technologies, product standards, and managerial regimes are relatively uncontroversial politically, especially when they can be expressed in terms of 'win-win' scenarios.

The much less familiar idea of "sustainable consumption" is more innovative and deserves further elaboration. Sustainable consumption, as it has been used in the academic literature in recent years, encourages consumers to conceive of products not as material objects, but as providers of services. In other words, people should no longer envision an automobile as a tangible item with intrinsic personal value, but rather as an artefact designed to provide mobility (Jackson 1996; Weizsäcker et al., 1997). Under such circumstances, to continue the example, a driver would pick up a car at a nearby parking facility and drop it off at the end of the journey — much like municipal bicycles are presently managed in some northern European cities. The driver would obtain another vehicle the next time (perhaps even later the same day) she needed to make a trip by automobile. The use of this terminology hints that policymakers in the UK are beginning to move away from purely productionist moorings and to develop a more sophisticated conceptual model of the connections between material consumption and the environment.

Second, this consultation paper contains the suggestion that ever-increasing volumes of consumption may not be consistent with conventional notions of the good life. The report remarks "[a] higher quality of life may be achieved with fewer but higher quality, more long lasting or satisfying products" (DETR 1998). Unfortunately, the document does not explain how this objective can be harmonised with an overarching posture of promoting the "maintenance of high and stable levels of economic growth" (DETR 1998). Presumably, in the absence of substantial restructuring, reductions of total material throughput would have to impact negatively on the prospects for continual economic expansion.[5]

---

[4]My investigations trace the origins of this term to a January 1994 workshop in Stockholm organised by the Nordic Council of Ministers. See Nordic Council of Ministers, 1995 and Norwegian Ministry of Environment, 1994.

[5]Presumably, a country could only reduce its material through-put without cutting into economic growth by stemming its purchase of imported goods and services, while strictly maintaining its purchases of locally-produced goods. Such an approach suggests that consumers would be able to distinguish carefully between indigenous and foreign items and only curtail their consumption of the latter. Moreover, the document provides no suggestion that sustainable consumption would require more fundamental changes in contemporary processes of material acquisition, say, by reducing the overall volume of goods and services purchased.

8. The Role of the Organisation for Economic Cooperation and Development

Although it does not have power to actually implement policy, the Paris-based Organisation for Economic Cooperation and Development (OECD) serves important facilitating and co-ordinating functions for the world's wealthiest nations.[6] In the wake of the UNCED Summit, the OECD established a working group on sustainable consumption and production. Much of the organisation's work to date on this broad topic has concentrated on the production side of the equation. However, the OECD has begun more recently to inquire into the "factors that determine consumption patterns and levels, including welfare and lifestyle considerations" (see, in particular, OECD 1997a, 1998a, 1998b, 1999). In an effort to establish the rationale for addressing consumption explicitly a recent OECD report notes

> [Our] Work Programme focuses on *consumption issues and demand-side management*, seeking to identify measures to address the wider economic system and the problems caused by millions of individual consumer decisions ... [I]t reflects a shift away from a purely supply-side perspective, the traditional focus of environmental policy. It permits a more comprehensive view of the economy as a "system" causing environmental stress and provides the means to take a systems view of both the micro-economic influences on firms and households, as well as the macro-economic influences on the economy (italics in original) (OECD 1997:8).

As part of this programme of work the OECD is seeking to develop its

> [u]nderstanding of both the driving forces behind specific consumption patterns, and the implications of using different policy instruments to try to change them ... [s]tudies by the OECD and other institutions agree that, in many areas, innovative approaches to modifying consumer behaviour — particularly those which involve community and private sector stakeholders — can have positive environment, social and economic impacts (OECD 1997).

Personal transport is a specific area of consumption that has drawn the attention of the OECD. The organisation's work is generating insights that move the policy discourse beyond customary perspectives of consumer information and fiscal instruments. A recent summary report notes that "[e]vidence from the social sciences (e.g., anthropology, geography, psychology, sociology, etc.) indicates that many of the approaches typically used in transport policy development and evaluation are inadequate to deal with the complexity of

[6]The OECD includes a number of countries not typically considered to be part of the world's economic elite, namely Greece, Ireland, Portugal, Spain, Turkey, Mexico, the Czech Republic, Hungary, Poland, and the Republic of Korea.

the problem". Accordingly, the OECD has begun to draw more extensively on such expertise. This new orientation has led to recommendations that favour "mobility" (rather than
transport) and that recognise the value of experimental initiatives involving, for example,
car-sharing.

However, the organisation is quite clear about the overarching framework within which
this initiative will be pursued. Though the OECD observes that member-countries
currently have "unsustainable consumption patterns," it does not intend to promote "*de
facto* an agenda for reducing consumption in general." The working group is not blind to
the complexity of this particular problem definition and they set themselves an ambitious
agenda that emphasises

> the need for better knowledge of present consumption patterns; the chal-
> lenges remaining to define a framework and set of goals for government to
> address consumption patterns as a coherent issue; the opportunities to influ-
> ence lifestyles and consumption through practical, value-neutral measures;
> the importance of influencing the broader network of actors and institutions
> which shape individual consumption patterns; government measures to
> empower the individual consumer to make positive changes; and the need
> for the underlying macro-economic framework to encourage rather than
> obstruct progress towards more sustainable consumption and production
> patterns (OECD 1997).

9. Discussion and Conclusions

This survey of environmental-policy documents suggests that the discourse on consumption has gone through a sharp transformation during the past three decades, with the most
dramatic changes coming about since the 1992 UNCED Summit. A recent OECD report
acknowledges this conversion.

> [T]here have been important shifts in thinking in both OECD and non-
> member countries, which have reduced geopolitical tension that has
> emanated from the *consumption versus population* debates of the preceding
> two decades. In the OECD, a growing number of countries have [sic]
> acknowledged that rethinking ways in which environmental resources are
> utilised to meet human needs is both a moral obligation and in their enlight-
> ened self-interest (italics in original) (OECD 1997:41).

During the 1970s, the dominant view attributed global environmental problems to
uncontrolled population growth in developing countries and extrapolated the impacts of
demographic trends onto the availability of natural resources. Policymakers in the affluent
nations devoted some attention to the so-called design flaws of modern industrial societies,
but managed to suppress more substantive critiques of their consumption practices. Such
framing had the effect of displacing responsibility for change onto the production sphere
and developing countries. While this perspective did not exculpate advanced nations from

total engagement, it did provide them with the rhetorical means to avoid some very tricky political decisions. Western Europe, North America and Japan exported development aid abroad and created national regulatory regimes to control their most obnoxious forms of pollution.

Clearly a joint-statement from two esteemed scientific associations, a UK government consultation paper, and a work programme within a secondary policymaking organisation do not have the same significance as official pronouncements by individual nation-states and tangible accomplishments on the ground.[7] Nonetheless, there can be little question that within policy circles the discourse concerning the relationship between consumption and the environment is rapidly evolving. Influential organisations are now beginning to fix responsibility for global environmental problems on the provisioning practices of affluent consumers — a population that encompasses residents of both developed and developing nations.

From the standpoint of achieving environmental improvements the current emphasis on informational campaigns and fiscal instruments is unlikely to promote unambiguous movement toward "sustainability." The popularity of policy programmes predicated upon consumer-driven reform derives from the fact that such approaches enable the state to avoid confronting the essential contradictions between stewardship and economic growth. The consumer model most prevalent among influential policymakers is based on a dubious characterisation of human behaviour that assumes it is principally a lack of authoritative information and appropriate price signals that are preventing people from acting on what are otherwise strong personal commitments with respect to the environment. To its credit the OECD appears to realise that the modification of contemporary consumption is more complex than its constituent national governments would like to believe. The organisation confesses

> Although using economic instruments to ensure that prices of goods and services consumed fully reflect their true environmental costs remains fundamental to changing consumption patterns, price is only one variable influencing those patterns, and in some cases may not be the most important (OECD 1997:50).

In part because of allegations of "state failure" in the environmental arena, governments have been under considerable pressure to delegate their policy responsibilities to other actors (e.g., industry, non-governmental organisations) (see, for example, Jänicke 1990). Environmental certification and eco-taxation schemes make it possible for the state to discharge itself from some very intractable situations and these subtle moves are becoming

---

[7]A large gap exists between policy documents of the sort described above and actual strategic interventions. Progress moving toward greater "sustainability" has to date been, by virtually any meaningful measure, quite limited. There are serious reasons to question whether existing institutional forms are adequate for such an arduous process of transforming the physical and mental architecture of (post)modernity. Accordingly, we must view the activities of international advisory commissions, transnational policymaking bodies, and scientific societies with care. The extent to which more sustainable lifestyles are actually achievable is still very much an open question.

increasingly common across a wide range of policy domains. In the current case, we see consumers inheriting the regulatory responsibilities that the state has cast off. It is not at all clear that the public cares enough about protecting ecological integrity, or that individuals left to their own devices will make environmentally appropriate consumption decisions. Sociologist Peter Dickens (1996) argues persuasively that the key institutional features of modern society (industrialism, capitalism and science) have undermined lay and tacit forms of knowledge, leaving people alienated and without the capacity to relate to the environment.

The inadequacies of using consumers, rather than the state, as change agents to force the production sphere to act with greater environmental responsibly are apparently becoming evident. The UK government's consultation paper observes

> [Consumers] need help to make choices. Existing consumer information could be improved: voluntary "green claims" are not always trusted, while official schemes, such as the European eco-label, have sometimes been slow to have an impact. In the short term, efforts may need to focus on simpler, standardised information on key products and key issues, such as energy consumption. Labelling and information schemes also need to be supported by improved general awareness levels and consumer education (DETR 1998).

We thus see that environmental-certification schemes, even at this early stage of their implementation, may not be the panacea that the state is seeking and will require supplementation from other sources. In the meantime, governments are likely to have a more difficult time than they presently anticipate absolving themselves of these stubborn — and perhaps irreconcilable — dilemmas.

The implementation of more aggressive proposals, especially interventions that might endanger economic-growth mechanisms, are difficult to envision.[8] In the absence of confirmation in future statements, the suggestion in the UK government's consultation paper that the road to personal satisfaction might be paved with less consumption must be viewed sceptically and as not representative of a more committed policy position.[9] Outside

---

[8]This is notwithstanding the seemingly tentative steps contained in the DETR consultation paper. The experience of ex-US President Jimmy Carter is burned on the political consciousness not only in the United States but in other countries as well. In 1979, Carter gave a nationally-televised speech in which he encouraged the American public to practice restraint. He said,

> In a nation that was proud of hard work, strong families, close-knit communities, and our faith in God, too many of us now worship self-indulgence and consumption. Human identity is no longer defined by what one does but by what one owns ... [O]wning things and consuming things does not satisfy our longing for meaning. We have learned that piling up material goods cannot fill the emptiness of lives which have no confidence or purpose. Quoted in Shi (1985:270–272).

[9]There would thus appear to be a growing recognition, at least in some public policy circles, of the need to shift affluent societies onto a footing in which they were no longer singularly focused on maximising consumption. This need for a notion of self-sufficiency is also a theme of growing importance in some social theoretical work with respect to the environment (see, for example, Gorz 1987), as well as among certain ecological economists (Princen 1997; Lintott 1998).

of the exigencies of war, few liberal democracies have been inclined to advance *overt* propositions to manage consumption (see Chapters 4 and 5 in this volume).

Nonetheless, we should not fail to realise that states have extensive experience in this area. National bank and treasury officials regulate consumption daily as part of the pursuit of macro-economic objectives such as managing inflation, unemployment, and foreign exchange. All modern governments have at their disposal the means both to stimulate and to suppress material acquisition, and during times of economic emergency have not been indisposed to relying on these tools. Additionally, it is useful to recall that sumptuary laws were, prior to the eighteenth century, frequently used to limit consumption — at least of certain segments of the population (see Hunt 1996). Present-day fiscal instruments, such as taxes on luxury goods, while promoted politically as a means of "penalising" wealthy individuals for certain forms of conspicuous consumption, essentially serve the same purpose. In a different vein, the state actively intervenes to regulate activities deemed to be social vices such as smoking and alcohol consumption, as well as access to other potentially harmful goods (e.g., guns, drugs). It is useful to keep these precedents in mind when the charge rings out that the liberal state has no legitimate grounds to interfere with personal consumption.

It is however unreasonable to expect the prevailing policy discourse around sustainable consumption to include in the foreseeable future unequivocal calls for restraint. If experience serves as an instructive guide, substantive interventions in the short and medium term will be thwarted by demands for further research into the environmental impacts of particular forms of consumer behaviour. Despite justifiable enthusiasm for life-cycle analysis and other modes of ecological auditing, "scientific" evaluation of the environmental impacts of individual consumption decisions is an extraordinarily complex enterprise and contemporary methodologies are insufficient for making unambiguous determinations. While the task might be relatively simple for some agricultural items originating from single, discrete locations, it becomes unwieldy for goods such as automobiles or computers that are built with components sourced from multiple sites and have intricate and rapidly shifting supply chains. Under circumstances characterised by a paucity of incontrovertible causal evidence it will prove difficult for even the most resolute policymaker to justify claims for more austere lifestyles.

At the same time, proponents of the emerging "sustainable consumption agenda" realise that social-science knowledge is important and indispensable. For instance, the OECD recognises that a major barrier to further progress in this domain stems from the fact that "it is difficult to piece together in a comprehensible framework all the influences which shape what and how societies consume" (OECD 1997:46). The extant situation provides a major opportunity for the social sciences to influence the way in which policymaking around sustainable consumption develops. Incisive understanding of the extent to which changes in prevalent patterns of material acquisition are practicable awaits the infusion of the more expansive understanding of consumption that has been developing over the past ten years within a number of individual social science disciplines (see, among others, Miller 1995; Slater 1997; Corrigan 1997). The situation is presently very fluid:

> A defining framework and set of goals has not yet been defined by governments to comprehensively address consumption issues and evaluate

potential policy responses ... [Governments can] improve their dialogue
with the public, by drawing on expertise from a wider range of disciplines
(particularly the non-economic social sciences) (OECD 1997:47, 50).

The very challenging task at present is to devise a means to synthesise the wide array of
new perspectives on consumption into a more unified and coherent paradigm. Furthermore, the social sciences' ability to contribute meaningfully to emergent modes of
environmental policymaking hinges on a dialectic process that can overcome the estrange-
ment that has existed between the two domains for much of the past two decades (Grove-
White 1996; see also Bauman 1987).

On one hand, policymakers will have to realise that social-science knowledge cannot
simply be distilled down to instrumental rules for scoring quick political points and maintaining social control. On the other hand, social scientists will need to lower the "guildish"
barriers that have been erected to protect their specific brands of esoteric expertise. Moreover, they will have to develop ways to communicate their abstract knowledge that are
both publicly accessible and sensitive to the requirements of particular locales.

References

Bauman, Z. (1987), *Legislators and Interpreters: On Modernity, Post-Modernity and Intellectuals.*
   Cambridge: Polity Press.
Corrigan, P. (1997), *The Sociology of Consumption.* London: Sage.
Dickens, P. (1996), *Reconstructing Nature: Alienation, Emancipation, and the Division of Labour.*
   London: Routledge.
European Commission. (1992), *Fifth Programme of Policy and Action in Relation to the Environ-
   ment and Sustainable Development.* Luxembourg: Office for Official Publications of the
   European Communities.
Gorz, A. (1987), *Ecology as Politics.* London: Pluto Press.
Grove-White, R. (1996), "Environmental knowledge and public policy needs: On humanising the
   research agenda." In S. Lash, B. Szerszynski & B. Wynne (eds) *Risk, Environment, and Moder-
   nity: Towards a New Ecology* (pp. 269–286). London: Sage.
Hajer, M. (1995), *The Politics of Environmental Discourse: Ecological Modernization and the
   Policy Process.* Oxford: Clarendon Press.
Heap, B., & Kent, J. (eds). (2000), *Towards Sustainable Consumption: A European Perspective.*
   London: The Royal Society.
Hunt, A. (1996), *Governance of the Consuming Passions: A History of Sumptuary Law.* Basing-
   stoke: Macmillan Press.
Jackson, T. (1996), *Material Concerns: Pollution, Profit, and Quality of Life.* London: Routledge.
Jänicke, M. (1990), *State Failure: The Importance of Politics in Industrial Society.* Cambridge:
   Polity Press.
Lintott, J. (1998), "Beyond the economics of more: The place of consumption in ecological
   economics." *Ecological Economics 25,* 239–248.
Meadows, D., Meadows, D., Randers, J., & Behrens, W. (1972), *The Limits to Growth: A Report for
   the Club of Rome's Project on the Predicament of Mankind.* New York: New American Library.
Miller, D. (ed.). (1995), *Acknowledging Consumption: A Review of New Studies.* London:
   Routledge.

Myers, N., & Simon, J. L. (1994), *Scarcity or Abundance: A Debate on the Environment.* New York: W. W. Norton.

Nordic Council of Ministers. (1995), *Sustainable Patterns of Consumption and Production: Reports from the Seminar on Instruments to Promote Sustainable Patterns of Consumption and Production.* Copenhagen: Nordic Council of Ministers.

Norwegian Ministry of Environment. (1994), *Report of the Symposium on Sustainable Consumption.* Oslo: Ministry of Environment.

Organisation for Economic Cooperation and Development. (1997), *Sustainable Consumption and Production.* Paris: OECD.

Organisation for Economic Cooperation and Development. (1998a), *Sustainable Consumption and Production: Clarifying the Concepts.* Paris: OECD.

Organisation for Economic Cooperation and Development. (1998b), *Towards Sustainable Consumption Patterns: A Progress Report on Member Country Initiatives.* Paris: OECD.

Organisation for Economic Cooperation and Development. (1999), *Education and Learning for Sustainable Consumption,* Working Paper, 7(43). Paris: OECD.

Princen, T. (1997), "Toward a theory of restraint." *Population and Environment 18* (3), 233–254.

Royal Society of London and the United States National Academy of Sciences. (1997), *Towards Sustainable Consumption.* London: The Royal Society.

Schmidheiny, S. (1993), *Changing Course: A Global Business Perspective on Development and the Environment.* Cambridge: MIT Press.

Shi, D. (1985), *The Simple Life: Plain Living and High Thinking in American Culture.* Oxford: Oxford University Press.

Slater, D. (1997), *Consumer Culture and Modernity.* Cambridge: Polity Press.

Stern, P., Dietz, T., Ruttan, V., Socolow, R., & Sweeney, J. (eds). (1997), *Environmentally Significant Consumption: Research Directions.* Washington, DC: National Academy Press.

UK Department of Environment, Transport, and the Regions. (1998), *Sustainable Development: Opportunities for Change* (Consultation Paper on a Revised UK Strategy). London: DETR.

United Nations Conference on Environment and Development. (1992), *Report of the United Nations Conference on Environment and Development.* New York: United Nations.

Weale, A. (1992), *The New Politics of Pollution.* Manchester: Manchester University Press.

Weizsäcker, E. von, Lovins, A., & Lovins, H. (1997), *Factor Four: Doubling Wealth, Halving Resource Use.* London: Earthscan.

Welford, R., & Gouldson, A. (1993), *Environmental Management and Business Strategy.* London: Pitman Publishing.

World Commission on Environment and Development. (1987), *Our Common Future.* Oxford: Oxford University Press.

Worster, D. (1985), *Nature's Economy: A History of Ecological Ideas,* 2nd ed. Cambridge: Cambridge University Press.

Chapter 3

From Production to Consumption: Environmental Policy in the European Union

Joseph Murphy

1. Introduction

In advanced industrial countries environmental policy has been an accepted part of public policy for well over one hundred years. Throughout this period a key area has been the regulation of production via emission-limit values and technology standards. However, particularly in Western Europe, a fundamental shift is underway. It is beginning to be accepted that no matter how strictly production is regulated important environmental problems will remain. This is particularly the case because many problems are closely related to consumption and lifestyles and do not result directly from dangerous or inefficient production processes. Consequently policymakers are starting to think about the regulation of consumption to achieve environmental goals. This chapter examines how the European Union (EU) is dealing with the issue.

The first two sections of this chapter describe the EU's approach to production and consumption-related environmental problems. The former involves, for example, dealing with aqueous emissions from production processes, whereas the latter includes such things as solid waste resulting from the disposal of end-of-life consumer goods. In each case I discuss policy documents and specific regulations and directives. These sections show that since the early 1990s production-focused environmental policy has been justified by the argument that public policy can be used to drive innovation and technological change and that if this is done effectively it will simultaneously produce improved environmental performance and more efficient production processes. However, evidence suggests that the EU has found it difficult to develop legislation that actually builds on this argument. With respect to consumption-related environmental problems I show that the EU is in the process of extending the approach it takes to production. Consumption-related environmental problems are being understood as technical problems, largely related to products, which can be solved in a way that will bring economic gains for all concerned.

To explain the EU's approach to production and consumption-related environmental problems the third and fourth sections of this chapter describe various ideas and concepts from environmental social science. In section three I introduce and develop ecological modernisation theory. The discussion shows that the European Commission began to promote the ecological modernisation of production in the early 1990s, but the current

Exploring Sustainable Consumption: Environmental Policy and the Social Sciences, Volume 1, pages 39–58.
Copyright © 2001 by Elsevier Science Ltd.
All rights of reproduction in any form reserved.
ISBN: 0-08-043920-9

approach to consumption is not consistent with widely understood notions of ecological modernisation. In the fourth section I examine actual policy outputs using a structural-institutional approach to environmental policy analysis (Jänicke 1992; Jänicke 1997) and a discourse analysis approach (Hajer 1995; Hajer 1996). Taking the case of the European Union as one example, the conclusion considers how public-policymaking institutions more generally are likely to engage with consumption-related environmental problems in the short to medium-term.

2. The European Union, Environmental Policy and the Regulation of Production

Industrial-environmental policy has evolved through at least three phases, although dates vary in different countries and with respect to distinct environmental media (see Andersen 1994:17–24). In its first phase policymakers encouraged, or at least permitted, the dispersal of pollution. A common response by industry was the construction of tall chimneys or long out-fall pipes at sea. The second phase was associated with an emphasis on the control of pollution rather than its dispersal. On the whole the implementation of legislation in this phase resulted in the installation of so-called "end-of-pipe" or "control" technologies, such as waste water treatment plants and flue-gas scrubbers. In both phases influential industry groupings argued that protecting the environment was financially costly and could compromise economic competitiveness, particularly at the international level, if firms based in other countries were not subject to the same requirements. However, at least in the case of the European Union, it is clear that in the late 1980s and early 1990s industrial-environmental policy began to move into a third phase. Evidence of this can be found in various policy documents, directives and regulations.

The most important European environmental policy document of the 1990s was the Fifth Environmental Action Programme *Towards Sustainability* (Fifth EAP) (CEC 1993a). This report was prepared by the Environment Directorate of the European Commission and adopted by the Council of Ministers in February 1993.[1] The Fifth EAP attempted to provide guidance to all actors in the EU on issues of the environment and manufacturing industry was one of five economic sectors discussed in detail.[2] In this area the document attempted to outline a new relationship between production, public policy, environment and competitiveness. It argued that industry could be part of the solution to environmental problems and that economic development and environmental protection need not be mutually antagonistic. Instead, the Fifth EAP argued, effective environmental policy may benefit the private sector and could be viewed as an opportunity.

To realise this opportunity the Fifth EAP suggested that policymakers should work constructively with industry and that environmental policy should aim to improve the

---

[1]Three institutions dominate policymaking in the European Union. The Council of Ministers is composed of relevant ministers from the member states. The European Parliament is the directly-elected assembly comprised of Members of the European Parliament (MEPs). The European Commission is the EU's civil service.

[2]The other areas covered were energy, transport, agriculture and tourism.

management and control of production processes. The minimisation of waste should be the primary concern rather than simply the control of harmful emissions. The Fifth EAP also argued that demanding environmental standards could be used to stimulate innovation. This in turn would enhance competitiveness provided that waste minimisation (efficiency improvement) was the way in which environmental problems were addressed. The following passage from the Fifth EAP illustrates the point:

> ... there has been a tendency to view industrialization or economic development and environmental concern as being mutually hostile ... [However] on the question of international competitiveness, the perceived conflict between environmental protection and economic competitiveness stems from a narrow view of the sources of prosperity and a static view of competition. Rather than reduce competitive advantage, stringent environmental requirements can actually enhance it by triggering upgrading and innovation. Those countries which have the most rigorous requirements mostly lead in exports of the affected products and technologies. (Chapter 4 Section 4.1)

The Fifth EAP also argued that if environmental policy was going to enhance competitiveness it would have to be more sophisticated, focusing on processes rather than emissions and making use of a variety of instruments, not just standard command-and-control approaches.[3]

In the early 1990s similar ideas were also being discussed in mainstream economic policy documents such as the EU's White Paper on *Growth, Competitiveness, Employment: The Challenges and Ways Forward into the 21st Century* (The White Paper) (CEC 1993b) (Gouldson and Murphy 1996). The White Paper was developed by the European Commission to consider how the EU might stimulate economic growth and reduce unemployment. Chapter 10 of the White Paper, entitled "Thoughts on a New Development Model for the Community" offered an assessment of the links between environment and economy. The Chapter starts by identifying two problems, namely that the European Union was suffering from high unemployment (under-use of labour resources) and an overuse of environmental resources. The document uses this and related issues, such as the ongoing substitution of labour by capital, to call for a new development model:

> The new development model for the Community therefore has to address the inefficient use of available resources in a wide perspective, i.e., taking into consideration the overall quality of life of the citizen. (CEC 1993b:146–47)

According to the Commission:

---

[3]The term "command-and-control" is commonly used in environmental policy circles although in practice very little may actually be commanded. The reality of implementation is likely to involve negotiated compliance between the regulator and the regulated. As a result there is some risk that the term promotes a false view of the nature of regulation.

> A major element of the new development model will be to decouple future economic prosperity from environmental pollution and even to *make the economic-ecological relationship a positive instead of a negative one*. The key for doing this will ultimately lie in the creation of a new "clean technology" base. (Emphasis original) (CEC 1993b:147)

Concerning the economic implications of this novel approach the Commission was quite clear:

> This new clean technology is likely also to generate, apart from a substantially improved environment, considerable *secondary benefits* for the Community ... In competitiveness terms ... the Community would improve the overall strength of the economy through optimal use of its resources and the prevention of costly clean-up operations, while a first-mover advantage can be exploited; the latter element is not to be underestimated as the new technology is not only a necessity in the industrial world but also in the NICs and LDCs. (CEC 1993b:147)

This argument is very similar to that made in the Fifth EAP. And as was the case with the Fifth EAP, the White Paper saw a positive role for public policy:

> The decoupling of economic prosperity from environmental deterioration through the creation of a new clean technology base is unlikely to happen without ... active and imaginative policy support. (CEC 1993b:148)

A number of specific directives and regulations can be linked to this new policy agenda. Two examples of "active and imaginative policy support" are the Integrated Pollution Prevention and Control (IPPC) Directive and the Eco-Management and Audit Scheme (EMAS) Regulation.

The IPPC Directive was agreed in 1996 and is the best example of European command-and-control type legislation in a new style.[4] The objective of the directive is to prevent or minimise air, water and soil pollution by emissions from industrial installations. The emphasis in the Directive is on the management of industrial processes themselves rather than associated wastes or the receiving environment. The legislation is designed to avoid the movement of waste from one media to another, something that in the past has been associated with media-specific approaches to industrial-environmental legislation. It also encourages (but does not require) the creation of a single pollution inspectorate with sole responsibility for implementation of environmental regulations. The assumption is that various gains will be associated with such an institution in the form of less bureaucracy and cheaper costs associated with implementation (see Haigh & Irwin (1990) for influential arguments in this area).

---

[4]Council Directive 96/61/EC of 24 September 1996 concerning integrated pollution prevention and control.

For a variety of reasons, therefore, the IPPC Directive is quite innovative. However, in some key areas, it is not entirely consistent with the new approach to environmental policy that the Commission began promoting in the 1990s. During the negotiations that led to the IPPC Directive the most contentious issue was the extent to which the Directive would be used to implement European best available technology standards and to drive innovation and technological change. The European Parliament was keen to have a technology-forcing piece of legislation and Germany argued for this in the Council of Ministers. However, what emerged leaves specific technological requirements largely to the discretion of implementing institutions in member states. The IPPC directive focuses mainly on the procedures through which the regulating institutions should proceed. Competent bodies in member states are required to take into consideration best available technology guidance documents prepared at the European level, but it is left to their discretion whether or not they actually require these standards of the companies they are regulating. In this key area the IPPC Directive arguably fails to put into practice the approach to environmental policy outlined in broader strategy documents.

A second example of specific action that can be linked to the new approach to environmental policy is the European Eco-Management and Audit Scheme Regulation (1993).[5] With this piece of legislation the EU attempted to move away from traditional command-and-control approaches to industrial-environmental regulation. It establishes an EU-wide scheme that allows companies to register an independently-audited environmental-management system as long as it is producing continuous improvement in environmental performance and satisfies other requirements of the scheme. The EU justifies and encourages the adoption of EMAS in a variety of ways. It argues, for example, that improving management systems in companies alone will result in economic and environmental gains. It claims that some companies are increasingly interested in being proactive on environmental problems and a voluntary scheme such as EMAS allows them to demonstrate this strategic posture to a variety of stakeholders. Finally, voluntary self-regulation holds out the possibility of changing the relationship between the public and private sectors over the medium to long term. Arguably, therefore, EMAS is consistent with the broader approach to policy outlined in documents like the Fifth EAP. And, compared to the IPPC Directive, EMAS was a relatively uncontroversial piece of legislation.

3. The European Union, Environmental Policy and the Regulation of Consumption

The EU began to experiment with consumption-focused environmental legislation in the early 1990s as consumption-related environmental problems became more acute — particularly the growing mountain of domestic solid waste (see below).[6] However, by the

---

[5]Council Regulation (EEC) No 1836/93 of 29 June 1993 allowing voluntary participation by companies in the industrial sector in a Community eco-management and audit scheme.

[6]Like most governments the EU has a long history of attempting to manipulate consumption for macroeconomic reasons. However, manipulation of consumption for environmental reasons is a new departure. Even energy efficiency, which is a slightly older concern and which has environmental aspects, emerged largely for economic reasons.

mid-1990s it was clear that it was developing pieces of legislation in an ad hoc way, without a clear underlying framework or rationale. At this point the European Commission began to fund research projects with the aim of crafting a more coherent approach (for an early example see Oosterhuis *et al.*, 1996). In the late 1990s, a special report on the topic was commissioned from the Science and Policy Research Unit (SPRU) of the University of Sussex (SPRU 1998). SPRU has been particularly influential in establishing the broad approach to consumption-related environmental problems and in promoting the idea of Integrated Product Policy (IPP).

The SPRU report on IPP analyses recent product-policy developments at national and international levels with the aim of establishing the elements of a European policy in this area. For the purposes of the report IPP is defined as follows:

> Integrated product policy addresses the whole life-cycle of a product, thus avoiding shifting environmental problems from one medium to another, as opposed to specific product policy, which addresses one particular environmental effect. (SPRU 1998:1).

> ... [IPP is] public policy which explicitly aims to modify and improve the environmental performance of product systems. (SPRU 1998:9).

The report justifies the idea of IPP environmentally by claiming that the relative importance of consumption-related environmental problems has been rising over the past two decades. Obvious examples are the growth of domestic waste and local air-quality problems related to private automobile use.

The main conclusion of the report is the proposal that IPP can be created around five IPP building blocks. Each block should be composed of a cluster of policies with a common objective and, it is argued, IPP will be achieved by the "structured accumulation of measures" in each area over time. The five IPP building blocks are:

- Measures to reduce/manage waste generated by the consumption of products;
- Measures targeted at the innovation of more environmentally sound products;
- Measures to create markets for more environmentally sound products;
- Measures for transmitting information up and down the product chain;
- Measures which allocate responsibility for managing the environmental burdens of product systems.

One of the practical recommendations of the SPRU report was that the European Commission should hold a conference to launch a debate on IPP. Such a workshop was held at the beginning of December 1998, though very little was actually agreed about the content of IPP beyond its coverage of all product systems and environmental effects. Nonetheless, participants accepted that life-cycle analysis would be important (as already developed in association with the Eco-Labelling Regulation).

More recently, the Commission discussed the idea of IPP in its *Global Assessment* (CEC 1999) of the Fifth EAP. The period of implementation of the Fifth EAP ended in 2000 and the *Global Assessment* was designed to be a review of its achievements. It was also intended to launch a debate on the content of the Sixth Environmental Action Programme, which is likely to have a major impact on the direction of EU-environmental policy in the years ahead. The *Global Assessment* clearly links waste and consumption practices by focusing on products and states that IPP should be a key part of the Sixth Environmental Action Programme:

> The problems of waste in the EU are still growing faster, due to consumption patterns, than the implementation of measures to control and prevent them ... priority in the future will need to be given to promoting an active product policy in order to make products recyclable from their design phase as well as further preventing waste generation. (CEC 1999:11–12)

As mentioned above the EU had actually begun the ad hoc accumulation of measures in the area of consumption before the idea of Integrated Product Policy was fully developed. The eco-labelling scheme and the packaging-waste directive are two examples, although these are now being understood in the context of IPP.

The European Eco-labelling Scheme Regulation was agreed in 1992 and aims to promote the design, production, marketing and use of products that have a reduced environmental impact throughout their entire life cycle.[7] The main idea is that such an approach will be achieved by encouraging producers to redesign products and by providing consumers with better information about their environmental impacts. The scheme is voluntary, but producers can have their products assessed against specific criteria to establish whether or not they qualify for a European eco-label. The criteria are developed by national eco-labelling boards in close collaboration with industry. In theory the eco-label can be applied to most products and criteria currently exist for such things as washing machines, photocopy paper and mattresses.

The primary motivation for the eco-labelling scheme was the Commission's desire to harmonise the provision of environmental information on products throughout Europe. In each member state of the Union there currently exist a variety of environmental labels and theory suggests that this could compromise the operation of the single market. However, in practice the European eco-label has not been particularly successful. Companies in some sectors have shown little enthusiasm and whole sectors have effectively boycotted the scheme for a variety of reasons. At the same time, consumers show minimal awareness of the label itself and it is now accepted by the Commission that the European eco-label will not replace existing schemes at the national level (Nadäi 1999).

In 1994, the EU developed another piece of consumption-focused environmental legislation with the Packaging and Packaging Waste Directive (PPW Directive).[8] The origin of this Directive was the need to deal with the market-distorting implications of German domestic-packaging legislation. The objective of the PPW Directive is to harmonise national measures concerning the management of packaging and packaging

---

[7]Council Regulation (EEC) No 880/92 of 23 March 1992 on a Community eco-label award scheme (Official Journal L 99, 11.04.1992).
[8]Council Directive 94/63/EC of 15 December 1994 on packaging and packaging waste (Official Journal L 365, 31/12/1994).

waste. It covers all packaging placed on the market in the Community and all packaging waste, whether it is used or released at industrial, commercial, office, shop, service, household or any other level, regardless of the material used. It thus applies to intermediate, as well as end consumers. The PPW Directive requires member states to take measures to prevent the formation of packaging waste. For example, they must introduce systems for the return and/or collection of used packaging to attain specific targets. The Directive also lays down essential requirements as to composition, reuse, recovery and recycling of packaging. However, perhaps most important of all, the PPW Directive began to introduce the idea of extended producer responsibility into European environmental law establishing that key obligations in the Directive rest with the producers of packaging rather than consumers. Extended producer responsibility is central to more recent proposals for legislation on waste electrical and electronic equipment, and end-of-life vehicles.

4. The Ecological Modernisation of Production and Consumption in Europe

It is clear from the above that in the 1990s the EU began to endorse a new approach to environmental policy. This was developed first with respect to production-related environmental problems, but is now being explored as a way to deal with consumption-related issues. In this section I discuss ecological modernisation theory and use this perspective to analyse these recent developments. Ecological modernisation theory is useful because it critically analyses the relationship between environment and society in advanced industrial countries and, at the same time, allows prescriptions to be derived from it relatively easily. The theory has also been developed largely in the western European context and is therefore appropriate for this discussion.

The ecological modernisation debate began in the early 1980s (see Murphy 2000 for a history). Proponents of the theory have argued that environmental problems in advanced industrial societies are largely caused by wasteful and inefficient production processes, and, as a result, argue that new technologies will play a major role in dealing with them. Joseph Huber, for example, promoted superindustrialisation where "... the dirty and ugly industrial caterpillar will transform into a[n] ecological butterfly" (Huber 1985:20 as quoted in Mol 1995:37). More recently, Gouldson and Murphy have examined the nature of industrial innovation and technological change in more detail. They draw attention to the fact that changing management techniques may be as equally important to this evolutionary process as developing new technologies. They also argue that ecological modernisation in practice will involve the incremental improvement of existing approaches to production in combination with less frequent radical change. With respect to the *immediate* environmental impacts of industrial processes, they argue that innovations (technological and managerial) can result in environmental and economic gains simultaneously (Gouldson & Murphy 1998; Murphy & Gouldson 2000).

Arthur Mol (1995) has been responsible for establishing a broader vision of ecological modernisation. Based on research in the Dutch chemicals industry, Mol has demonstrated that ecological modernisation involves the transformation of the institutions of modernity via the integration of environmental priorities. According to Mol (1995:394)

> Economic institutions such as the commodity and labour markets, regulating institutions such as the state and even science and technology are redirected in the sense that they take on characteristics that cause them to diverge from their productivity-oriented predecessors ... Ecological modernization can thus be interpreted as the reflexive (institutional) reorganization of industrial society in its attempt to overcome the ecological crisis.

Consumption has received relatively little attention in the context of ecological-modernisation theory, but it is possible to establish what the ecological modernisation of consumption might involve. One obvious starting point is technological change. This might involve redesigning products based on life-cycle analysis of environmental impacts or more fundamental changes such as the promotion of tele-working (if this does in practice result in reduced environmental impacts). However, such technological changes on their own do not involve or require the integration of environmental concerns into consumption practices themselves. As a result, technological change may be a necessary part of the ecological modernisation of consumption, but there must be more involved.

Gert Spaargaren has done the most to develop a broader perspective on the ecological modernisation of consumption (see Spaargaren 1997, Chapters 5 and 6). Although he acknowledges that technology has a significant role to play, and he endorses Huber's maxim that "all roads *out of* the environmental crisis lead us further *into* the industrial society", he argues for a different approach. It is necessary, he claims, for consumption to be understood in its own terms and not as determined by technology and therefore by producers. To achieve this understanding he draws on the literature from a variety of social science disciplines. This analysis confirms that beyond a basic level consumption is no longer entirely (or even largely) explained by issues of material well-being and utility and that consumers are not simply duped by producers into consuming. Researchers aligned with the fields of cultural studies, sociology and anthropology have established that identity formation, status- seeking, group communication, and a variety of other contextual influences are central to understanding consumption practices (see for an overview Lury 1996; Corrigan 1997). Therefore, Spaargaren argues, the ecological modernisation of consumption must involve "... focus[ing] on the social processes that are hidden behind the changes in consumer behaviour" (Spaargaren 1997:169). The integration of environmental concerns into these social processes is therefore central to the ecological modernisation of consumption.

From a public-policy perspective this outline of the ecological modernisation of production and consumption raises the question of the extent to which it is possible to actively encourage such changes. In other words, what is the role of government in promoting and facilitating more sustainable consumption patterns? Although it is clear that many transformational processes are operating beyond government control, most authors have argued that governments and public policymakers are still central to ecological modernisation. Most of the existing work has focused on the relationship between governments and producers (see Weale 1992; Boehmer-Christiansen & Weidner 1995; Gouldson &

Murphy 1998).[9] I argue here that intervention is required to make sure that companies overcome the short-term barriers to innovation that prevent them from realising medium- to longer-term economic and environmental gains (Gouldson & Murphy 1998). In terms of actual policies, empirical work suggests that the integration of the environment into production will require the establishment of demanding medium- to long-term environmental targets and standards to encourage the invention, innovation and diffusion of new technologies. At the same time, a variety of policy instruments will need to be used — such as voluntary agreements and market-based approaches — to complement more traditional approaches to regulation. Overall, this is a reregulation rather than a deregulation agenda.

In comparison, very little work has considered the role of the state and public policy in the ecological modernisation of consumption. However, the essential approach that a policy programme must take can be derived from the above. Policies to encourage and require product-oriented techno-fixes will be part of any programme, but a much broader approach is necessary. To actually restructure consumption practices via the integration of environmental concerns public policy will have to recognise at least three issues: the role that consumption plays in identity formation; the relational characteristics of consumption practices; and the structural-infrastructural constraints on consumption. This definitional framing of the consumption and environment nexus suggests that instruments such as the provision of environmental information on product labels or the manipulation of prices may be involved, but that a much wider range of approaches are required. Influencing the context of consumption may involve changes to education curricula and public debate on the relationship between consumption and quality of life. More radically, and more problematic in the context of liberal democracy, action to control advertising messages could be necessary. However, regardless of the nature of specific actions, it is clear that a genuine attempt to encourage the integration of environmental concerns into consumption practices will place significant demands on the policy process.

This brief discussion of ecological modernisation theory provides some tools that can be used to assess the EU's approach to environmental policy. In the area of production-related environmental problems it is clear that in the early 1990s the EU began to endorse a programme of action that has much in common with the ideas discussed above. The Fifth EAP in particular reveals these connections. The analysis underpinning the document essentially argues that many environmental problems are linked to wasteful production processes. It also argues that this inefficiency represents an environmental, as well as an economic, opportunity. However, contrary to free-market ideas, the Fifth EAP does not accept that rational economic actors will necessarily exploit these opportunities. Instead the report claims that public policy is required to ensure that environmental targets are met and economic opportunities realised. This contention is essentially the same as the argument that underpins ecological modernisation theory in this area.

---

[9]This discussion will not consider the transformation of the institutions of government themselves, although this is important. Instead it will focus on the external actions institutions take in an attempt to transform production and consumption. Clearly, however, these are not unrelated and more effective, or at least better informed, external actions are likely to be related to greater success at integrating environmental issues internally.

With respect to more specific proposals and actual policy outputs, the Fifth EAP is careful to avoid endorsing old-style central planning. Instead, in common with the ecological modernisation debate, it argues for an innovative approach to public policy and the use of a variety of policy instruments. The EMAS Regulation establishing a voluntary scheme that companies can join at their discretion is an example of the EU actually putting this into practice. And, consistent with the theory of ecological modernisation, evidence suggests the management techniques involved will result in environmental and economic gains for those companies that register under the scheme. However, the IPPC Directive is not as convincing as a piece of environmental legislation consistent with the broader policy position. IPPC provided the EU with an opportunity to introduce a technology-forcing piece of legislation consistent with the position adopted in broader policy documents. Instead, the IPPC Directive that has emerged will at best result in the wider adoption of existing production technologies rather than the rapid development of new ones.

EU environmental policy in the area of consumption-related environmental problems can also be analysed using ecological modernisation theory. It is clear from the description of Integrated Product Policy that the EU is basing policy on the assumption that consumption-related environmental problems exist largely as a result of poorly designed products. Thus, strictly speaking, environmental problems are product-related rather than consumption-related and they are traced back to producers. On the basis of this narrower problem definition the specific actions that flow from the IPP framework aim to encourage the redesign of products and the consumption of products with less of an impact on the environment. In practice this involves extended producer responsibility, eco-labelling, differential pricing of products and so on. And, as an extension of the previous argument, the EU argues that this may simultaneously result in reduced production costs, cheaper products and environmental gains.

With the discussion of the ecological modernisation of consumption in mind, the EU appears to have adopted a very limited consumption and environment agenda. By exclusively focusing on products the EU is failing to engage with consumption itself and why people are consuming in particular ways. This raises some doubts about key policy principles such as extended-producer responsibility (EPP). EPP appears logical if the main problem is product design because it can be used to encourage producers to reconceptualise and refashion products so they have less of an impact on the environment. However, alternatives, such as combined responsibility or consumer responsibility, may actually be a better starting point if the aim is to achieve the integration of environmental considerations into consumption practices rather than simply encouraging technological changes to products. Related to this is the problem that where the EU is actually targeting the act of consumption all of its actions are focused on the immediate encounter between the individual and the product. Little attention is being directed toward interventions that might influence the context within which consumption takes place. The eco-labelling scheme is a good example. There is no evidence to suggest that the EU has engaged with the relational aspects of consumption or the structural-infrastructural influences on consumption practices.

5. Environmental Capacities and Discourses in the European Union

Using ecological modernisation theory as a framework the previous section critically assessed the EU's approach to production and consumption-related environmental problems. Particularly in the area of consumption this chapter has raised some doubts about the approach currently being adopted. However, the discussion so far has not attempted to actually account for the EU's approach to environmental policy. This section takes up this task using structural-institutional and discourse approaches to environmental-policy analysis.

The structural-institutional approach to policy analysis is common in environmental policy studies. This perspective emphasises the institutional and other structural influences on the policy process. Martin Jänicke has made several valuable and influential contributions in this tradition (see particularly Jänicke 1992 and 1997). He argues that in advanced industrial countries actors develop environmental-policy strategies while being influenced primarily by:

- the economic performance of the country/region concerned;
- the structure of the problem being addressed;
- the framework conditions including institutional, economic and informational factors;
- the short-term situative context.

Although it is not possible to develop a very detailed analysis here the structural-institutional approach does help to explain a number of the characteristics of environmental policy in the EU.

Considering the impact of economic performance on environmental policy in Europe draws attention to the economic imperative that explains the existence of the European Union.[10] From the 1950s onward, as described by Williams (1994:4):

> The powerful logic of capital accumulation ... exposed the critical need for economic reorganization [in Europe]. Production was becoming increasingly globalized and required the assemblage of capital and labour at the international scale. The logic of market access and scale economies also pointed to the need for transnational strategies in both sales and production.

Therefore, the *raison d'être* of the European Union is economic growth and international competitiveness, particularly with respect to the United States. Projects such as the creation of the European single market and the launch of the single currency are practical examples and failure to achieve economic growth places the whole European project in doubt.

Compared to economic growth, and despite its inclusion in recent European treaties, environmental protection is still a marginal issue in Europe. Arguably this is one of the

---

[10]The economic explanation for the existence of the EU is the most convincing, but the desire to promote cohesion in post-war Europe is also important and a political goal.

biggest influences on environmental policymaking. As Boehmer-Christiansen (1995:174) has argued:

> The overriding goals of the EU are economic growth and political integration, both are to be advanced by environmental regulation. Only when both promise to be satisfied, can an active and effective Community policy be expected.

Viewed in such terms, the European Commission's adoption of a new approach to environmental policy toward the end of the 1980s and into the 1990s is understandable. At this time, despite its main priority being economic growth, much of the EU was suffering from slow growth and structural unemployment as described in the White Paper on *Growth, Competitiveness and Employment*. Environmental policymaking under these conditions was difficult particularly given the prevailing assumption that addressing environmental problems was financially costly. In this situation an underpinning argument suggesting that environmental and economic priorities are compatible was arguably a necessary condition of environmental action.

From the EU's perspective waste is often the structure of the problem being addressed. Clearly waste is related to economic performance, but there are a variety of structural influences on the policy process that tend to ensure that environmental problems are understood in this way. First, when the unit of analysis is Europe it is likely that waste, rather than an alternative such as resource use, will emerge as the key policy problem. In most cases, developed economies use up the resources of other countries, but production and consumption wastes often have to be disposed of locally. The impact of the unit-of-analysis problem is clearly seen in European state-of-the-environment reports — for example *The Dobris Assessment* — that emphasise waste-related problems of various kinds (solid, liquid, gaseous) (EEA 1995). Second, as a result of the diminishing number of landfill sites, and opposition to building new incinerators, solid waste is particularly problematic for some powerful member states of the European Union. It is easy to imagine how domestic priorities are communicated and prioritised at the European level where waste is seen as a key structural environmental issue. Third, presenting environmental problems as related to waste is appealing to policymakers who typically have technical/ engineering or neo-classical economic backgrounds and emerges out of policy networks dominated by associated worldviews. Finally, engaging with environmental problems from a waste perspective reinforces a win-win type of argumentation because it is the wasteful nature of production in particular that creates the opportunity of realising environmental and economic gains simultaneously. Waste is therefore appealing to European environmental policymakers and not surprisingly dominates many policy documents and pieces of legislation.

The structural-institutional approach to policy analysis also establishes the need to understand specific outputs as influenced by framework conditions and situative context. The IPPC Directive, as described above, is a good example. I argued above that the IPPC Directive is not consistent with the broader position adopted in the Fifth EAP and other policy documents in the area of production-related environmental problems. This is particularly the case because of its failure to implement the idea of technology-forcing legislation, for example, via pan-European technology standards. However, this outcome is easily explained because some EU-member states did not accept the underpinning argument that supports technological change driven by public policy. Also, some countries were sceptical about the motivations behind its endorsement by countries such as Germany, fearing that they were attempting to establish foreign markets for environmental technologies developed at home. The UK was one of the dissenters and due to prior experience with integrated environmental legislation, and well-placed staff in the European Commission, it ensured that the IPPC Directive reflected an alternative approach to industrial environmental policy. In contrast the EMAS regulation is consistent with the ecological modernisation position, but the successful adoption of this instrument needs to be explained with care. Even those actors sceptical about the ecological modernisation argument could endorse this proposal because it involved establishing a voluntary scheme. In fact, those in favour of a deregulation agenda could view this as a positive step because it opened up the possibility of self-regulation by industry at some point in the future.

EU consumption-related environmental policy can also be explained by bearing in mind framework conditions and situative context, particularly the Integrated Product Policy approach. Here, there are two issues (1) the reduction of the scope of the consumption-environment debate to the design and purchase of environment-friendly products and (2) the approach being adopted within IPP, particularly extended-producer responsibility. The first of these points is also partly explained by the EU's commitment to growth. This makes questioning consumption, and more specifically increasing levels of consumption, difficult. Doing so would immediately be antagonistic to the central project of the EU and focusing on products rather than consumption is much less problematic. At the same time, like all institutions of government, questioning consumption is difficult because of the link between consumption, consumer sovereignty and ideas of freedom and liberty. And, more practically, because of its areas of competence, the EU actually has limited ability to develop a very expansive policy programme in the area of consumption. For example, the discussion above outlined the linkage between consumption and infrastructure, but the EU has very little power to influence planning decisions for physical facilities in member states. EU environmental impact assessment legislation does exist, but it would be difficult to address the affects of development projects on consumption practices through this mechanism.

With the focus on the design and purchase of more environment-friendly products, the actual approach being adopted is in part explained by the existence of policy networks dominated by two communities. The first community is composed of scientists and engineers and the second community is controlled by traditional neo-classical economists. People with scientific/engineering backgrounds tend to view environmental problems as technical issues that can be addressed with technical solutions. From this perspective, with an environmental concern such as waste, the obvious technical solution is to make production and consumption more efficient via new process technologies and products. Extended-producer responsibility appears to provide the most logical route to this objective, regardless of who is actually accountable for consumption-related environmental problems, because producers have the capacity to use their research and development expertise to develop new products. With respect to encouraging people to buy less environmentally damaging products, arguably the most influential group is economists who make certain assumptions about markets and consumers, which then influence the policy proposals they make. For example, it is assumed that consumers are autonomous rational economic agents motivated by personal welfare and that access to information is fundamental to the functioning of a market (refer to Chapter 5 of this volume).

The idea of IPP and its associated proposals can be explained largely in these terms. Like many parts of the European Commission the Environment Directorate is poorly staffed for the task it has to carry out. A small staff relies heavily on contracted work and seconded employees. When faced with an emerging issue, such as consumption-related environmental problems, the Environment Directorate will tend to turn to research organisations with which it is familiar for guidance. Sussex University's Science Policy Research Unit is a group that enjoys such a relationship and, as outlined above, has done much of the most influential work for the Commission in the IPP area. Without commenting on the quality of the effort, the long-standing relationship between the Commission and SPRU means that the Commission is sympathetic to the general approach that SPRU applies to problems. This approach typically involves a technical/engineering view of environmental problems that is underpinned by innovation and network theory. With respect to society, public-policy proposals from SPRU are commonly based on an analysis that is grounded in neo-classical economic assumptions. As a result SPRU's analysis of consumption-related environmental problems for the Commission was always likely to result in something similar to IPP. Extended-producer responsibility seeks to encourage innovation and technological change. Regarding consumers, SPRU recommends the provision of information and price signals to make sure the market functions correctly. The analysis in the area of consumers is particularly weak because it fails to take into account the identity formation and relational characteristics of consumption.

An alternative and less traditional approach to policy analysis involves focusing on the language of policy itself. The discourse-analysis approach for the study of environmental policy is particularly associated with the work of Maarten Hajer (1995, 1996) (but also see Hannigan (1995) and Dryzek (1997)). Hajer aims to explain environmental policy outcomes not by focusing on the reality of the problem or the structural influences like staffing and institutions, but by assessing the power of the arguments that underpin policy documents.

Hajer (1995:44) defines discourse as:

> ... a specific ensemble of ideas, concepts, and categorizations that are produced, reproduced, and transformed in a particular set of practices and through which meaning is given to physical and social realities.

In association with this perspective Hajer has argued that environmental policy is determined by the particular policy discourse that is dominant at a point in time. A hegemonic discourse is composed of specific "story-lines" that are attractive to a majority of actors who then form a "discourse coalition" in support of a specific approach. When a discourse is translated into institutional arrangements and policies "discourse institutionalisation" has been achieved. This approach can help to refine the understanding of EU environmental policy developed above.

From the late 1980s onward environmental policy debates in advanced industrial countries began to be influenced by a variety of new concepts and theories. Many of these novel
approaches made the same or similar points, but the most influential has probably been the
concept of *eco-efficiency*, introduced by the World Business Council for Sustainable
Development (WBCSD) as the private sector's contribution to the 1992 Earth Summit (see
Schmidheiny 1992; De Simone and Popoff 1997). WBCSD state that eco-efficiency

> Involves the delivery of competitively-priced goods and services that
> satisfy human needs and bring quality of life, while progressively reducing
> ecological impacts and resource intensity throughout the life cycle, to a
> level at least in line with the Earth's estimated carrying capacity (WBCSD
> web-site 20 April 2000).

Proponents of the concept argue that a company wanting to become more eco-efficient
should strive to reduce the material intensity of its goods and services, reduce the dispersion of any toxic materials, extend the durability of its products and so on. Case studies
show that a firm that follows such a programme will get an economic payback. Other
concepts making the same or similar claims are "Factor Four" and "Factor Ten" (von
Weizsäcker *et al.*, 1997), "industrial ecology" (Socolow *et al.*, 1997) and "the Porter
hypothesis" (Porter 1991; Porter and van der Linde 1995).

These ideas introduced new storylines into environmental debates from the late 1980s
onward. Taken as a whole they helped to create a new discourse that involved rethinking
the relationship between production, environmental problems and public policy. This in
turn allowed new discourse coalitions to form. Since the early 1990s, for example,
WBCSD has become a key coalition partner with the Organisation for Economic Cooperation and Development (OECD) in part because of the eco-efficiency concept. This is seen
in the OECD's adoption of eco-efficiency in the mid- to late- 1990s, at which point the
organisation arguably began a process of discourse institutionalisation (OECD 1998).

By the end of the 1990s to be considered a legitimate voice in environmental policymaking it was necessary to make use, at least to some extent, of the "win-win" type
language associated with all the concepts outlined above. As Hajer (1995) points out, the
new discourse involved more than just new arguments, it transformed the perception of
environmental problems for policymakers. It is clear that the EU, and particularly the
European Commission, has influenced and has been influenced by the creation of this new
environmental discourse. It is also clear that the new discourse was used initially in the
area of production-related environmental problems, but from the early 1990s onwards it
began to be applied to consumption-related problems as well.

The ready availability of the win-win eco-efficiency discourse therefore made it less
likely that a new approach to environmental policy would be developed around consumption itself. Instead, eco-efficiency has simply been extended. However, reflecting its
origins in supply-side debates, the eco-efficiency discourse has very few concepts within it
that can actually be used to underpin consumption-related environmental policy in any
significant way. Although it may indicate ways of integrating environmental concerns into
production practices it cannot suggest ways of integrating them into consumption practices. As a result the EU in this area is falling short of what would be consistent with an

ecological modernisation of consumption programme and policy appears to be somewhat simplistic.

6. Conclusion

This chapter has developed two arguments. In the first part of the discussion I introduced ecological modernisation theory and used this perspective to analyse the EU's approach to production and consumption-related environmental problems. In the area of production it was concluded that the EU appears to be endorsing a programme of ecological modernisation. Characteristic of this emphasis is the prominence of technological innovation, the view that environmental and economic gains may result from public policy interventions and the idea that businesses should integrate environmental concerns into their business practices. However, in the area of consumption the EU's approach is not consistent with ecological modernisation. EU policymakers have simply focused on products and extended the existing technology-focused strategy. The ecological modernisation of consumption as developed in this paper would involve much more than this, in particular public policy aimed at integrating environmental concerns into consumption practices.

The second part of this chapter sought to explain the EU's approach to environmental policy in these areas. At the broadest level, the EU has clearly been influenced by the emergence of a new environmental policy discourse at the international level. Ideas of eco-efficiency and "win-win" solutions to environmental problems have resulted in a new understanding of the role of environmental policy. However, the EU's current stance is not simply explained by discourse. A variety of structural and institutional influences on the policy process also help to explain recent policy outputs. Perhaps most important of all is the need to reconcile environmental protection with the EU's core project of economic growth. Other important influences are the tendency to view environmental problems from a waste perspective and for policy debates to be dominated by technologists and economists.

It is in the area of consumption that the EU's approach to environmental policy seems to be most compromised by these influences. Although consumption-related environmental problems are not solely the result of poorly designed products or poorly informed consumers, the EU seems unable to develop a more sophisticated approach. These ideas are production-oriented and provide little guidance in the area of consumption. A more promising policy agenda would involve thinking about the role that consumption plays in identity creation, the relational characteristics of consumption practices, and the structural/ infrastructural constraints on consumption that people experience everyday. However, developing environmental policy from this perspective would involve overcoming a variety of very significant influences on the policy process.

It is also worth reflecting upon some of the wider implications of this chapter. Many environmental policymakers and institutions are currently starting to think about consumption-related environmental problems and "sustainable consumption". The OECD and the United Nations Environment Programme (UNEP) both have groups working on the issue and it has been an ongoing theme in the United Nations Commission on Sustainable Development. Although the EU has a number of unique characteristics it also shares a number of common features with these secondary policymaking groups. The OECD, for example, has a tendency to prioritise economic growth over environmental protection. Environmental policymaking in all of these organisations is dominated by the engineering and economic worldviews. Not surprisingly, therefore, all of these institutions are endorsing product-focused strategies and technological solutions in the area of consumption. At the same time they are finding it difficult to engage with consumption on a broader and more thoughtful basis. Scholars interested in the politics of environmental policy can play a useful role in drawing attention to the inherently conservative nature of these policymaking processes. In this sense, the EU is simply a case study and other institutions are likely to show similar characteristics. For social scientists of consumption more generally, in disciplines that have in many cases distanced themselves from normative and prescriptive policy-relevant work, there is an opportunity to influence an emerging debate.

Acknowledgment

An earlier version of this paper was presented at a seminar organised by the Environmental Change Institute of Oxford University. I would like to thank everyone who offered thoughts and criticisms — particularly Tina Fawcett.

References

Andersen, M. (1994), *Governance by Green Taxes: Making Pollution Prevention Pay*. Manchester: Manchester University Press.

Business Council for Sustainable Development (BCSD). (1993), *First Workshop on Eco-Efficiency*. Antwerp, Business Council for Sustainable Development.

Boehmer-Christiansen, S., & Skea, J. (1991), *Acid Politics: Energy and Environmental Policies in Britain and Germany*. London: Belhaven.

Boehmer-Christiansen, S., & Weidner, H. (1995), *The Politics of Reducing Vehicle Emissions in Britain and Germany*. London: Pinter.

Commission of the European Communities (CEC). (1993a), *Towards Sustainability: A European Community Programme of Policy and Action in Relation to the Environment and Sustainable Development (also The Fifth EC Environmental Action Programme), OJ 1993 C 138/01*. Office for Official Publications of the European Communities, Luxembourg.

Commission of the European Communities (CEC). (1993b), *Growth, Competitiveness, Employment: The Challenges and Ways Forward into the 21st Century, Bulletin of the European Community, Supplement 6/93*. Office for Official Publications of the European Communities, Luxembourg.

Commission of the European Communities (CEC). (1999), Communication from the Commission: *Europe's Environment: What Directions for the future? The Global Assessment of the European Community Programme of Policy and Action in Relation to the Environment and Sustainable Development, 'Towards Sustainability' (COM (99) 543/6)*.

Corrigan, P. (1997), *The Sociology of Consumption*. London: Sage.

De Simone, L., & Popoff, F. (1997), *Eco-Efficiency: The Business of Sustainable Development*. Cambridge, MA: MIT Press.

Dryzek, J. (1997), *The Politics of the Earth: Environmental Discourses*. Oxford: Oxford University Press.

European Environment Agency (EEA). (1995), *Europe's Environment: The Dobris Assessment.* Copenhagen: European Environment Agency.

Gouldson, A., & Murphy, J. (1996), "Ecological modernization and the European Union." *Geoforum 27* (1), 11–27.

Gouldson, A., & Murphy J. (1998), *Regulatory Realities: The Implementation and Impact of Industrial Environmental Regulation.* London: Earthscan.

Graedel, T. (1997), "Industrial ecology: Definition and implementation." In R. Socolow, C. Andrews, F. Berkhout & V. Thomas (eds) *Industrial Ecology and Global Change* (pp. 23–41). Cambridge: Cambridge University Press.

Haigh, N., & Irwin, F. (1990), *Integrated Pollution Control in Europe and North America.* Washington, DC: The Conservation Foundation and the Institute for European Environmental Policy Analysis.

Hajer, M. (1995), *The Politics of Environmental Discourse: Ecological Modernisation and the Policy Process.* Oxford: Oxford University Press.

Hajer, M. (1996), "Ecological modernisation as cultural politics." In S. Lash, B. Szerszynski & B. Wynne (eds) *Risk, Environment and Modernity: Towards a New Ecology* (pp. 246–268). London: Sage Publications.

Hannigan, J. (1995), *Environmental Sociology: A Social Constructionist Perspective.* London: Routledge.

Huber, J. (1985), *Die Regenbogengesellschaft: Ökologie und Sozialpolitik* (The Rainbow Society: Ecology and Social Politics). Frankfurt am Main: Fisher Verlag.

Jänicke, M. (1985), *Preventive Environmental Policy as Ecological Modernisation and Structural Policy.* Discussion Paper IIUG dp 85-2, Internationales Institut Für Umwelt und Gesellschaft, Wissenschaftszentrum Berlin Für Sozialforschung (WZB).

Jänicke, M., Mönch, H., Ranneberg, T., & Simnois, U. (1988), *Economic Structure and Environmental Impact: Empirical Evidence on Thirty-One Countries in East and West.* Working Paper FS II 88-402, Internationales Institut Für Umwelt und Gesellschaft, Wissenschaftszentrum Berlin Für Sozialforschung (WZB).

Jänicke, M., Monch, H., Ranneburg, T., & Simonis, U. (1989). "Economic structure and environmental impacts: East-West comparisons." *The Environmentalist 9* (3).

Jänicke, M. (1992), "Conditions for environmental policy success: An international comparison." In M. Jachtenfuchs & M. Strübel (eds), *Environmental Policy in Europe: Assessment, Challenges and Perspectives* (pp. 71–97). Baden-Baden: Nomos Verlagsgesellschaft.

Jänicke, M. (1997), "The political system's capacity for environmental policy." In M. Jänicke & H. Weidner (eds) *National Environmental Policies: A Comparative Study of Capacity-Building* (pp. 1–24). Berlin: Springer.

Liefferink, D. (1996), *Environment and the Nation State.* Manchester: Manchester University Press.

Liefferink, D. (1997), "The Netherlands: A net exporter of environmental policy concepts." In M. Andersen & D. Liefferink (eds) *European Environmental Policy: The Pioneers* (pp. 210–245). Manchester: Manchester University Press.

Lury, C. (1996), *Consumer Culture.* Cambridge: Polity Press

Mol, A. (1995), *The Refinement of Production: Ecological Modernization Theory and the Chemical Industry.* The Hague: CIP-Data Koninklijke Bibliotheek.

Murphy, J. (2000), "Ecological modernisation." *Geoforum 31* (1), 1–8.

Murphy, J., & Gouldson, A. (2000), "Environmental policy and industrial innovation: Integrating environment and economy through ecological modernisation." *Geoforum 31* (1), 33–44.

Nadäi, A. (1999), "Conditions for the development of a product eco-label." *European Environment 9* (5), 202–211.

National Society for Clean Air and Environmental Protection (NSCA). (1993), *1993 Pollution Handbook*. Brighton: National Society for Clean Air and Environmental Protection.

Organization for Economic Cooperation and Development. (1998), *Eco-Efficiency*. Paris: OECD.

Oosterhuis, F., Rubik, F., & Scholl, G. (1996), *Product Policy in Europe: New Environmental Perspectives*. London: Kluwer Academic Publishers.

Porter, M. (1991), "America's green strategy." *Scientific American*, April, 264.

Porter, M., & van der Linde, C. (1995), "Green and competitive: Ending the stalemate." *Harvard Business Review 73* (5), 120–133.

Schmidheiny, S. (1992), *Changing Course: A Global Business Perspective on Environment and Development*. Cambridge, MA: MIT Press.

Socolow, R., Andrews, C., Berkhout, F., & Thomas, V. (1997), *Industrial Ecology and Global Change*. Cambridge: Cambridge University Press.

Spaargaren, G. (1997), *The Ecological Modernisation of Production and Consumption: Essays in Environmental Sociology*. Thesis Landbouw, University of Wageningen.

Science Policy Research Unit (SPRU). (1998), *Integrated Product Policy*. Report for DGXI of the European Commission. SPRU/Ernst and Young, University of Sussex.

Weale, A. (1992), *The New Politics of Pollution*. Manchester: Manchester University Press.

Williams, A. (1994), *The European Community, 2nd Ed*. Oxford: Blackwell.

World Business Council for Sustainable Development (WBCSD). (1999), *Sustainability through the Market: A Business-Based Approach to Sustainable Consumption and Production*. Background Paper #11, Prepared by the World Business Council for Sustainable Development for the Seventh Session of the Commission on Sustainable Development, 19–30 April 1999, New York.

Von Weizsäcker, E., Lovins, A., & Lovins, H. (1997), *Factor Four: Doubling Wealth, Halving Resource Use*. London: Earthscan.

Part III

Values, Ethics and Sustainable Consumption

Chapter 4

Liberal Neutrality and Consumption: The Dispute Over Fur

Markku Oksanen

1. Introduction

Once it was rather popular to declare, as a response to ecological problems, that those forms of behaviour responsible should simply be banned and regulated effectively. But such an authoritarian view is undeniably out-dated today (see Taylor 1996; De-Shalit 1997:83; cf. Westra 1998). One reason for this turn is that liberal thinking emphasises that, as far as possible, the state should remain neutral, or agnostic, with regard to people's preferences and their fulfilment. This is the case unless the actions of one person are harmful to another, in which case state intervention is appropriate. The same view is directly applicable to people's patterns of consumption.

The assumption is that the commodities people choose to consume must not be subjected to censure by the government. Consumers are free to choose (in the same way they are free to form their own conception of the good life). This liberty can be called consumer sovereignty, and its counterpart — the right to supply commodities and services — producer sovereignty. However, these freedoms can cause many problems. An individual commuting in a car may not cause harm, but when most people do, it brings about undesirable consequences. So what can be done if some people do not regard their modes of behaviour and patterns of consumption as ecologically unsustainable (contrary to the evidence exposed to them)? Or, even if people realise this, they still decline to change their behaviour. This raises the question of coercion again, providing that external interference with consumer or producer sovereignty is conceived of as a form of coercion.[1]

For a political system that emphasises the plurality of values and deems coercion something to be avoided if possible, it is quite inevitable, but not necessary, that people will have profound disagreements over appropriate forms of, and reasons for, coercive action. Consumption can be a target of moral criticism, but is there a place in liberal theory to

---

[1]Of course, it is difficult to find a general agreement on what precisely counts as coercion. Consumption is already regulated in various ways. If the law forbids me to use unleaded petrol, does it illegitimately restrict the scope of free choice? If the government merely levies a larger tax on leaded petrol, does it force me to choose the unleaded alternative, or is it just trying to persuade me to make more environmentally responsible choices? Should different kinds of environmental taxation policies be regarded as forms of coercion, or are they nothing more than a politically neutral setting where action takes place? The view on interference taken here is a very broad one. A deeper discussion of this issue lies beyond the scope of this chapter.

Exploring Sustainable Consumption: Environmental Policy and the Social Sciences, Volume 1, pages 61–78.
Copyright © 2001 by Elsevier Science Ltd.
All rights of reproduction in any form reserved.
ISBN: 0-08-043920-9

make a shift from mere moralising about certain modes of consumption to regulation by legal means? In the spirit of this problem Mark Sagoff (1988) asks, "Can environmentalists be liberals?" Following Sagoff's view I shall answer positively. It is not my aim, however, to present a case for liberalism (or animal rights), but simply to state that there is some compatibility between liberal principles and environmental protection and to show that this compatibility depends on our understanding of liberalism and environmental objectives. By doing so I shall show that an appeal to liberal neutrality cannot justify — in a sense of giving permission to — environmental degradation and cruelty to animals.

I shall consider whether it is up to consumers what kind of things can be consumed or whether the government can legitimately act to control supply and demand. Of particular interest here is work by John Rawls (1993) in *Political Liberalism*. As a case study I shall focus on the dispute over the moral rightness of fox farming and the right to consume fur-products. How should the conflict between pro- and anti-fur groups be understood? How can it be solved within the confines of liberal-democratic society and the market economy, or can it? However, unlike much of the criticism targeted at consumption, the thrust of the animal issue relates to the quality, not the quantity, of consumption. In other words, the problem is not excessive consumption, but that the form of consumption is wrong. For the defender of animal rights, there is no need to refer to statistical figures to establish immorality.

I begin by examining how the idea of neutrality has been defined in liberal political theory. In the third section, I focus on anthropocentric elements in liberalism, and then, in the fourth section, on what are the limits and conditions of formation of environmental ethics within liberal doctrines. The fifth section is an analysis of the case of fox farming and fur wearing and how to decide about controversial issues. In the end, I summarise the results of my discussion and briefly describe the applicability of it to other cases of disputed modes of consumption.

2. The Idea of Liberal Neutrality

In modern liberal-democratic societies one of the most heated on-going discussions focuses on environmental degradation and the treatment of non-human animals. The debate stems from questioning whether liberal society allows, or even encourages, modes of behaviour that actually should be outlawed because they threaten the physical basis of life. Consumption, in its relentless form, is often given as a manifestation of human arrogance and negligence of the natural world and as a form of organised cruelty to animals. As a solution many green thinkers have advocated what is known as "post-materialism" (Inglehart 1977; cf. Goodin 1992:55). In the same way, when we pay attention to our treatment of animals, the defenders of animal rights claim "the ultimate objective of the rights view is the total dissolution of the animal industry as we know it" (Regan 1988:348); this includes banning fur farming. But if consumers have a morally justified sovereignty regarding their consumption patterns, does this requirement then undermine the legitimacy of external interference in individual consumption? Such questions are topical and get at the issue of whether people can be compelled not to buy and use furs. Or, can people be enjoined to follow a vegetarian diet instead of a carnivorous one? Such requirements are not today considered categorically commanding and so do not receive full legal and political recognition. They are things that cannot be discussed within the bounds of liberal society. It may even be the case that these are challenges that should be answered mainly by individuals themselves. The reason for this assessment can be found in principles that are constitutive to the liberal society.

A paramount doctrine in liberal thinking is the idea of the neutral state (Dworkin 1978:127; Coglianese 1998:44), and one of the most important applications of this principle resides in the idea of consumer sovereignty. Advocates of liberalism who hold to this idea — libertarians and egalitarian liberals particularly (Raz 1988:110) — typically regard neutrality as the only possible understanding of the state that is compatible with the idea of individual autonomy. Although there is virtually no consensus on every detail of neutrality in practice, how neutrality should be defined, or even on whether this is the ideal term to capture the idea it stands for, there is an intuitive shared notion. This approximate consensus seems to suggest that the state should allow individuals to constitute their own plans of life. This includes a conception of the good life based on their values, wants and beliefs that they have a *prima facie* right to seek to realise (Rawls 1993:191–93; Dworkin 1978:127).

The idea of a neutral state can also be understood so that ideally the state exists to safeguard the individual's sphere of autonomous decision-making. The decisions made within this sphere are *prima facie* legitimate and final and therefore individuals can be authors of their own lives. In a liberal society, it is then up to individuals on their own to decide what religion to follow, what to wear, what form of transportation to use, and what to eat. Wissenburg (1998:7) has argued "liberal democracy is totally incompatible with attempts to dictate peoples' tastes and preference". However, alternatives are possible. John Rawls has called the ethical and political view that rejects the ideal of the neutral state perfectionism. According to perfectionism, following Rawls' definition, what the state should do is promote a certain view of the good life and discourage people from following other views (Rawls 1972:325). In recent discussions of political theory, perfectionism has usually been seen as a part of communitarian thinking (see Mulhall and Swift 1990; Baxter 1999).

Although liberals do not think that the state should give people a model of the good life, the state apparatus is not unnecessary. In fact, they are likely to endorse a perspective that is quite the opposite. In spite of different views on the legitimate tasks of the state among liberals, there is consensus at least on one thing, namely that the state is to protect the rights of individuals. Thus the power of government is limited (Raz 1988:107). The fundamental basis for legitimate external interference is found where a person's actions would violate the harm principle (the classical presentation of this view is Mill (1910:73)). As Joel Feinberg (1984:11) has put it, "the need to prevent harm is always an appropriate *reason* for coercion." But the harm principle is inaccurate and dependent on supplementary principles that specify how to solve a situation where interests are in conflict (Feinberg 1984:187). The state can thus be understood to have quite a large set of social responsibilities. These obligations may include the fostering of policies that help to maintain liberal society. For Rawls it is legitimate that the state promotes "the virtues of toleration and mutual trust, say by discouraging various kinds of religious and racial discrimination" (Rawls 1993:195; cf. Raz 1988:136; O'Neill 1998:92–6). In practice, therefore, the harm principle can be interpreted in numerous ways. Just consider the diversity of the responses of actual liberal-democratic societies and how they have defended themselves against those forces that aim to demolish them.

Individuals live in societies that are nation-states. A state has a public sphere, in which matters of common interest are decided. Nevertheless, it is inherent to the liberal society — especially if it has been as deeply divided by religious, philosophical and moral doctrines as Rawls (1993:1–2) assumes — that the members of society will be in constant debate about the limits of the public sphere. The purpose of these debates is to determine in which cases external interference into individual behaviour is legitimate and what form it will take. But still, despite all these controversies, in a pluralistic, liberal society, deeply conflicting philosophical, moral and religious beliefs and modes of behaviour can coexist. How this can happen is the puzzle that Rawls (1993) examines in *Political Liberalism*.

The key idea in Rawls' account is that in a liberal society there is a political consensus, or "overlapping consensus", and this consensus concerns "the basic structure of a constitutional democratic regime." Rawls claims that the consensus can be achieved without accepting any "comprehensive religious, philosophical, or moral doctrine" as a constitutional basis of a society. Because this kind of consensus does not extend to all aspects of human life, it allows individuals to follow their own personal inclinations. Accordingly, Rawls (1993:175) specifies that his theory of political liberalism is a presentation of "the main institutions of political and social life," not of "the whole of life". For him a comprehensive conception of justice also includes "nonpolitical values and virtues."[2] A society that has reached an overlapping consensus on constitutional essentials without expelling any reasonable view has thus reached a stable state of neutrality. At first sight it is easy to say that as far as the state does not try to suppress, say, any religious group or promote one at the cost of others, it acts impartially and sustains neutrality.

There are, nevertheless, many difficulties in formulating a consensus that would be truly neutral. I will discuss these problems in the remainder of this chapter. The first difficulty in Rawls' analysis is that the constitution is not wholly independent of people's actual beliefs, but it reflects them. The second issue is how to separate the political from the nonpolitical or social and to determine what precisely is the scope of overlapping consensus. A third problem, because of its vastness, lies beyond the scope of this chapter, but is enmeshed with the question of whether the neutral state is in itself a contested idea that requires a justification, and there might not be a consensus that it is a worthwhile goal (O'Neill 1998:27; Raz 1988:118). Concern about the environment and animal welfare seems in this respect to put liberal neutrality into a wholly new light. This is so because for some liberal thinkers (e.g., Wissenburg 1998:98) these matters, and their related requirements, are examples of a perfectionist attitude. By extension, they do not deserve full legal and political recognition, and may even be something that cannot be discussed within the bounds of liberal society. As we shall see in the next two sections, reasons for holding such views can be found both in the actual moral beliefs of liberal thinkers and in liberal

---

[2]Formally, Rawls (1993:15) defines overlapping consensus as follows: "Such a consensus consists of all the reasonable opposing religious, philosophical, and moral doctrines likely to persist over generations and to gain a sizeable body of adherents in a more or less just constitutional regime, a regime in which the criterion of justice is that political conception itself".

ideology itself. In other words, liberal theorists subscribe to anthropocentric ideas that are regarded by environmentalists and animal rights activists as the main cause of existing problems.

3. Anthropocentrism in Liberalism

In this section I shall describe liberal views of environmental ethics generally, and try to relate them to the Western tradition. The subsequent section is devoted to a more detailed study of them with particular attention being given to Rawls' views.

Fundamental liberal ideas conform to the larger anthropocentric tradition in Western philosophy.[3] This is so because liberalism has strongly emphasised the notion of human exceptionality and denied the idea that the natural world, or any non-human living being, in itself is intrinsically valuable. Consider a few examples. In his *Two Treatises of Government* John Locke (II §43) thought that the value of natural objects is primarily attributable to human labour, and there are many others who have followed this labour theory of value. Immanuel Kant (1996a:564) in turn said that we have direct duties merely to other persons, not to animals or inanimate objects. Moreover, Kant (1996b:84–5) made a sharp distinction between the concepts of worth (dignity) and price. He claimed that human beings, as moral persons, are to be regarded as bearers of dignity, whereas in regard to non-human beings the value standard is that of price or market value, which is related to human desires and inclinations. Generally speaking, with respect to the valuation of non-human things, modern-liberal thinking follows a robust subjectivism. This means the value of non-human entities is something that humans attribute to them. Moreover, it is something that humans may, and even should, do as individuals and not as a collective body. So "value is in the eyes of the beholder," and nature as such is devoid of value (Wissenburg 1998:97).

Consider also the idea of the social contract. It is hard to imagine contracts with animals or plants, since the making of a contract requires an explicit mutual recognition of each other's interests. (This is the standard view and both advocates and opponents of animals rights tend to subscribe to it although it has been questioned (see, for example Rowlands 1997) Therefore, Thomas Hobbes (1962:152) claimed that "to make covenants with brute beasts, is impossible" because, for instance, they do not recognise other beings' rights and "without mutual acceptation, there is no covenant." Others have followed Hobbes's route. For instance, John Rawls in his *Theory of Justice* (1972:512) says "it does not seem possible to extend the contract doctrine so as to include them [animals] in a natural way." In *Political Liberalism* Rawls (1993:246) is explicitly anthropocentric when he claims "the status of the natural world and our proper relation to it is not a constitutional essential or a basic question of justice" (see also Wissenburg

---

[3] This is the case particularly with respect to those forms of liberalism that do not rest on utilitarian thinking. For utilitarians from Jeremy Bentham to Peter Singer, the criterion of moral considerability has been sentience — those beings that are capable of feeling pleasure and pain have interests that matter morally. It seems plausible that there are sentient beings other than humans. Certainly, one may deny the moral considerability of animals by denying that they are sentient, but it is rather difficult to defend this position (see Singer 1990).

1998:102).[4] As we shall see in the next section, both the historical aspects — what liberal thinkers have actually said and what people have thought — and ideological commitments are merged in Rawls' account of the reasons for, and the implications of, the exclusion of non-human forms of life from the moral community.

The institutional status of different environmental goods has, of course, varied in time and place, and so have the norms of appropriate treatment. Considering privately-owned tracts of land, trees or animals, it is a personal matter, to a great extent, what people may do with them. The approximate meaning of ownership is that there are no restrictions in so far as the owner does not harm other people. Richard Routley (1973) has called this liberal conception of the human-nature relationship *human chauvinism*, describing the view that considers non-human nature as inferior to humanity and regards it primarily as something that can be dominated by humans to meet their needs and desires. Not questioning Routley's view wholly, there are, however, some difficulties when we focus on animals and the kind of restrictions we can place on their treatment. History is more blurred and generalisations are often half-truths at best. To assert that animals are not moral persons, and therefore can be treated in any way one pleases, is to present an untrue statement from the mainstream liberal point of view. Although we may not have direct duties to animals, concern for their well-being and condemnation of ruthless treatment can still be fully justified. Locke, Kant and Rawls, to mention a few, plainly disapproved of cruelty to animals, and from this we can derive the moral doubtfulness of fox farming. Why they did so, and how the requirements they present can be understood, I shall return to later on. For the time being let us conceive of liberal theory as anthropocentric.

4. Liberalism and the Possibility of an Environmental Ethic

The purpose of this section is to scrutinise more closely the relationship between liberal principles and the formation of an environmental ethic and to explain why liberal theorists are reluctant to expand the moral community to cover animals. Consider the following questions: if we deny the justifiability of anthropocentric-ethical theory, and replace it with some form of biocentrism,[5] are we also rejecting liberalism? In what sense can the defenders of animal rights be liberals? There seems to be a deep divide between these opposing views because most defenders of animal rights do not assume they are rejecting liberalism when they defend their view; their objective is somewhat different. What is of relevance here is to address why some liberal theorists have answered the first question

---

[4]History is, of course, not without exceptions. See, for example Nozick (1974:35–42). Although Regan (1988, see in particular p. 341) does not directly address larger political issues, he does not seem to be antagonistic to certain fundamental liberal ideas.

[5]In environmental ethics it is a commonplace to distinguish between different positions according to what are morally considerable beings. For my purposes here it is enough to make a rough distinction between anthropocentrism and biocentrism (non-anthropocentrism). Presumably, all kinds of non-anthropocentrists are critical of fox farming as far as it prevents foxes from living a satisfactory life. For a review of different positions in environmental ethics see Oksanen (1997).

positively, and claimed that animal rights, as realised throughout the whole of society, and liberalism, cannot go hand in hand.

Ethics and Human Reciprocity

Marcel Wissenburg (1998:65) has suggested that the most likely environmental ethic of liberal democracy is anthropocentric egalitarianism, the view that only human beings have moral standing and this is equal by its nature. One reason why liberals are reluctant to acknowledge the moral status of non-humans as full members of the moral community is embodied in Rawls' views on society and the constitution of public morality. He argued morality results from human reciprocity and it basically covers common affairs. As Simon Hailwood (1999:271) puts it, Rawls' liberal political theory is above all an "account of *political* morality, specifically justice, not of morality as such." Hailwood (1999:272) further states that the common understanding of Rawls' theory of justice, and this includes what Rawls explicitly says himself, is such that it can accept aims like species preservation and other forms of environmental protection on the basis of concern for human well-being, but to go beyond these limits of prudentiality would imply the adoption of an "attitude of natural religion" (Rawls 1993:245–6; cf. also Rawls 1972:267–8). In the case of Rawls, the rationale for this position stems from his understanding of society "as a fair system of social co-operation between free and equal persons viewed as fully co-operating members of society over a complete life" (Rawls 1993:9). This view is intuitively appealing and it is rather difficult to see how non-human animals can participate in the construction of such a thing as society that consists of abstract entities, such as institutions. To say this is to make, in the first place, an ontological statement on the existence of society, not an ethical statement on the appropriate treatment of excluded beings, but it seems to have some ethical implications.

It is clear that like any other form of government that is not fully arbitrary, a liberal democracy is explicitly constructed upon certain common values and commitments, and the content of political consensus reflects these values. Rawls says that the construction of systematic views of what is just and unjust involves as its starting point what people actually think is just and unjust. He writes that:

> We start, then, by looking to the public culture itself as the shared fund of implicitly recognized basic ideas and principles. We hope to formulate these ideas and principles clearly enough to be combined into a political conception of justice congenial to our most firmly held convictions (Rawls 1993:8).

If the answer to this question is in actual moral beliefs, then we have to find out what these beliefs are and have been. In fact, the first question in environmental philosophy to be systematically studied is whether we can find ethical ideas to respond to the ecological crisis from within Western intellectual traditions or whether we need to create a fully new ethical system.[6] Opinions are, naturally, rather divided. One of the most considered positions has

---

[6]Although Aldo Leopold noted the lack of ecological ethics in Western morality in his *Sand County Almanac* (1949) a major stimulus in this debate was the article by Lynn White (1967).

been developed by the British philosopher Robin Attfield. Although defending a version of biocentrism, Attfield finds the Western (Judaeo-Christian) tradition as capable of reacting to environmental problems. Moreover, Attfield argues that the total rejection of actual morality would not work and actually is not even desirable: "the most that is possible is a revised normative theory accommodating and enlarging upon accepted judgements" (Attfield 1983:225). Rawls (1993:175) thinks in much the same way about the significance of actual moral values: "Political liberalism ... must have the kind of content we associate with liberalism historically". It does, then, leave some room for environmental concern, but this is contingent, of course, on our understanding of past morality.

In sum, for Rawls the idea of what are morally considerable beings results from the system of social cooperation. But the content of public morality, that is the ethical norms and prescriptions, should also depend on shared moral beliefs. For theoretical and historical reasons, this morality governs directly the relations between the individuals who are members of the system and indirectly their relationship with the natural world. As far as animals are merely parts of the external world, our duties to them can be indirect. So liberalism in this form is essentially bound to be anthropocentric at the most fundamental theoretical level, but the endorsement of this does not by logical necessity imply the acceptance of cruelty to animals.

Reasonability and Tolerance

As Attfield suggests, reliance on historical interpretations does not exclude the possibility of change. Rawls also, although defending moral conservatism, entertains the possibility of revising common moral standards. If morality and publicly-shared conceptions of right and wrong ultimately rest on the way people think, then it is rather difficult to see why liberalism has to be necessarily anthropocentric and why it could not adopt the idea that animals, alongside humans, are morally considerable beings (cf. Hailwood 1999). For example, if non-human animals are regarded by the majority of the people as having moral standing, and if this view is compatible with the constitutive principles of a society, or at least tolerable, then there is room for general recognition of the rules that govern the treatment of animals as parallels with those rules that govern interhuman relationships. These rules would then have a firm, politically relevant philosophical basis in people's moral beliefs. This is a challenge to liberalism that is perhaps best put forward by those environmental ethicists who subscribe to biocentric individualism. Both are individualist positions and attempt to establish the value of non-humans by using as an analogue the concept of human dignity and its defence; these philosophers include Paul W. Taylor (1986) and Tom Regan (1988). The moral principles employed to defend animals are the conventional ones, such as utilitarianism and Kantianism. In this respect these reasons for animal rights are similar to the reasons presented in support of the rights of humans.

Can these claims about animals really be put into practice in a liberal society? The answer seems to be negative for the following reason. For sure, on the one hand, it is unreasonable to suggest that biocentric views are irrational, logically unsound and fully unreasonable. They are, to use Rawls' (1993:114) expression, "universally communicable"[7] and the idea of animal rights can be explained to other people so that it makes sense to them. But, on the other hand, it may be too much if a biocentric ethic was among the basic ethical standpoints of a society and eating meat and wearing fur were legally-forbidden practices. The reasonability of this is further stressed when it is remembered that for some people there really is no alternative to a carnivorous diet or furs. In certain cases natural conditions reduce individual autonomy to a bare minimum of survival. Let us ignore these cases in which there are no real choices and focus on the situation in affluent liberal democracies.

It seems to be so that those who refute the rights of animals can live with the fact that there are people defending animal rights and not eating meat. However, it is not so that the defenders of animal rights can always tolerate the habits and inclinations of those who eat meat and dress in fur, because to them such habits and inclinations are immoral. Whether or not this is the case in reality, it is useful, if not necessary, to also distinguish between liberal and non-liberal conceptions of animal rights. The distinctive mark is the attitude of the advocates of these conceptions to anthropocentrism — whether or not they hold the views of those people who deny the claim that animals have rights. Consequently, non-liberals would require that the principle of animal rights and all the secondary norms are legally recognised and implemented. There are rules to be followed by a society as a whole, without exception. Contrary to this, according to liberal conception — and this is a view that Rawls might think of as compatible with political liberalism — the recognition of animal rights, and of the normative implications of it, are matters of individual choice as far as these views are *reasonable*. In other words, the espousal of the philosophy of animal rights is voluntary and no-one should be compelled to not use animal products if they want to. This is because "[i]t is unreasonable for us to use political power … to repress comprehensive views that are not unreasonable" (Rawls 1993:61).

The inability of animal-rights defenders to tolerate the views of their opponents can also be understood in terms of neutrality — the legal recognition of rights of animals or plants is perfectionism. As these liberals see it, the neutral state should not rank different conceptions of the good and the right or, therefore, what kind of nature is valuable and what kind of use of it can fulfil an individual's ideals and wants. Accordingly, they claim that doctrines like the intrinsic value of nature or animal rights inescapably lead to a certain conception of the good and may restrict "access to resources for those individuals with alternative visions of the good life" (Coglianese 1998:54). For this reason, non-anthropocentric ideas cannot be part of the value basis of a society.[8] Therefore, a person is to be permitted to wear a mink coat if he thinks it will satisfy his preferences optimally.

---

[7]Rawls (1993:127) also says that, "Political constructivism does not criticize, then, religious, philosophical, or metaphysical accounts of the truth of moral judgments and of their validity. Reasonableness is its standard of correctness, and given its political aims, it need not go beyond that" and that "Political liberalism does not question that many political and moral judgments of certain specified kinds are correct and it views many of them as reasonable." (Rawls, 1993:63) (cf. Raz 1988:108).

[8]Consider for example the comprehensiveness of deep ecology. As formulated by Bill Devall and George Sessions (1985:65) it "attempts to articulate a comprehensive religious and philosophical worldview." However, in his well-known ecophilosophical theory Arne Naess does not attempt to suppress diverse religions and views of the world. Rather he says that his aim is to create a theory in which the principles of action ("the deep ecology platform") can rest on different ultimate premises — Christian, Buddhist or philosophical for example. So there could be more in common between deep ecology and Rawlsian liberalism than may appear at first sight.

The appeal to neutrality is closely related to the claim that acceptable modes of environmental valuation are generally private matters. To be acceptable it is enough that the view is reasonable and consistent with constitutional essentials (Rawls 1993:127, 153). In practice the denial of the compatibility of liberalism and non-anthropocentrism means that at the level of individuals a non-anthropocentric valuation of nature is appropriate. These are matters of personal moral choices. But at the level of the overall political and economic system the liberal state holds to anthropocentrism (Wissenburg 1998:98–9; cf. Sagoff 1988:165). The reasons for this can be found in liberal views on the formation of public morality in general.

Providing that this analysis holds, it does not seem to be an open question what kind of environmental-ethical commitments a democratic state can logically and politically adopt, but the commitment to neutrality sets certain limits. These limits cannot be transcended without rejecting the principle of liberal neutrality. It is equally true that for the majority of people certain modes of treatment of non-humans can appear morally intolerable even if society does not regard animals as moral persons or subjects. Liberal societies have criminalised (some forms of) cruelty to animals and these societies can regard some forms of exploitation as too brutal to be tolerated. The actual moral beliefs seem then to be rather complicated. Which set of rules in regard to animals should be adopted?

5. Neutrality in Practice

It is inevitable that a liberal-democratic society, like any other decent society, has to decide what kind of things or states of affairs are to be secured by the fundamental laws of the state. This means that it has to adopt some kind of environmental ethic, with or without a direct concern for other living beings. Often there is, however, no consensus. Despite this fact, it is clear that no society, including a liberal democratic one, necessarily petrifies into a state of indecisiveness or drifts into a violent conflict. It can in practice follow a certain policy, either formally or informally. A liberal-democratic society has manifold methods to accommodate views. These include referenda, decisions in a legislative assembly, governmental decisions and decisions made by state officials. The decisions can also be such that no universal decision is made and this means, in many cases, that they are left to the market.

Theoretically, the basic divide is between approaches that emphasise either politics or economics. Accordingly, liberals may claim that the neutrality requirement gives us two basic options — either to leave these things open, unresolved, or to make statutes that are the outcome of democratic deliberation, often being in practice some kind of compromise. John O'Neill argues that these alternatives stem from different understandings of neutrality — the former follows from a non-dialogical, and the latter from a dialogical, conception of neutrality. According to a dialogical conception of neutrality it is possible to reach a rational solution in matters of moral disputes by means of open debate. The defenders of non-dialogical neutrality say this is not possible. For a dialogical conception, the public forum is the site where debate takes place, whereas for non-dialogical conception of public life controversial moral issues can be decided upon in the market (O'Neill 1998:18). Let us take a closer look at how these two distinct understandings of neutrality lead to different policy models with regard to fox farming.

The Case of Fox Farming

It is a hot moral issue at the moment whether fox farming and the fur industry in general are morally acceptable or whether they represent a form of organised cruelty to animals that must be outlawed. The views are seriously conflicting and incompatible, and they seem to be, independent of whether one is a committed liberal or something else. This example is topical (this chapter was written in the winter of 2000) because of the British Labour government decision to ban fox farming as a cruel form of industry. Animals live their lives in small cages where they have little opportunity to fulfil their natural inclinations and needs. The decision, as well as widespread speculation over its possible implications for European Union policymaking, has upset representatives of the fur industry in Finland. The production of fur, particularly fox fur, is an important source of livelihood in some rural parts of Finland. It employs directly about 6–7,000 persons in small family firms, and indirectly a few thousand more individuals. Most of the pelts are exported, the total value being approximately 250 million Euros. There are altogether about five million animals living in cages, and the species include fox, mink and polecat.[9]

The Finnish government will make an official appeal to the European Commission arguing that the British decision should be understood as an illegitimate intervention into the freedom of industry.[10] What it tries to claim is that if consumers demand fur, the production of them should be allowed, otherwise it interferes with the market mechanism and prevents people from meeting their lawful wants. In other words, the argumentative strategy is to allege that there is no significant difference between the following two statements:

(S1) It is as acceptable to run a fox farm as it is to oppose the idea that there is a right to farm and breed foxes.
(S2) It is as acceptable to wear fur clothes as it is to refrain from wearing them.

The statement (S2) expresses something that is related to a person's private life. Everyone is free to choose his or her own mode of dressing, whether to wear a fur or an anorak or something else. And if the demand for fur products is legitimate, the production has to be also. The non-dialogical form of neutrality says that there is no politically relevant difference between these two statements. We should leave it up to consumers to decide whether fox can be farmed and bred and doing otherwise is to coerce them to act against their own will. The fox farmers might say to the opponents of their industry that, privately, you may make consumptive choices that do not support fox farming, but as a form of industry fox farming is legitimate and, therefore, you have no right to otherwise interfere in our businesses. In other words, they require that opponents of fox farming tolerate the actual preferences of consumers and the right to produce furs. Defenders of the dialogical form of neutrality have a different opinion. They suggest when we conceive of

---

[9]For statistics see the web-site of the Finnish fur breeders association at: http://www.stkl-fpf.fi.
[10]See *Helsingin Sanomat* from 13 February 2000. The debate in the Finnish *Eduskunta* (Parliament) echoed much of the debate in the UK Parliament. For an account see the web-site: http://www.parliament.the-stationery-office.co.uk/pa/cm199900/cmhansrd/cm000628/debtext/0062833. htm.

fox farming as a form of industry — something the statement (S1) refers to — we are not speaking about a purely private matter, or one that should be left to the market to decide. Rather it is a matter that has general moral significance.[11]

The fundamental questions concerning fox farming then become:

(Q1) Is it in the first place morally acceptable to produce and to consume fur-products?[12]
(Q2) Providing that it is permissible to wear fur, how may they be produced?

Let us consider each of these in turn. Is it morally acceptable to produce and to consume fur-products? The moral acceptability of producing and wearing fur is at issue in Western societies. There are people who think of furs as an expression of human arrogance towards the rest of nature, and there are those who regard it as just one category of garments among others. In every society, there must be some decision about this matter because even no decision is a decision in effect as it allows the continuation of the practice of wearing furs. Meta-theoretical views on neutrality give different answers about the possibility of reaching a solution that would satisfy everyone. The dialogical view defends the possibility of a rational decision, whereas the non-dialogical view is sceptical about the possibility of consensus. The non-dialogical view requires that the decision be left to the market because it is the only possible way to settle the controversy given that there is no rational and socially acceptable solution.

Let us assume that the members of society are feeling increasingly dissatisfied with fox farming and want to see a radical change. Growing numbers of people in Western Europe and elsewhere may have such anti-fur sentiments. To express this change of attitude in economic terms, we might say that the actual preferences of people have transformed. Typically, the market is thought of as having a feedback mechanism such that if there is a change in preferences and, consequently, in demand, this information will be conveyed to producers. If the demand for furs collapses, sooner or later the same will occur to the supply. Therefore, it might be said, there is no need to ban this form of industry. Furthermore, were it so that governmental neutrality as an ideal regulates the relations between the citizens and the state in an adequate way, only this kind of protection policy — the one that consumer behaviour produces — would be regarded as acceptable. But it is plausible that the minority that is deeply attracted to furs is able to keep this industry alive, although the majority would look down on it. So, according to the dialogical concept, although the two statements (S1) and (S2) are often confused, they should be kept separate. The dialogical view requires that if people feel fox farming is morally repulsive, there should be an

---

[11]There are many examples of objects and services of which production, use and/or even possession is more or less under strict governmental control or totally banned. Just consider the following examples: drugs, guns, child pornography and prostitution.

[12]To be precise, the regulation of consumption and production are different things. While regulation always serves some societal aim, it is debatable what part of the whole process should be targeted for realising the aim. For example, Sweden has outlawed the use of prostitutes' services in spite of the fact that traditionally it is the supply of these services that has been outlawed. However, as I see it, it is not necessary for my purposes here to keep them distinct, because they both are constituents of the problem.

open debate on the acceptability of this industry. Such public deliberation would then lead to the most satisfactory solution.

As I see it, the non-dialogical conception of neutrality fails to settle the dispute, simply because the conflict over fur stems, at least in part, from the claim that the market model is in this case inadequate and, worse still, immoral. Fox-farming opponents claim that what is at issue is the moral acceptability of fox farming *per se* and the patterns of consumption on which it depends. For them the core of the problem does not rest with (inappropriate) individual choices. According to the opponents, it is this kind of treatment of animals, and the related industry, that is a public affair calling for a public decision on its acceptability. Furthermore, they regard a ban on fox farming as the only acceptable alternative because it is evident that a lifestyle based on exploiting other forms of life in such a cruel way is not a good life. By implication, the worldview on which it is based cannot be reasonable, in the sense of being tolerable.

The defenders of animal rights are also critical of the use of the market mechanism as a compromise because it leads to monetary valuation of animals and, finally, to the idea that the value of morally considerable beings is reducible to how they have actually been evaluated. Animals are, then, a mere category of commodity. Thus, it still sticks to anthropocentrism and cannot be, in this respect, neutral for an animal-rights advocate. To express Regan's view of the moral standing of animals in other terms, what he opposes is the commodification of animals. When something is commodified, it becomes a marketable object, the value of which is determined in the marketplace and expressed in monetary terms (see Radin 1996). For Regan (1988:343–44) animals have inherent value and they have this value independent of their use value and how people actually value them. Inherent value is something that animals either have or have not; it is categorical. For Elizabeth Anderson (1993:193) the market is in this respect defective, because "markets are responsive only to given wants, without evaluating the reasons people have for wanting the goods in question, which may be based on ideals or principles."

The reason underpinning this objection to universal commodification is the fact that we are accustomed to classifying things and to evaluating them by means of various different standards. Consider for example Kant's distinction between the notions of worth and price, and the assertion that human beings are bearers of dignity, whereas for non-human entities the value standard is that of price or market value. To be able to use the market as a compromise in a way that accords with the idea of neutrality, there should be a consensus on the applicability of this method. However, the case concerning the moral justifiability of fox farming is not closed. Even if money was generally regarded as an appropriate form of valuing commodities, that is, in determining their price, there would be a problem since not all things that are of value are merely commodities, as something that can be consumed as we see best.

But if the government forbids one way of using animal resources, does it then violate the principle of neutrality? It seems unavoidable that the precise content of the practice of neutrality finally depends on the shared views of right and wrong and on our conception of neutrality. Moral views can alter, and the more people who resist fox farming as a form of industry the more pressure there is to change government policy and to bring the practice under governmental control. If liberals hold rigidly to the idea that banning fox farming violates the principle of state neutrality and the liberal idea of the right to establish a firm freely, we seem to encounter two incompatible options. Either the liberal model of government should be rejected or fox farming as an industry should be allowed. To put the problem so is, however, to present it in a pointed way. My intent here is that there are other possible positions, like that of the dialogical conception of neutrality, according to which the norms that govern our relations to other animals are an outcome of democratic deliberation.

Providing that it is Permissible to Wear Furs, How May They Be Produced?

The tradition of wearing fur clothes can remain alive, even if the production of fur is regulated. Directives condition how, where, by whom and which animal species can be farmed for these particular purposes. Finding such a compromise to a disagreement might actually be something that Rawls would applaud as he says that "A constitutional regime does not require an agreement on a comprehensive doctrine: the basis of its social unity lies elsewhere" (Rawls 1993:63). But what is the proper role for the state in realising and implementing the agreement?

The non-dialogical conception of neutrality emphasises the private nature of environmental decision-making and, as a result, the continuity of ecologically unsound forms of consumption depends on individual preferences and related patterns of behaviour. So it is not fully clear that even the production of fur needs to be regulated; after all the market can take care of it. Just consider how many different kinds of eggs are available in an ordinary supermarket: organic, free-range, low-cholesterol and "normal" eggs, to mention a few. Consumers may express their concern about the well-being of chickens, or the lack of it, through their choices. In the same way, fur farmers could attach a label to their pelts that would give relevant information to the consumer, for example, a description of the life and killing of the animal(s). This would allow consumers to decide what kind of animal treatment constitutes cruelty and what is acceptable. The alternatives might be numerous: ordinary fur, "animal-friendly" fur, free-range fur or wild fur.[13] Moreover, if people want to refrain from using any furs at all, they have all the possibilities to do so by expressing that preference in the marketplace. But does either of these two options leave it open to ban fox farming? My claim is that there are cases where it is not in conflict with the principle of neutrality to ban a form of industry if it appears to us as immoral. To ban fox farming we do not even have to appeal to the radical doctrines of the rights of animals.

Even though Rawls denies the possibility of a non-anthropocentric ethic, there is a place for critique with respect to human behaviour and the natural world and animals. Typically, this evaluation employs as a standard of criticism the question of whether action is harmful or is believed to be harmful to other people (Coglianese 1998:47). This is an important reason why many eminent philosophers, including many liberals, have taken a disapproving stance on cruelty to animals. Perhaps the most famous of all, Kant, condemned it as leading to cruelty toward other persons. We may also think that being cruel to others

---

[13]In practice, there are many problems associated with eco-labeling, particularly with regard to the reconciliation of the interests of various actors. However, these matters are not germane to the current discussion.

somehow degrades or corrupts our sense of the value of life (Raz 1988:210–3). However, the main reason for many other liberals, like Locke and Rawls, for disapproving of cruelty is not instrumental, at least not in such a direct manner. Rather, as they see it, cruelty is wrong because animals are conceived of as suffering from callous treatment. As Rawls (1972:512) expresses his "considered belief" that "[t]he capacity for feelings of pleasure and pain and for the forms of life of which animals are capable clearly impose duties of compassion and humanity in their case." Theoretically the duties we owe to animals can thus be understood as duties of charity, not as duties of justice (Clark 1987).

So a liberal can admit that it is our duty to minimise cruelty to animals — even though they are not recognised as full members of the moral community. And this can be of significance regarding our practical relationship to animals; as Wissenburg (1998:112) puts it, the exclusion of animals "does not imply that *all* human interests necessarily take precedence over *all* animal interests." The problem with the market compromise is that it tolerates too much, too much from the perspective of mainstream liberal advocates. So if fox farming is a particularly cruel form of fur production, it is not justifiable by appealing to the non-dialogical principle of neutrality. In other words, the liberal position is a kind of compromise. It will not silence the advocates and the opponents of animals' rights from criticising it, but it can still avoid a kind of moral nihilism that allows people to behave in any way they like and to disregard the pain of others.

6. Concluding Remarks

My primary purpose in this chapter has been to examine why the idea of consumer sovereignty is so deeply embedded in liberal thinking and why it is difficult to impose rigid rules with respect to consumption. If the state promotes a vegan lifestyle it privileges one mode of living over others. This may mean that people are being treated in unequal ways according to their "tastes". It would be perfectionism. At first sight, liberalism does not necessarily give any definitive answer to the question of what kind of beings are morally considerable. It is therefore fully feasible to imagine "a vegan state" that would rely on liberal doctrines. However, such a state accords with the Rawlsian ideal state only if this philosophy of life is accepted by a clear majority of the people in their considered moral beliefs, and if the views are based on traditional beliefs. And even in this context it is difficult to marry a biocentric view on ethics with a Rawlsian view, because according to the latter morality emerges from interpersonal relationships in a society and thus must be anthropocentric. But this does not fully undermine the possibility of environmental and animal-welfare policies, and these policies may include forbidding certain forms of behaviour.

The most plausible case for state-based, or collective, environmental protection is the one that aims at the protection of public goods. Even though Rawls denies the possibility of a non-anthropocentric ethic, there is room for criticism of human behaviour with respect to the natural world and animals. Environmental protection that is prudentially motivated may justify coercion when it is regarded as the protection of public goods. As Rawls (1972:267–68) says, "Assuming that the public good is to everyone's advantage, and one that all would agree to arrange for, the use of coercion is perfectly rational from each man's point of view". This principle can be even more significant for environmental protection when extended to future generations (see Wissenburg 1998:127–36). This is one way to solve the free-rider problem, where a person does not pay for his or her use of public goods, and other liberals deem it applicable to cases in which there is a risk of harm (Coglianese 1998:47). But it is common to all these cases that environmental regulation is derived from the harm principle. In other words, an external intervention into individual behaviour is acceptable if it serves the interests of the larger community. The reason for recognising animals was argued to be different as animals themselves matter.

Should we leave the decision on what is right and wrong in our relationship to animals to the market? I assume that it is a widely-shared opinion that cruelty to sentient beings is always a public affair and has to be examined according to the standards of public morality. Certain issues are simply too important, regarding the whole of society, to be left open. When we leave it to the market to govern the treatment of animals it opens up the legitimate possibility to subject them to all kinds of cruelties. The situation would be intolerable to anyone who cares for animals. If the production of fur by means of farming (of wild animals) is a truly cruel form of treatment, then it should not be allowed. A more moderate version of this claim requires the fulfilment of certain humane conditions where these animals are raised.

To provide a solution to the controversy over fox farming we should pay attention to the ethical points of departure of animal-welfare protection. It is questionable in what sense the concern for animal welfare constitutes a "comprehensive" moral theory. Imagine a society in which the respect for animals is firmly based on religious doctrines and it is one instance of religious correctness to show this respect in one's own behaviour. Should we think in this case that everyone should follow these religious rules? I think many of the defenders of animals I characterised earlier as non-liberal would also give a negative answer to this question and would argue for pluralism. This is so because the freedom of religion has at least since Locke's influential writings on toleration been regarded as a major dimension of liberal pluralism. Therefore, it is important to emphasise that the actual ethical basis of the modern animal-rights movement is not religious in kind, but correlates with the fundamental ethical commitments of liberal-democratic society as it is.

If fox farming is thought of as a cruel form of treatment of animals, it can be banned without transgressing the principle of neutrality and it is not an unbearable violation of consumer and producer sovereignties. When it comes to finding a solution to a controversy, if the "leave-it-to-the-market" position is unsatisfying, we should find alternative methods. One such method is discussion that takes place in public. Then we can evaluate in the best possible way whether fox farming accords with our moral thinking; neutrality and pluralism are not and should not be excuses for cruelty to innocent living beings.

Acknowledgement

Many thanks to Marcel Wissenburg for his insightful comments on the manuscript of this chapter. This chapter was prepared during a year-long visit at the Institute for Environment, Philosophy, and Public Policy, Lancaster University for which I am most grateful.

References

Anderson, E. (1993), *Value in Ethics and Economics*. Cambridge: Harvard University Press.
Attfield, R. (1983), "Western traditions and environmental ethics." In R. Elliot & Gare, A. (eds) *Environmental Philosophy* (pp. 201–230). Milton Keynes: The Open University Press.
Baxter, B. (1999), *Ecologism: An Introduction*. Edinburgh: Edinburgh University Press.
Clark, S. (1987), "Animals, ecosystems and Liberal ethic." *The Monist 70*, 114–133.
Coglianese, G. (1998), "Implications of Liberal neutrality for environmental policy." *Environmental Ethics 20* (1), 41–59.
De-Shalit, A. (1997), "Is Liberalism environmentally-friendly?" In R. Gottlieb (ed.) *The Ecological Community* (pp. 82–103). London: Routledge.
Devall, B., & Sessions, G. (1985), *Deep Ecology: Living as if Nature Mattered*. Salt Lake City: Gibbs Smith.
Dworkin, R. (1978), "Liberalism." In S. Hampshire (ed.) *Public and Private Morality* (pp. 113–143). Cambridge: Cambridge University Press.
Feinberg, J. (1984), *Harm to Others*. Oxford: Oxford University Press.
Goodin, R. (1992), *Green Political Theory*. Cambridge: Polity Press.
Hailwood, S. (1999), "Towards a Liberal environment?" *Journal of Applied Philosophy 16*, 271–281.
Hobbes, T. (1962), *Leviathan*. J. Plamenatz. (ed.). London: Collins.
Inglehart, R. (1977), *The Silent Revolution*. Princeton: Princeton University Press.
Kant, I. (1996a), "The metaphysics of morals." In M. Gregor (ed.) *Practical Philosophy*. Cambridge: Cambridge University Press.
Kant, I. (1996b), "Groundwork of the metaphysics of morals." In M. Gregor (ed.) *Practical Philosophy*. Cambridge: Cambridge University Press.
Leopold, A. (1949), *Sand County Almanac*. New York: Oxford University Press.
Locke, J. (1988), *Two Treatises of Government*. Peter Laslett (ed.). Cambridge: Cambridge University Press.
Mill, J. (1910), *On Liberty*. London: Everyman's Library.
Mulhall, S., & Swift, (1990), *Liberals and Communitarians*. Oxford: Blackwell.
Naess, A. (1995), "The deep philosophical movement: Some philosophical aspects." In G. Sessions (ed.) *Deep Ecology for the Twenty-First Century* (pp. 64–84). Boston: Shambala.
Nozick, R. (1974), *Anarchy, State and Utopia*. Oxford: Blackwell.
Oksanen, M. (1997), "The moral value of biodiversity." *Ambio 26*, 541–545.
O'Neill, J. (1998), *The Market: Ethics, Knowledge and Politics*. London: Routledge.
Radin, M. (1996), *Contested Commodities*. Cambridge: Harvard University Press.
Rawls, J. (1972), *A Theory of Justice*. Oxford: Clarendon Press.
Rawls, J. (1993), *Political Liberalism*. New York: Columbia University Press.
Raz, J. (1988), *The Morality of Freedom*. Oxford: Clarendon Press.
Regan, T. (1988), *The Case for Animal Rights*. London: Routledge.
Routley, R. (1973), 'Is there a need for a new, environmental ethic?' *Proceedings of the XV World Congress of Philosophy* (Varna) 1, 205–210.
Rowlands, M. (1997), "Contractarianism and animal rights." *Journal of Applied Philosophy 14*, 235–247.
Sagoff, M. (1988), *The Economy of the Earth: Philosophy, Law and the Environment*. Cambridge: Cambridge University Press.
Singer, P. (1990), *Animal Liberation*. 2nd ed. New York: Avon Books.

Taylor, B. (1996), "Democracy and environmental ethics." In W. Lafferty & J. Meadowcraft (eds) *Democracy and the Environment: Problems and Prospects* (pp. 86–107). Cheltenham: Edward Elgar.

Taylor, P. (1986), *Respect for Nature: A Theory of Environmental Ethics*. Princeton: Princeton University Press.

Westra, L. (1998), *Living in Integrity. A Global Ethic to Restore a Fragmented Earth*. Lanham, MD: Rowman and Littlefield.

White, L. (1967), "The historical roots of our ecological crisis." *Science 155*, 1203–1207.

Wissenburg, M. (1998), *Green Liberalism: The Free and the Green Society*. London: UCL Press.

Chapter 5

Economics, Ethics and Green Consumerism

Jouni Paavola

1. Introduction

This chapter examines green consumerism — the making of consumer choices at least partly on the basis of environmental concerns. I pursue here two different goals. First, I aim to clarify the promises and pitfalls of green consumerism as a way of transforming current consumption patterns in a more sustainable direction. Second, the chapter seeks to demonstrate that an economic approach can help us to understand the social and environmental dimensions of consumer behaviour.

Green consumerism is an interesting and important object of analysis for several reasons. First, consumer choices have a significant effect on the environment and, therefore, also have the potential to alleviate environmental problems. Second, green consumerism and lifestyles are becoming fashionable and the belief in their ability to improve environmental outcomes is increasingly widely shared (see, for example, Elgin 1993). Finally, as outlined in Chapters 2 and 3 of this volume academia and international policy arenas are focussing greater attention on consumption. It is felt that the potential of publicly regulating production is either not sufficient to remedy environmental problems, or is already largely exhausted (see Cogoy 1999; Crocker and Linden 1998; Georg 1999; Jackson and Marks 1999; OECD 1997a, 1997b, 1998; Røpke 1999).

For other social scientists economics is not by any means an obvious discipline to use to gain a deeper understanding of consumer behaviour. After all, economic theorising in its usual form builds on narrow and counterfactual assumptions concerning human behaviour that render consumption as an object of analysis without symbolic and social dimensions. In essence, the traditional economic approach views consumption as a string of rational choices which individuals make to maximise their personal welfare without regard for the consequences of their choices for other humans and non-humans and without considering the choices made by others and their consequences. Even economists themselves have sometimes considered the theory of consumer choice to be an area that has not progressed since the mid-twentieth century.

Yet some relatively recent developments in economics promise to make it less naïve and more useful for the kinds of inquiries into consumption that interest other social scientists. These developments include the recent revival of interest in the study of interdependent consumer choices, originally pioneered a century ago by Thorstein Veblen (Corneo and Jeanne 1997; Frank 1985, 1991; Veblen 1899). Another area of research at the interstices

Exploring Sustainable Consumption: Environmental Policy and the Social Sciences, Volume 1, pages 79–94.
Copyright © 2001 by Elsevier Science Ltd.
All rights of reproduction in any form reserved.
ISBN: 0-08-043920-9

of economics and philosophy has made space for non-welfarist behavioural motivations and examined their implications for economic analysis (Sen 1977, 1979; Anderson 1993; Kavka 1991, 1993). Finally, increasingly popular game-theory provides a heuristic framework that can be used to integrate these new trends in economics.

In essence, as I seek to demonstrate in this chapter, at its best economics enables us to analyse consumer choices as the decisions of agents with plural values who act on socially constructed identities and knowledge. Often their choices are interdependent, in other words they are bound up with the choices made by others. Some agents may seek to display their wealth in the Veblenian (1899) fashion, while others may seek status in their subcultures by actually resorting to green consumerism or lifestyles. This chapter also demonstrates that we can gain policy-relevant insights by analysing consumption games characterised by plural motivations.

In the following discussion, the first section describes the understanding of consumption in conventional economics — a series of independent and welfare-seeking consumer choices — and discusses the limited potential of green consumerism if this model is accepted. The second section demonstrates how the standard model can be expanded to accommodate plural values and a broader notion of green consumerism. The third section examines the significance of accepting the interdependence of consumer choices through the use of game theory and the fourth section works out the implications of value pluralism for interdependent consumer choices. The chapter's final section examines in greater detail the implications of green consumerism when value pluralism prevails.

2. The Standard Model of Consumer Choice

The model of rational choice (see Hargreaves Heap *et al.*, 1992) is a useful starting point for understanding how economics has traditionally approached consumption and, therefore, how it must treat green consumerism. The rational choice model contends that consumers are interested exclusively in their own utility or welfare and that they rank choice alternatives according to how they would enhance individual welfare. The model also assumes that consumers have limitless cognitive capabilities and can obtain perfect knowledge about the choice alternatives they face and that they make choices that do maximise their welfare. Additionally, consumers are not understood to have any control over the available alternatives: market forces generate the menu of choice alternatives they face.

There coexist within economics three different views of how items of consumption relate to the utility or welfare of the choosing agent:

- Items of consumption somehow directly translate into enhanced utility or welfare. This "naïve" view collapses consumption into acquisition.
- Items of consumption have characteristics that are useful for consumers (see Lancaster 1966). This approach is more useful and is able to treat the act of consumption as distinct from the act of buying. However, it still usually incorporates a narrow and problematic notion of consumption as an isolated and individual activity.

• Items of consumption such as steak, wine and candles generate utility only indirectly after being transformed into final goods like candlelight dinners through household production (see Becker 1976; Stigler and Becker 1977).

The third of these approaches can form the basis of a rich and elaborate view of consumption if it is accompanied by the notion of socialised agents acting on plural motivations. However, this is not usually the case (see, for example, Stigler and Becker 1977).

All traditional economic theories assume that consumers are motivated only by the improvement of their personal utility or welfare. These traditional theories also usually fail to make a distinction between utility and welfare and assume that whatever values underpin agents' preferences; the choices made on the basis of them must improve the choosing agent's welfare. Early economic theory justified this close association of utility and welfare. It provided a strong link between utility, welfare and the preferences of agents by associating utility with pleasure or usefulness: agents simply preferred things that made them happier and better off (see Georgescu-Roegen 1968; Sen 1991). However, in the early twentieth century utility came to be redefined as the satisfaction of an agent's preferences, whatever they may be (see Broome 1991; for the original argument see Hicks and Allen 1934). This redefinition left utility without substantial content and severed its connection to the choosing agent's welfare (see Sen 1973).

Therefore, there is no reason why the choices of agents should improve their welfare when the broad notion of utility is accepted: agents may deliberately choose to pursue some other goals. These kinds of motivations are likely to explain why at least some agents engage in green consumerism. However, this discussion cannot adopt the broad notion of utility as the satisfaction of preferences because it aims to understand the implications of different value positions for preferences and choices. It therefore needs to be able to distinguish between them. In what follows, utility will be understood in the classic sense as pleasure or usefulness closely connected with a narrow understanding of the individual's welfare. To put it differently, the agents of the standard economic model are informed by self-centred welfarism, a form of utilitarian values.

Although the rational-choice model suggests that consumers choose between alternatives to maximise their welfare within the constraints of their budgets, this does not necessarily make them short-sighted hedonists. In contemporary scholarship it is usually understood that agents seek to maximise their utility or welfare over their whole lifetime (Deaton and Muellbauer 1980). This may entail postponing consumption, for example when saving for a home before buying one. At other times it may be better to incur debt. However, while lifetime utility or welfare maximisation provides a richer view of consumption than a view that does not consider agents as forward-looking planners, it also overestimates their actual capabilities and downplays the significance of mistakes.

The standard model has another noteworthy feature: no effects are understood to exist between one agent's consumption and another agent's welfare. These kinds of interpersonal effects are called consumption or positional externalities (see Frank 1985, 1991; Hirsch 1995; Leibenstein 1950) and, to put it mildly, the assumption of independent consumer choices is unrealistic. We all know that relatives, neighbours and peers do care about each other's consumption: they may feel better or worse off depending on whether they do or do not have the items of consumption possessed by others. At best we may start with the assumption of independence, because independent consumer choices form the necessary first step in understanding before we expand the economic analysis of consumption.

No matter what preferences self- and welfare-centred consumers have, the assumption is that they are always better off if they exhaust their budgets, either by consuming now or in the future. Moreover, it is understood that it is better for them to spend their budgets to maximise their welfare regardless of the impact on other humans and non-humans. But this does not mean that the consumers of the standard model of rational consumer choice cannot engage in green consumerism: personal welfare and environmental protection are compatible in a number of choices. For example, consumers may well choose environmentally benign non-material services, such as going to an art exhibition or theatre, if they think doing so will improve their welfare more than material consumption. Consumers may also choose environmentally friendly products, such as organically-grown produce or vegetarian meals if they believe that doing so will be welfare enhancing.

To put it differently, the rational-choice model assumes that all agents revealing environmental preferences obtain welfare gains from expected improvements in environmental quality. It also understands that the seeking of these welfare gains exhausts motivations for environment-friendly behaviour, such as engagement in green consumerism. Monetary valuation of the environment is based on this idea: rational consumers are thought to be willing to pay at least the value of changes in environmental quality to secure these changes for themselves. This line of reasoning suggests that the value of environmental quality or its change could be determined by measuring consumer willingness to pay.

However, positions that suggest consumers engage in environment-friendly behaviour and support environmental protection only because they expect welfare gains are problematic. First, it is difficult to explain all environmentally informed behaviour such as green consumerism as self-interested welfare maximisation because the improvement of personal welfare and desirable environmental outcomes are incompatible in a number of cases. For example, forgoing the use of a car often imposes significant burdens on those who commit themselves to cycling or public transport. The case of dutiful recycling is similar. Finally, the choice of more expensive environment-friendly products may increase expenditure more than is compensated for by any additional welfare benefits. Economists usually explain away these apparent contradictions by claiming that agents obtain some sort of psychological satisfaction from what they do. However, this ploy does not do justice to all consumer choices: individuals do sometimes consider that certain goals are more important than their own welfare. Moreover, references to "satisfaction" do not improve our understanding of what actually motivates people to engage in more environmentally responsible behaviour.

The existence of non-welfarist motivations, therefore, should be taken seriously. Our understanding of our own behaviour tells us that our choices are not always determined by decisions to improve personal welfare. There is also evidence of non-welfarist motivations and behaviour from surveys that aim to determine the monetary value of environmental quality. For instance, respondents sometimes express strong commitments to environmental protection, but refuse to offer willingness-to-pay estimates (Jorgensen *et al.*, 1999; Spash and Hanley 1995). A number of philosophical and theoretical objections have also been levelled against exclusively welfare-based explanations of human behaviour and choices (Foster 1997; Sagoff 1988; Sen 1995; Vatn and Bromley 1995). Finally, contemporary research on ethics and economics provides a sound foundation for recognising non-welfarist behavioural motivations. The next section develops the idea of value pluralism, incorporates it into the standard model of rational choice and examines the implications for our understanding of green consumerism.

3. Green Consumerism and Value Pluralism

Extending the rational-choice model to accommodate value pluralism requires us to redefine the idea of rationality. The conventional view in economics is that rationality involves strictly welfare-maximising behaviour. We must substitute for this perspective a wider notion of rationality as deliberated, intentional action (see Elster 1983; Simon 1978). As agents may well base their deliberations and intentions on value positions other than self-centred welfarism, value pluralism can be accommodated only within this wider conception of rationality.

In this chapter I emphasise the formal plurality of values, in addition to their substantial plurality. Two self- and welfare-centred consumers may value taking a bus instead of a car quite differently. They may also hold different views with respect to the consumption of vegetarian meals. At the same time their assessments can still both be based on what they consider is most likely to enhance their welfare (substantial). However, other kinds of values may lead agents to consume in ways that do not improve and may even reduce their welfare (Sen 1977). For example, social welfarists may make personal sacrifices for the common good, however they understand it. Other-centred welfarists may choose so as to maximise the welfare of other humans or non-humans, even at the expense of their own welfare. Similarly, non-utilitarian consequentialists will make personal-welfare sacrifices to achieve the outcome they feel is intrinsically valuable. Moreover, agents may not attach value to the consequences of their choices at all: they may attach it to acting in a particular way. For example, a rule-following Kantian consumer will not consider some choice alternatives because she thinks choosing them is simply wrong. Instead of following rules, consumers may also feel certain choices are virtuous.

Preferences can thus be based on welfarist, non-utilitarian consequentialist or deontological ethical foundations. The preferences of a self-interested welfarist, as depicted in the standard model of rational choice, mean she cannot choose in a way that decreases her welfare. However, preferences based on social or other-centred welfarism, non-utilitarian consequentialism and deontology could allow this. Ethical premises capable of inducing welfare-reducing behaviour do not influence behaviour towards the environment only: they influence many choices and especially institutional ones. For example, attitudes relating to the freedom of private enterprise or freedom from government interference imply that these freedoms are often felt to be intrinsically rather than instrumentally valuable. They may thus be pursued and/or defended even to the detriment of the individual's welfare.

As a result of value pluralism an agent is likely to hold different values each of which could inform choices in a given choice situation (Kavka 1991, 1993). It can be argued that agents deliberate and choose between values when their values are in conflict. Anderson

(1993) argues that we make choices to realise the ideal person we want to be. When values are plural, different agents may also choose on the basis of different values in the same choice situation. This may result in similar or different choices (Anderson 1993). That is, the choice of an alternative, say a vegetarian diet, may be based on different ethical premises. Some may choose vegetarianism to improve their own welfare, while others may base their choice on animal-welfare considerations. Still others may select vegetarianism simply because they consider it a virtuous thing to do. Similarly, agents choose to engage in green consumerism or to adopt green lifestyles for various reasons.

The incorporation of value pluralism into the model of rational choice is relatively straightforward at a general level. In the standard model, an agent's preferences can be understood as that ranking of choice alternatives that maximises her welfare (Sen 1973). When the motivational basis of human behaviour is broadened, it simply means that an agent's preferences do not reflect exclusively her personal welfare any more. Rather her preferences reflect her moral convictions, whatever they are. A consumer that is rational in the wider sense thus chooses so as to realise her values (Anderson 1993).

The acknowledgement of non-welfarist behavioural motivations in the expanded model of rational choice gives green consumerism more depth. The consumers of the expanded model are sometimes willing and able to make choices that do not improve, and may actually reduce, their welfare. Many of these choices are not dramatic or extraordinary in any way. For example, consumers sometimes choose environment-friendly products that are costlier than ordinary products. Their choices may not bring about welfare improvements that would compensate for their diminished ability to buy other items, and to obtain the welfare gains promised by them. Still, consumers can make these welfare-reducing choices deliberately to realise their non-welfarist values. Green consumerism will thus be more potent when values are plural. Under conditions of value pluralism consumers will choose in an environmentally-sounder way more frequently than when everybody is concerned only about his or her own welfare. Some consumers will also reduce their ability to consume as a result of the choices they make at the expense of their personal welfare.

However, green consumerism remains a problematic strategy for reducing the environmental impacts of consumption for various reasons. First, although green consumerism will deliver general environmental improvements, the costs are borne exclusively by those who care the most. In some cases the most concerned consumers may obtain no welfare improvements in return for the costs they incur and, moreover, the most concerned consumers are unlikely to be the ones most responsible for environmental impacts. Leaving non self- and welfare-centred consumers to finance environmental improvements for all relieves other parties of responsibility. It allows them to avoid financial penalties in a way that violates the polluter-pays principle and clearly raises free-rider issues. Second, to be effective green consumerism requires environmental concerns to be widely held. It is not clear that this is currently the case in rich countries. Third, potential public policies could reduce the environmental impact of consumption at a lower overall cost compared to that associated with countless individual consumer choices. Finally, relying exclusively on green consumerism to reduce the environmental impact of consumption does not provide agents with the opportunity to agree collectively that they do not wish to be repeatedly confronted by certain moral dilemmas as they act as consumers. Keeping this possibility open could result in public policies to remove certain choice alternatives.

4. Consumption for Display and Distinction

When one consumer's choices or welfare are affected by how others choose, consumer choices are said to be interdependent. Departing from standard consumer theory to recognise the interdependence of consumer choices adds realism to economic analysis because a number of our consumption decisions are actually affected by how others choose. The interdependence of some choices also influences choices that are not themselves interdependent. For example, Robert Frank (1985) has argued that people spend more on items of interdependent consumption such as cars and houses and save on items that are not readily observable by others, such as food. This kind of behaviour is not by any means irrational from the individuals' viewpoint, because one's relative position in certain areas of life may have important consequences. For example, even if one has a good education, it may not be enough for success if others have an even better one. Physical presentation and attire also often serve as proxies for skills and prowess. Poor relative performance in any of them may eliminate opportunities and prove costly. Yet, from the society's viewpoint, competition for relative position may result in excessive investments in some areas — appearance, for example.

Consumer choices can be interdependent in different ways. Competition for relative position or merit has already been mentioned (see Hirsch 1995). Many of us also want to be fashionable: we sometimes choose a good because others do so and it adds to the value of the good for us. Witness, for example, how the use of personal palm-held organisers has spread in certain walks of life just like the use of mobile phones did earlier. This is called a bandwagon effect in economics (Leibenstein 1950). Others, called "snobs" in economic parlance, deliberately choose differently from others: the fact that others choose a good diminishes its value for them. For some people, the most important dimension of goods like Swiss wristwatches or Italian sport cars may be their price because this communicates to others their ability to consume and hence confers status. This phenomenon is typically known as the Veblen effect (Bagwell and Bernheim 1996; Leibenstein 1950), named after Thorstein Veblen who developed a theory of consumption as a behaviour primarily concerned with establishing status (see Veblen 1899).

Various strands of research in economics explain and treat the interdependence of consumer choices differently. For Becker (1976), for example, consumer choices are interdependent simply because an agent's welfare depends on the income, wealth, welfare or choices of other agents. That is, consumer choices are interdependent because agents have sometimes "nosy" preferences (Sen 1970). Despite its departure from more mainstream modes of treatment, this approach is still unable to treat consumption as a social phenomenon because it individualises the inter-personal dimension of consumption. In other words, there is nothing outside an individual that explains her having so-called nosy preferences in the first place. Because they dress interdependent consumption in the garb of consumer sovereignty approaches that ignore the relational characteristics of consumption make it difficult to justify public policies aimed at alleviating problems that stem from the conditional and contingent qualities of consumption. It is argued that consumers do truly prefer what they choose when they are interdependent with others and will suffer a loss of welfare if they are denied an opportunity to exercise their preferences.

In comparison, other economists argue that the interdependency of consumer choices results from the characteristics of certain consumer goods. For example, items that satisfy our preferences as self-interested, welfare-centred and independent agents are called non-positional goods (Frank 1985). Other goods such automobiles and dwellings may signal status and wealth and thereby affect the choices or welfare of others. Goods that have this signalling capacity are called positional goods (Frank 1985; Hirsch 1995). Still, as Dugger (1985) has argued, a good does not by itself communicate anything about the status of its owner. It must be understood in the society to be a positional good to function in such a capacity. The bottom line is that consumption involves interdependent consumers and there are important relational aspects.

Some contemporary economists (see Corneo and Jeanne 1997) consider that positional goods do not contribute to the welfare of their consumers. This problematic argument suggests that there are altogether superfluous goods that only serve to make distinctions and other goods that serve "genuine needs" intimately related to the agents' welfare. The familiar concepts of "necessities" and "luxuries" reflect this understanding. Yet it is diffi-cult, if not impossible, to separate the symbolic use of goods from their mundane use for satisfying needs. Therefore, the desire to distinguish oneself should be understood to enter into all consumption choices. This includes those forms of consumption that appear to be primarily linked to the satisfaction of "needs". As a result, we spend more money on all items of consumption than would be necessary to obtain their basic services. The extra increment is linked to characteristics that have symbolic importance.

Paying a premium for the symbolic functions of consumer goods does not alone raise environmental concerns as it amounts to taxing oneself and cutting back on one's ability to engage in material consumption. Given that adverse environmental impacts are usually directly related to the quantity of material consumption this may be a good thing from an environmental perspective. However, the situation is different if consumption for status causes more adverse environmental impacts than ordinary consumption. This is true in the case of many positional goods, such as cars and houses. Competition for status also influ-ences the life span of many goods, such as clothes, furniture, household appliances and cars. Furthermore, it may cause environmentally adverse structural changes in consump-tion if consumers maximise the public display of their possessions or expenditure (see Veblen 1899).

Interdependent consumer choices can be analysed as games in which self- and welfare-centred agents seek to distinguish themselves. In these games agents make their choices aware of the alternatives faced by others, but without being able to communicate or collab-orate with them (Kreps 1990). The competition for status and distinction follows the logic of the Prisoners' Dilemma game exemplified below in Table 5.1. If Consumer A chooses to distinguish herself when Consumer B does not, she earns a high pay-off of four in comparison to the low pay-off of 1 received by B, and vice versa. If both try to distinguish themselves at the same time they fail to do so and both earn a relatively low pay-off of two. Had both decided not to distinguish themselves they would each have earned a payoff of three and the maximum joint outcome in this game (see Kreps 1990; Schelling

Table 5.1: Payoffs in the consumption game among self- and welfare-centred agents.

A \ B	Does not signal	Signals
Does not signal	(A = 3, B = 3)	(A = 1, B= 4)
Signals	(A = 4, B = 1)	(A = 2, B = 2)

1978:216–17). This outcome would also have been the most desirable one from the environmental viewpoint, if the assumption that consumption for status has worse environmental impacts than ordinary consumption is accepted.

The game's expected outcome is that both Consumer A and Consumer B try to distinguish themselves, because it is the best choice for both of them individually, regardless of whatever the other does. However, it is the game's worst outcome in welfare and environmental terms. The self- and welfare-centred consumers of the standard rational-choice model are not able to avoid this outcome within the accepted constraints of the usual two-person, one-shot Prisoners' Dilemma-type game. The same applies in a multi-person Prisoners' Dilemma game that better characterises status seeking in real societies (see Schelling 1978). However, the consumers can avoid status competition in an endlessly repeated game (see Axelrod 1984). In this game the players can discipline those who do not conform to the jointly best strategy through their choices. This action amounts to rudimentary communication and collective action that is ruled out of the two-person, one-shot Prisoners' Dilemma game in the beginning.

The recognition of the interdependence of consumer choices highlights problems related to choosing green consumerism and lifestyles in societies where competition for status is rife. In the standard model of independent rational choice, individuals informed by self- and welfare-centred values could choose in an environment-friendly way if it improved their welfare. When we recognise the interdependence of consumer choices, the very same choice by the same agent may have significant adverse consequences for her. She may face high costs or forgo important opportunities if she attains a poor relative performance in important areas of interpersonal competition and comparison when seeking to realise welfare improvements related to the environment. This also means that there may be a number of agents who would view environmentally benign behaviour as welfare improving for themselves, but who are discouraged from acting according to their preferences. For these agents, public policies requiring changes in consumption or lifestyles and eliminating the sanctions linked to competitive status consumption could be welcome. The next section examines the implications of value pluralism for interdependent rational choice.

5. Interdependence and Value Pluralism

The two-person consumption game introduced in the previous section also enables us to examine the implications of non-welfarist environmental values and value pluralism for interdependent consumer choices. It also helps us to draw some conclusions concerning green consumerism more generally when agents' consumption choices are interdependent.

Since we do need two consumers for their choices to be interdependent, there are two different kinds of situations to analyse. On one hand, both consumers may have non-welfarist environmental concerns. On the other hand, one consumer may have these non-welfarist environmental concerns while the other consumer is informed by the self- and welfare-centred values that are usually assumed in economic analysis. I will address the situation where both consumers share non-welfarist environmental concerns first and after that will move on to discuss the situation where consumers hold formally different value positions.

It is necessary to modify the consumption game slightly before analysing the situation in which two consumers have non-welfarist concerns for the environment. First, as these two consumers are not motivated by their personal gain when making their choices, the term "pay-off" is not really a satisfactory way to describe the desirability of choice alternatives. It is more useful to talk about index values that reflect the desirability of an outcome from the viewpoint of a particular player in the game, given her motivations. Second, non-welfarist consumers assess and rank choice alternatives differently compared to welfarist agents as will be indicated below.

When Consumers A and B have non-welfarist concerns for the environment the best outcome for both is the one where neither of them distinguishes themselves. The second best outcome for both is to not distinguish themselves when the other player does so. The third best outcome for Consumers A and B is to distinguish themselves when the other does not. Clearly, the second and third outcomes are equal in environmental terms, but for a rational agent an outcome brought about when she acted according to her moral convictions must be preferable to a similar outcome that was brought about when she did not so act. The worst outcome for both Consumers A and B is the one in which they both try to distinguish themselves. The desirability index values for the different outcomes are depicted below in Table 5.2 by integers four, three, two, and one, listed in order from the best outcome to the worst one.

Table 5.2 indicates that consumers who have non-welfarist concerns for the environment are able to avoid competitive consumption for status and its environmentally adverse consequences in a two-person, one-shot consumption game. Committed agents are able to achieve this solely on the basis of their individual deliberated consumer choices, without government assistance or intervention. The result indicates that green consumerism is potentially a very powerful way to change aggregate outcomes and partly explains the increasingly shared confidence in different forms and expressions of green consumerism and lifestyles.

However, Table 5.2 presents a rather typical analysis in game theory that understands another set of values to dissolve the relationship of interdependence. Therefore, the above described one-shot, two-person game does not shed adequate light on the potentially

Table 5.2: Consumption game with universal non-utilitarian environmental concerns.

A \ B	Does not signal	Signals
Does not signal	(A = 4, B = 4)	(A = 3, B= 2)
Signals	(A = 2, B = 3)	(A = 1, B = 1)

Table 5.3: Payoffs in a non-welfarist green consumption game.

A \ B	Does not signal	Signals
Does not signal	(A = 3, B = 3)	(A = 1, B= 4)
Signals	(A = 4, B = 1)	(A = 2, B = 2)

problematic consequences of a game for distinction on non-welfarist merits among green consumers. This game is described below in Table 5.3 with the pay-offs from the standard consumption game presented in Table 5.1. The index values indicate that this game is likely to lead to undesirably stoic conduct among competing green consumers, a phenomenon that finds empirical support from the behaviour of environmentalists: some of them drift towards more extreme positions in a (usually undisclosed) search for status, esteem and authority.

The game-theoretic result confirming the capability of committed individuals to resolve the dilemma of interdependent consumption without government intervention is theoretically and practically important and is replicated in game-theoretic analyses of many other interdependency situations as well. It is also important to recognise that a new set of values may simply result in undesirable competition in another direction. Yet these games do not characterise well the interdependency issues involved in actual societies. After all, they do consist of numerous consumers who have both formally and substantially different values. Therefore, I will now examine a two-person game in which values are plural and that goes one step further towards a more realistic understanding of the actual social dilemma posed by interdependent consumer choices.

Values are plural in the formal sense when Consumer A is informed by self- and welfare-centred values and Consumer B would, because of her values, protect the environment or behave in an environmentally-benign way, even at the expense of her personal welfare. Table 5.3 describes a game between these two consumers that have different values. Consumer A's pay-offs can be obtained from Table 5.1 and Consumer B's ranking of alternatives is available in Table 5.2. The pay-offs and the desirability index values are indicated below in Table 5.4 by integers four, three, two, and one in order from the best outcome to the worst.

Table 5.4 indicates that in this game the right column's outcomes would never be chosen, because they are inferior for both agents. The game's worst outcome in welfare and environmental terms could thus be avoided on the basis of deliberated individual consumer choices even when value pluralism prevails. However, if the self- and welfare-centred Consumer A always seeks to distinguish herself, as she is thought to do under the usual assumptions, she would bring about, of the two remaining alternatives, the environmentally more undesirable one. On the other hand, a good question is whether the green consumer would "qualify" as a participant in competition for status for Consumer A. That is, she might not be able to successfully distinguish herself from the green consumer by choosing goods that have signalling capacity. The choices of Consumers A and B may thus not continue to be interdependent. As a result, Consumer A may reassess her valuation of outcomes to reflect their contribution to her welfare as an isolated consumer. This could mean that Consumer A would also choose not to signal, if doing so would improve her welfare.

Table 5.4: Consumption game with value pluralism.

A \ B	Does not signal	Signals
Does not signal	(A = 3, B = 4)	(A = 1, B= 2)
Signals	(A = 4, B = 3)	(A = 2, B = 1)

To conclude, the analysis of the implications of value pluralism for interdependent consumer choices indicates that the existence of consumers who are committed to non-welfarist environmental goals could dampen the competition for status in consumer choices. That is, green consumerism could also influence the choices of those consumers who act on self- and welfare-centred values, by creating an incentive for them to make their choices as isolated individuals rather than as participants in status competition. Of course, the degree to which this could actually happen depends on the relative numbers of welfarist and non-welfarist consumers and how welfarist consumers respond to non-welfarist ones. The ordinary two-person, one-shot consumption game does not shed light on these issues. The next section seeks to remedy the problem by examining the implications for interdependent consumption choices under value pluralism of a greater number of consumers.

6. Multi-Person Games, Plural Values and Sub-Cultures

A multi-person game describes the interdependence of consumers in society more realistically than the two-person games analysed above. However, as the multi-person game is significantly more complex, and usually entails quite technical analysis, this section only seeks to draw out some heuristic lessons to enrich the discussion. In what follows, an analysis will first be conducted assuming that all consumers are informed by self- and welfare-centred values. The implications of introducing consumers informed by non-welfarist values into the game are discussed at the end.

In multi-person games pay-offs linked to choosing particular alternatives are depicted by lines or curves. The horizontal axis represents the number of individuals making the choice. The vertical axis describes the magnitude of the pay-off (Schelling, 1978). For example, Figure 5.1 below shows an interdependence situation in which consumption for status yields a higher pay-off (Curve S) than ordinary consumption (Curve N) no matter what others do, and in which consumption for status yields a higher pay-off when fewer consumers choose it. This is indicated by the fact that the right end of the pay-off Curve S yields a higher pay-off than the left end. The collective outcome in welfare terms is shown by the dotted line that lies between the pay-off curves. It indicates that in welfare terms it would be better if nobody signalled.

Consumption for status is the dominant choice in the multi-person game described in the Figure 5.1. Correspondingly, the game has an equilibrium that is represented by the left-hand end of the collective outcome curve: everybody engages in consumption for status to the detriment of private and collective welfare. Not consuming for status results in a welfare loss before a critical number (K) of consumers choose it. The critical coalition size

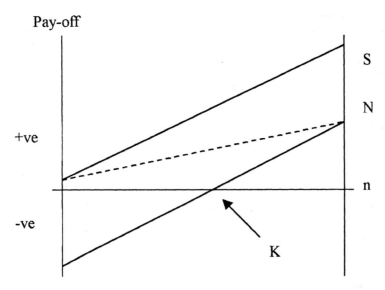

Figure 5.1: The consumption game among n players.

K is found at the intersection of the Curve N and the horizontal axis. When more than K consumers do not consume for status, their choices result in a positive individual pay-off. If everybody chooses to withstand status consumption, it will be a better outcome in terms of both collective and individual welfare compared to the case where everybody signals. This is indicated by the fact that the right-hand end of the collective pay-off curve is at its highest while the right-hand end of Curve N is at a higher level than the left-hand end of Curve S. However, this outcome is difficult to attain. Everybody is inclined to consume for status when it is not a common strategy because it yields a very high pay-off.

Although this brief analysis of a multi-person consumption game is based on assuming welfarist agents, it is easy to assess the implications of value pluralism because signalling is an equilibrium solution that is difficult to dispense with. A sizeable coalition of consumers is required not to signal before it can become a viable strategy in welfare terms. That is, the environmental vanguard engaging in green consumerism may suffer significant welfare losses if they cannot enlist enough support. The self- and welfare-centred consumers assumed in standard economic analysis do not voluntarily choose to the detriment of their personal welfare. Therefore, they cannot form the critical coalition.

In contrast, the consumers that hold non-welfarist concerns for the environment are able and willing to make personal welfare sacrifices for the environment. The crucial question is, are they numerous enough to make withstanding status competition a preferable choice also for welfarist agents. This is an important question. An outcome in which a small minority (N < K) of non-welfarist consumers withstands status competition while a large majority (N > n–K) of welfarist consumers engages in it may not differ significantly from the "everybody does it" outcome from an environmental viewpoint.

Green consumerism may also result in elitist green sub-markets and lifestyles because of non-welfarist status competition. In this scenario, deeply committed green consumers make their choices at the expense of their personal welfare to realise their values. While seeking to earn status in their own sub-culture by exhibiting non-welfarist environmental concerns and consumer choices that are compatible with them, they continually revise the standards of conduct that confer esteem. Over time, this leads to the widening of the gap between the green sub-culture and the mainstream consumer culture, making it increasingly difficult to move across the cultural divide.

The emergence of an elitist green culture is a problematic possibility, because demanding environmental lifestyles and sub-markets may not be able to command enough support to successfully transform a whole society. Broader use of environmental alternatives could lower the cost of environmental choices, turn them potentially into welfare-improving choices, and invite consumers who are informed by self- and welfare-centred values to alter their level and pattern of consumption.

The analysis raises the question of whether it is wise to leave determination of the feasibility of creating a critical coalition of green consumers to uncoordinated individual action. Collective action could modify the alternatives and/or pay-offs in order that agents realise collectively the most desirable outcome. For example, one can contrast a consumer boycott of an environmentally harmful product versus the establishment of formal institutional rules that prevent it from being offered altogether. Being able to act morally may satisfy the informed consumer, but it may not prevent an undesirable outcome that is preventable by collective action.

7. Conclusion

This chapter has examined green consumerism and its implications for human welfare and the environment. The analysis began with a simple model of rational choice. This was gradually expanded to take into account the fact that our choices are not informed exclusively by our concerns for our own personal welfare, and that sometimes our consumption choices are interdependent with those of others. The aim was in part to demonstrate that economics can yield insights into consumption that are not as simplistic as those built into many conventional models.

The standard model of rational choice, and its expansion to take into consideration non-welfarist concerns for the environment, yields a somewhat optimistic view of green consumerism and its potential to deliver more sustainable consumption patterns. In essence, it contributes an overly optimistic understanding, according to which sensitising consumers to environmental values and concerns, or otherwise bringing about a change of values, will be enough to change behaviour. Models that recognise the interdependence of consumer choices substantiate the promise of green consumerism perhaps even more powerfully. It is evident that we could fundamentally transform our consumer choices if only all of us shared non-welfarist concerns for the environment.

On the other hand, the models that recognise the interdependence of consumer choices also equally strongly remind us of the fragility of the promise of green consumerism. To begin with, universally shared non-welfarist values are unlikely in pluralist societies. Moreover, the models demonstrate that it may be costly for consumers to change their consumption patterns, as long as relative performance in certain areas of consumption matters. Values would thus need to change more broadly to bring about any environmentally benign changes in consumption. The other alternative these models remind us about is public policy, which may expand opportunity sets and alter the relative costs and benefits of alternatives.

Perhaps the most worrying aspect of green consumerism is its potential transformation into an elitist alternative lifestyle. In this case what are traditionally understood as welfare sacrifices become a sub-culture's means for distinction. This politics of distinction would prevent the expansion of the lifestyle and the incorporation of the bulk of consumer households into it. Under such circumstances, green consumerism might not be able to deliver environmental benefits, although it could deliver moral satisfaction for the alternative minority.

References

Anderson, E. (1993), *Value in Ethics and Economics*. Cambridge: Harvard University Press.

Axelrod, R. (1984), *The Evolution of Cooperation*. New York: Basic Books.

Bagwell, L., & Bernheim, B. (1996), "Veblen effects in a theory of conspicuous consumption." *American Economic Review 86* (3), 349–373.

Becker, G. (1996), *Accounting for Tastes*. Cambridge, MA: Harvard University Press.

Becker, G. (1976), *The Economic Approach to Human Behavior*. Chicago: The University of Chicago Press.

Broome, J. (1991), "Utility." *Economics and Philosophy 7* (1), 1–12.

Bromley, D. (1989), *Economic Interests and Institutions: The Conceptual Foundations of Public Policy*. Oxford: Basil Blackwell.

Brown, T., & Gregory, R. (1999), "Why the WTA-WTP disparity matters." *Ecological Economics 28* (3), 323–335.

Cogoy, M. (1999), "The consumer as a social and environmental actor." *Ecological Economics 28* (3), 385–398.

Corneo, G., & Jeanne, O. (1997), "Conspicuous consumption, snobbism and conformism." *Journal of Public Economics 66* (1), 55–71.

Crocker, D., & Linden, T. (eds). (1998), *The Ethics of Consumption: The Good Life, Justice and Global Stewardship*. Oxford: Rowman and Littlefield.

Deaton, A., & Muellbauer, J. (1980), *Economics and Consumer Behavior*. Cambridge: Cambridge University Press.

Elgin, D. (1993), *Voluntary Simplicity: Toward a Way of Life that is Outwardly Simple, Inwardly Rich*. New York: Morrow.

Elster, J. (1983), *Sour Grapes: Studies in the Subversion of Rationality*. Cambridge: Cambridge University Press.

Foster, J. (ed.). (1997), *Valuing Nature? Economics, Ethics, and Environment*. London: Routledge.

Frank, R. (1991), "Positional externalities." In R. J. Zeckhauser (ed.) *Strategy and Choice* (pp. 25–47). Cambridge: Harvard University Press.

Frank, R. (1985), "The demand for unobservable and other nonpositional goods." *American Economic Review 75* (1), 101–116.

Georg, S. (1999), "The social shaping of household consumption." *Ecological Economics 28* (3), 455–466.

Georgescu-Roegen, N. (1968), "Utility." In D. Sills (ed.) *International Encyclopedia of the Social Sciences*, Vol. 16 (pp. 236–267). New York: Macmillan.

Gowdy, J. (1997), "The value of biodiversity: Markets, society and ecosystems." *Land Economics 73* (1), 25–41.

Hargreaves Heap, S., Hollis, M., Lyons, B., Sudgen, R., & Weale, A. (1992), *The Theory of Choice: A Critical Guide*. Oxford: Blackwell.

Hicks, J., & Allen, R. (1934), "A reconsideration of the theory of value." *Economica 1*, 52–76 and 196–219.

Hirsch, F. (1995), *Social Limits to Growth*. London: Routledge.

Jackson, T., & Marks, N. (1999), "Consumption, sustainable welfare and human needs: With reference to UK expenditure patterns between 1954 and 1994." *Ecological Economics 28* (3), 421–441.

Jorgensen, B., Syme, G., Bishop, B., & Nancarrow, B. (1999), "Protest responses in contingent valuation." *Environmental and Resource Economics 14*, 131–150.

Kavka, G. (1991), "Is individual choice less problematic than collective choice." *Economics and Philosophy 7* (2), 143–165.

Kreps, D. (1990), *Game Theory and Economic Modelling*. Oxford: Clarendon Press.

Lancaster, K. (1966), "A new approach to consumer theory." *Journal of Political Economy 74*, 132–157.

Leibenstein, H. (1950), "Bandwagon, Snob and Veblen effects in the theory of consumers' demand." *Quarterly Journal of Economics 64* (2), 183–207.

Organisation for Economic Cooperation and Development (1997a), *Sustainable Consumption and Production*. Paris: OECD.

Organisation for Economic Cooperation and Development (1997b), *Sustainable Consumption and Production: Clarifying the Concepts*. Paris: OECD.

Organisation for Economic Cooperation and Development (1998), *Towards Sustainable Consumption Patterns: A Progress Report on Member Country Initiatives*. Paris: OECD.

Røpke, I. (1999), "The dynamics of willingness to consume." *Ecological Economics 28* (3), 399–420.

Sagoff, M. (1988), *The Economy of the Earth: Philosophy, Law and the Environment*. Cambridge: Cambridge University Press.

Schelling, T. (1978), *Micromotives and Macrobehavior*. New York: Norton.

Sen, A. (1970), "The impossibility of a Paretian Liberal." *Journal of Political Economy 78* (1), 152–157.

Sen, A. (1973), "Behaviour and the concept of preference." *Economica 40* (159), 241–259.

Sen, A. (1977), "Rational fools: A critique of the behavioural foundations of economic theory." *Philosophy and Public Affairs 6*, 317–344.

Sen, A. (1991), "Utility: Ideas and terminology." *Economics and Philosophy 7* (2), 277–283.

Sen, A. (1995), "Environmental evaluation and social choice: Contingent valuation and the market analogy." *Japanese Economic Review 46* (1), 23–37.

Simon, H. (1978), "Rationality as a process and product of thought." *American Economic Review 68* (2), 1–16.

Spash, C., & Hanley, N. (1995), "Preferences, information and biodiversity preservation." *Ecological Economics 12*, 191–208.

Stigler, G., & Becker G. (1977), "De gustibus non est disputandum." *American Economic Review 67* (2), 76–90.

Vatn, A., & Bromley, D. (1995), "Choices without prices without apologies." In D. Bromley (ed.) *The Handbook of Environmental Economics* (pp. 3–25). Oxford: Blackwell.

Veblen, T. (1899), *The Theory of the Leisure Class: An Economic Study of Institutions*. London: Macmillan.

Part IV

Place, Space and Networks: Geographies of Sustainable Consumption

Chapter 6

Sustaining Foods: Organic Consumption and the Socio-Ecological Imaginary

David Goodman and Michael Goodman

1. Introduction

A central element in the social imaginaries of "sustainable consumption" and "green consumerism" is that the social values and everyday commitments that underpin consumer choice can be changed by the deployment of discursive resources. In this imaginary, changes in worldviews can transform consumption habits and cause significant shifts in market demand, creating profitable commercial opportunities for commodities produced more sustainably. As consumer values and habits of "getting and spending" are re-orientated toward "green" goods and services, producers of these commodities begin to enjoy competitive advantages over their less sustainable rivals. The process of capitalist competition, perhaps reinforced by state incentive policies and codes of ethical investment, will accelerate the transition of productive sectors, industries and, ultimately, capitalist economies to more sustainable development paths.

This standard, arguably reductionist, view conceives of sustainable consumption largely as a technological question, to be resolved within the parameters of capitalist instrumental rationality in a society where capitalist-exchange relations have penetrated all areas of economic and social life. In a second, less restrictive conception of sustainable consumption, premised on a different theorisation of capitalist society, alternative rationalities and social organisational forms could co-exist, and potentially restrict the scope of capitalist-exchange relations. This second conceptualisation clearly is implicit in arguments that consumer agency, even in the socially diffuse, incremental form of individual choice, can become a radical force for ecological and socially progressive change (Miller 1995). A wider analytical framework of co-existing social forms and different rationalities lends credibility to claims that "sustainable consumption" and "green consumerism" promise to achieve no less than the re-ordering of society's metabolic relations with nature via the growth of new producer-consumer networks cemented by shared social values and commitments.

The transformative potential of green consumerism is not predicated on social mobilisation in the sense conventionally associated with social movements and political activism. Nevertheless, the articulation of producer-consumer networks to advance green commitments must contend with hegemonic discursive regimes and economic and regulatory

Exploring Sustainable Consumption: Evironmental Policy and the Social Sciences, Volume 1, pages 97–119.
Copyright © 2001 by Elsevier Science Ltd.
All rights of reproduction in any form reserved.
ISBN: 0-08-043920-9

power. In this context, the conceptual repertoire and metaphors of actor-network theory (ANT) are helpful to describe the challenge of changing the present "ordering" of nature-society relations. In the lexicon of ANT, networks are relational co-productions of humans and non-human entities formed to advance actor projects, although agency is conceptualised as a collective property or "effect" of the network (Law 1992; Latour 1993). Networks are forged in processes of translation, which have various "moments", culminating in "mobilisation" when "a constraining network has been built" (Callon 1986:218–19).

Agro-food sectors and commodity systems fit easily into this conceptual framework of nature-society co-productions. In previous work, one of us has characterised food networks in terms of a dual combination of metabolic relations: between agricultural nature and social labour in production and the corporeal and symbolic act of human food consumption (D. Goodman, 1999). This approach places the relational materiality of agro-ecologies and human bodies at the centre of the analysis (FitzSimmons and Goodman, 1998). In this perspective, the discursive and material projects of organic agriculture and fair trade networks seek to re-configure this relational materiality by changing the under-lying metabolic relations and the social practices in which these are embedded. Human and non-human entities are "translated" into alternative production-consumption networks.

In turn, these alternative "orderings" of nature-society relations face competing networks in the struggle to translate actors and entities and so enhance their power. Trans-lation or alliance formation also is vital to the capacity of actor-networks to "act at a distance" across multiple scales of time and space (Latour 1993; Law 1986). As the case studies of food products reveal, standards, certification and other "immutable mobiles" (Latour 1987) are critical elements of this capacity to build networks of producers and consumers on multiple scales.

Our approach to organic agriculture, eco-labelling, and fair trade in food products is to map differences between their discursive claims and the material, ecological and social practices that constitute their respective imaginaries of sustainability. These networks make differing claims, for example, about local food security, provision of a living wage for farm workers and biodiversity conservation. This analysis thus distinguishes the various practices of producer-consumer networks making general claims of "sustainable consumption" in order to problematise this concept and its normative application.

Before we proceed, however, the notion of green or sustainable consumption requires further discussion, and especially in relation to its transformative claims. More specifi-cally, the radical content of these claims depends crucially on how capitalism is theorised. That is, the notion of sustainable consumption rests on hidden and largely unexamined assumptions about the nature of capitalism, its structural characteristics, and future devel-opment. One view of capitalism that underpins what may be termed the mainstream approach to sustainable consumption is the "universalization" thesis. This suggests that capitalism and its instrumental rationality now pervade all areas of human interaction, including social life, whose subsumption is characterised by Habermas (1987) as "the colonization of the lifeworld". Virtually all aspects of economic and social life are "commodified" and capitalist social relations are ubiquitous.

From this "universalist" viewpoint, green or sustainable consumption activities can be characterised essentially as a subset of generalised capitalist production-consumption rela-tions. A corollary of the universalist position is that the discourse of "sustainable consumption" is strongly, if not exclusively, focused on the technical relations or "forces" of production and their environmental consequences. Sustainable consumption does not propose any fundamental transformation of capitalist society and its distinctive rationality, but rather "running adjustments" to reorient the production-consumption nexus toward more environmentally friendly or "sustainable" production technologies.

By assumption, these alternative production technologies are efficient and consistent with the capitalist logic of exchange-value and the pursuit of profit. Here, sustainable consumption is mainly a form of technological competition, which adds a green gloss to capitalism, reifying its inherent dynamic and "tendencies".

The role of discourse in the "universalist" version of green consumption is to provide a mirror in which actors can clearly discern the environmental consequences of their individual and collective activity. The consequences of our "old" ways of getting and spending, hitherto obscured, are now made transparent by green discourse, with the aim of stimulating a reflexive, self-cognitive process that will lead to individual and societal demands for less environmentally degrading processes of production and consumption. These tropes are deployed in varying ways by the sustainable consumption networks examined below.

A second version of sustainable consumption can be distinguished, which is predicated upon a different implicit theorisation of capitalist society. Rather than "a totality of exchange relations", the underlying premise is that the instrumental rationality of the capitalist economy is not universal and, as a result, commodification is uneven. A theorisation of capitalism with this premise has recently been advanced by Jessop (1997:563), who argues that alternative forms of social organisation may co-exist, and even co-evolve, with the capitalist economy, since this "is not wholly self-contained". That is, "the capitalist economy is 'structurally coupled' to other systems with their own operational logics or instrumental rationalities and to the 'lifeworld' formed by various social relations, identities, interests and values not otherwise anchored in specific systems" (Jessop 1997:563).

A more open-ended, less totalising theorisation of capitalism, illustrated here by Jessop's formulation, is implicit in the practices and values advocated by some of the green or sustainable-consumption networks discussed in this chapter. Their social projects and imaginaries are not constrained by the straitjacket of capitalist criteria of rational behaviour and profitability. Sustainable consumption then may be conceived as an alternative project on its own terms, which can co-exist with the capitalist economy, and possibly expand at its expense. Once different operational logics are given space, analytically and concretely, sustainable consumption can extend beyond its "universalist" version and reductionist focus on green technology to interrogate the rationality, values and goals that structure social relations and society's relations with nature. In short, the concept of sustainable consumption can embrace social groups and organisational forms that do not all march to the same drummer.

From this standpoint, for example, sustainable-agriculture movements occupy "spaces of possibility" patterned by highly differentiated material eco-social relations and imaginaries. The analytical task is to provide a cartography of these spaces that reveals their diversity of form and diversity of practice. Organic food production-consumption networks in California are examined in Section 2 below, and international organic ecolabelling and fair trade are the focus of Section 3.

2. Organic Agriculture: California Dreaming

Diversity certainly is evident in Californian organic agriculture, but the patterns of number, practice and form encountered in that region prompt close interrogation of sustainable consumption and its meanings. California is the primary focus of an extraordinary "translation" of human and non-human entities into new metabolic networks of agricultural nature-social labour-food consumption. Very briefly, in the United States these networks grew from 2,753 certified organic farms and 479,000 acres in 1991 to 4,856 farms and 915,000 acres in 1995 (Klonsky 2000).[1] Sales of organic produce, admittedly starting from a low absolute level, have grown at an average annual rate of 20 percent since 1990, reaching an estimated $4.5 billion in 1998, including $3.5 billion in domestic sales, $5–600 million in exports, and $2–300 million in herbs and non-food products. Although still significantly less than one percent of United States retail food sales, this rapid scaling up has brought serious tensions, which have called sustainable agriculture *qua* social movement into question and clouded the transparency of its claims to sustainability, as we explain below.

Organic production-consumption networks have a storied past, whose history has yet to be written. In the United States, the many filaments extend from early pioneers of biodynamic agriculture and 1960s counter-culture movements, including back-to-the-land advocates, farm communes and alternative food-marketing initiatives (Belasco 1989), to projects to revitalise family farming and conserve farmland and sustainable-agriculture movements (SAMs). The metabolic co-productions of land and labour variously mobilised under the organic are heavily invested with ethical and philosophical values to constitute what Vos (2000) has characterised as a "moral ecology". This expresses certain "foundational values", including notions of stewardship, following Aldo Leopold's "land ethic", and intersubjective relational values based on reverence for nature. These values are drawn from and shape both the material or agroecological practices of organic farming *and* its operational logic to create a distinctive praxis or "way of life". In this discourse, organic praxis brings good husbandry to the land and healthy, nutritious food to consumers.

In actor-network terms, the organic discourse represents a specific "problematisation" of eco-social relations in agro-food networks, an initial though recurrent step in the process of translation. This discourse constructs the organic agro-food collective, where human and non-human entities — agricultural nature, sociotechnical artifacts, farmers, workers, consumers — are aligned and their identities defined in particular ways. For organic consumers, the discursive "imagined community" of shared metabolic values is materialised as a specific ordering of eco-social relations. This nature-culture collective acts at a distance through the "certified organic" label, the medium of trust and stamp of authenticity used to enrol other actors and intermediaries, human and non-human, extending the production-consumption spaces of the organic. In this field of narrative forces, the "biocidal" wasteland of conventional agriculture is restored by benign,

---

[1]Since these data are taken from private third-party certification groups, the number of organic growers, and particularly small operators, probably is significantly under-estimated. That is, growers who are registered as organic producers with state agencies, but not certified by third-party organisations, are excluded from these data.

transparent ecological practices and repopulated by family farms, and all effortlessly inscribed on the cartography of organic consumption.

From its inchoate beginnings, the organic production-consumption network gradually acquired certain industrial characteristics as SAMs moved towards self-regulation. In the 1970s, such groups as California Certified Organic Farmers (CCOF) and Oregon Tilth assumed state-level responsibility for certifying "organically grown" produce, initiating the legal construction of the organic. These efforts to further stabilise and coordinate the roles of human and non-human entities entered a decisive stage in 1990 with the passage of state and federal legislation, which is intended to establish legal minimum standards of organic production, including lists of allowable materials.

In this respect, such legislation represents a form of network coordination or "translation regime", that seeks to impose behavioural stability and give the appearance of irreversibility (Callon 1991). However, the features of this regime have been vigorously contested since the public outcry provoked by the National Organic Program Proposed Rule, which was released in 1997 by the United States Department of Agriculture (USDA) to regulate the federal Organic Foods Production Act of 1990. The rejection by the organic production-consumption collective of the roles and identities that the USDA had assigned was at the heart of this dispute, epitomised by the proposed enrolment of new hybrid entities, notably irradiation, municipal sewage, and genetically-modified organisms. The proposed rule was thus perceived as a threat to dilute the distinctive practices, material and discursive, of this alternative "mode of ordering" metabolic relations (Goodman 2000a).

Nevertheless, as Guthman (1998:141, 145) emphasises, "organic food has come to be defined by its regulation" and this, in turn, "has come to rely on gross simplification — an amazing irony considering the agronomic goals of organic agriculture". That is, organic is defined by the legally restricted materials and the exceptions, documented or illicit, that such codification implicitly encourages. This reductionism, and the associated levelling down of standards, arguably is the key source of the diversity of agronomic practice found in California organic agriculture.

Although the expository convenience of binary categories can be dangerously misleading, codification and economic expansion appear to have accentuated differences between "movement" farmers, who remain committed to the "moral ecology" and agroecological practices of organic farming, and "minimalist" farmers, whose practices and operational logic are more closely informed by legal input restrictions and profit maximisation. However, as will soon become apparent, the lines between these categories are imprecisely drawn, with each representing a diverse constellation of eco-social relations.

Both groups enjoy the refugial niche of organic production, protected by the costs of the conversion process from direct competition with conventional agriculture. Yet, in the context of rapidly growing organic markets, legal minimum standards have facilitated the scaling-up of production and drawn larger producers into the sector, including so-called "mixed" farm operators, who cultivate both conventional and organic crops. This configuration has two significant implications for the meaning of sustainable food consumption. First, the extension of organic production-consumption networks has provoked structural convergence with conventional agriculture, threatening the shared metabolic values that connect the "imagined community" of organic producers and consumers. Second, the bifurcation between "movement" and "minimalist" farmers problematises the notion of sustainable agriculture, even when this is understood purely in ecological terms.

Restructuring and Convergence

Recent research in California reveals that organic agriculture in important respects is not so much imitating natural systems — "farming in nature's image" as the textbooks have it — as industrial agriculture. Agroecological management involves the design of integrated farming systems, where organic matter, soil nutrients and biological pest control mecha- nisms, for example, are produced on-farm as use-values and recycled through the system. However, evidence from California indicates that farm production processes have been significantly eroded by industrial appropriationism (Goodman *et al.*, 1987). That is, there is considerable dependence on external inputs produced by specialist suppliers, allowing organic farmers to dispense with the recommended on-farm alternatives. Such input substitution, in turn, supports mono-cropping, sometimes at several production sites, and year-round multiple cropping (Guthman 2000; Buck *et al.*, 1997). As Altieri and Rosset (1997) observe, this recalls the "limiting factor mentality" that has dominated conven- tional agricultural research and practice for decades.

Critics of conventional agriculture have long drawn attention to the unsustainable, energy-intensive logistical patterns associated with agribusiness product sourcing. Thus Kloppenburg *et al.* (1996:34) cite an estimate that food products in the United States are transported 1,300 miles on average and are handled by six intermediaries before being consumed: "What is eaten by the great majority of North Americans comes from a global everywhere, yet from nowhere they know in particular". Yet California organic growers are approximating these conventional patterns via contract production for interregional markets, supermarkets and organic chain stores, such as Whole Foods Market, with 100 outlets in twenty states, as well as exports to international markets. These marketing struc- tures are a far cry from the development of local agro-food networks of farmers' markets and Community Supported Agriculture (CSA) schemes or integration in place-based "foodsheds" in support of community food councils and food security initiatives.

Finally, structural convergence is evident in the organisation of the labour process. The agronomic demands of intensive, specialist fresh vegetable crops and the recent scaling-up and concentration of production challenge the frequent conflation of organic production and family farms. Certainly these are generally not family-labour farms *strictu sensu*. Rather, the production process depends on casual non-unionised immigrant labour, which reproduces the exploitative wage relations of their counterparts in industrial agriculture.

The bimodal structure between "movement" and "minimalist" farmers, or what Melanie DuPuis (2000) characterises as "process" vs. "standards" approaches to organic produc- tion, was an implicit assumption of earlier research on California organic agriculture. Thus larger producers, including all-organic and "mixed" operators, were presumed to adhere to the codified criteria and be closely integrated with concentrated distribution and retail sectors, with smaller "process" farmers relying more on direct-marketing channels, notably farmers' markets, CSAs or subscription farming, and sales to sophisticated restau- rants (Buck *et al.*, 1997). However, following a comprehensive questionnaire survey, interviews and farm visits, Guthman (2000:18) has proposed some important qualifications to the bimodal hypothesis, suggesting "key variations in practices are related to variables quite separate from scale and grower commitment". Her research emphasises the significant influence of climatic and biophysical differences on agronomic practice, but the principal source of variation "is related to crop specificities and the availability of efficacious technologies and inputs to deal with crop-specific problems".

Differences emerge in the agronomic practices used by all-organic farmers and "mixed" operators, and "at least in some areas, there are clear gradations in practices between large-scale and small-scale growers" (Guthman 2000:18). However, the most singular finding is that "in almost all cases, organic farming practices fall notably short of agroecological ideals, although they remain within the letter of organic rules and regulations" (18). Guthman attributes these limitations in part to the contradictory effects of legal norms, which operate both as entry barriers and as a ceiling, giving "growers less incentive to incorporate an ideal practice when an allowable one will suffice" (19).

This research describes the wide diversity of agronomic practice and the malleable content of the organic in California. As Guthman (2000) emphasises, since her sample is not representative in terms of number of growers, there is uncertainty about how many certified small farmers remain committed to the philosophy and agronomic processes of organic agriculture. It is revealing, nevertheless, that of Guthman's sample of 77 all-organic growers, only four gained the highest agroecological ranking, as defined by basic principles of organic management drawn from the well-known text by Altieri (1995). While the median farm size of organic production of ten acres (Klonsky and Tourte 1998) leaves room for small "process" farmers, Guthman's survey "captures most of the acreage and sales in the sector" (Guthman 2000:2). In short, organic practices in California still may fall on a gradient but, for large and small producers alike, it is heavily tilted towards the minimalist or standards approach in terms of food sales and relations with agricultural nature.

This codified agricultural sustainability and the cost-oriented calculus of input substitution fit easily with capitalist logic, facilitating structural convergence and exposing organic agriculture to "translation" by other powerful actor-networks. This scenario describes the recent struggle of movement farmers and grassroots organisations with the USDA and its strong corporate agribusiness constituency. Sadly, the boundaries of this dispute have been defined largely by the USDA's framing of regulation in terms of production norms and market enhancement (Goodman 2000b). This discursive disciplining and capture of the regulatory process endangers other imaginaries that build on the nexus of philosophical values and agronomic practice as the foundation of alternative socio-ecological futures.

Codification, Organic Managerialism and Reflexive Green Consumerism

The codification of organic, and the structural change this promotes, problematises sustainable food consumption in various ways, principally by locating its political economy on the highly constrained terrain of technical criteria. The politics of sustainable food consumption can then be formulated as a choice between two forms of environmental managerialism. Both dovetail nicely with the "universalist" version of green consumerism discussed above. In this framing, the sustainability of organic food consumption is ascribed negatively by comparison with the unsustainable practices attributed to conventional agriculture. The organic is represented as a competing system of efficient resource management, and enframed by modernist epistemology and scientific knowledge claims (Allen 1993; Buttel 1993, 1997). This managerialist representation also privileges food safety and health claims. The organic is equated with the limited and controlled use of synthetic materials and substances, a reliable source of "chemical-lite" products. Sustainability as resource management is the hallmark of this techno-scientific discourse, which marginalises "moral ecology" and reifies the social division of labour.

With sustainable food consumption reduced to production standards and related food-safety claims, it is easily consigned to the neo-liberal terrain of individual market choice and consumer sovereignty. This terrain is populated by self-regulated bodies or reflexive consumers who, it is presumed, have the knowledge to evaluate food risks and the purchasing power to buy accordingly. In short, neo-liberal green consumerism pre-empts alternative conceptualisations of sustainable food consumption, which articulate social justice concerns and provide space for forms of food provisioning not disciplined by capitalist markets.

There seems little doubt that codification of organic, and the rapid scaling-up to "industry" status with the entry of larger growers, vertically integrated agribusiness, and retail chains, will reinforce technocentrism. Indeed, mainstream SAMs in the United States, by and large, have accepted this arena of legitimation and failed to elaborate a progressive socio-ecological politics that gives prominence to issues of social justice, food security, class, gender, and race (Allen 1999). The social agenda of sustainable agriculture has been subordinated to "the project of making agriculture sustainable" (Allen and Sachs 1991:571). By default, construction of food production-consumption networks to address this social agenda has fallen to community food security movements and anti-hunger activists.

Bridges to Progressive Green Consumerism

To expose these social "invisibilities", a more symmetrical understanding of sustainable food consumption is needed. The key requirement is the integration of sustainable agro-ecological processes — the conditions and forces of production — with social justice in the production and distribution of wholesome organic food. Discursive claims to transparency would then be systemic in scope, extending from farming practices to socially just relations in the labour process and equitable food access. Although embryonic and localised, more systemic, progressive agendas have recently emerged that challenge the erasures and silences of technocratic discourse. These initiatives to create sustainable agro-food networks are seeking to forge links between small-scale organic farmers and the working poor and other excluded groups in urban areas.

In California, the past decade has seen a remarkable groundswell of social movements and programs seeking to restructure regional and local food networks. Although often with strong historical roots, this organisational effervescence has created a rich array of new social forms at the food production-consumption interface. Mere labels do not convey the empirical diversity of form that embraces organic farmer movements, Community Supported Agriculture (CSA), farmers' markets, food policy councils, urban gardens, micro-food processing enterprises, therapeutic and rehabilitation projects, farmland-conservation trusts, food cooperatives, and myriad organic garden and meals projects in schools. Yet for all its creative energy, this wave of social innovation has made negligible inroads into agro-food networks at large. Organic food, as already noted, still represents less than one percent of retail food sales in the United States (Klonsky 2000).

As a general argument, the success of these progressive initiatives depends on the construction of "rural-urban bridges"[2] that promote expansion into spaces and production niches where non-capitalist operational logics can prevail. Sustainable food consumption otherwise will be defined in the technocentric lexicon of production norms and food safety, losing its credibility as a force for progressive structural change. However, these bridges are extraordinarily difficult to build in practice, as efforts to connect farmers' markets and CSAs with affordable food provision to low-income consumers have demonstrated.

These new institutional forms have grown spectacularly in recent years, with the number of farmers' markets in California rising from seven in 1977 and 250 in 1997 to over 300 currently (Perry, 2000). The livelihoods and social reproduction of organic "movement" or "process" farmers are closely linked to these regional and local markets. Thus the Community Alliance with Family Farmers (CAFF), a nonprofit membership organisation in California, "supports direct marketing as a key to economic viability for family farmers and as a way for city folks to get back in touch with the land and the people who grow their food" (CAFF 1998:3). "Economic viability" for operators in these marketing channels arguably is the simple reproduction of petty capitalists rather than the expanded reproduction of archetypal capitalist enterprise. Nevertheless, apart from extremely small holdings, fresh vegetable and fruit growers in California usually depend upon wage labour, as well as family members, and therefore have a structural requirement to earn an adequate economic return or "surplus product". Under these conditions, production for the market inevitably raises issues of exploitative class and gender relations within the labour process, as well as pricing practices.

This structural requirement has bedevilled efforts to reconcile market-based sustainable production with the community food security goal of providing equitable access for all consumers to organic food.[3] The short-lived Market Basket Project in Los Angeles, for example, supplied organic produce to low-income residents by purchasing from growers in local farmers' markets, who agreed to sell part of their output at a 15 percent discount below market prices. After two years, this project was phased out because of the economic difficulties of providing food to low-income families and logistical supply problems (Gottlieb and Mascarenhas 1997). In Santa Cruz, the grant and subscriber-supported Homeless Garden Project, which gives vocational training to homeless people in its CSA programme, contributes to local food security by allocating some CSA shares

---

[2]This phrase is used by the Community Alliance with Family Farmers to define its activities (CAFF 1998:3).
[3]For a general discussion critical of community food security movements and attentive to the limitations of localism, refer to Allen (1999).

to low-income households. However, this arrangement depends on a "cross-subsidy" from grant funds and donations from wealthier CSA subscribers.

The social exclusion that these CSA projects seek to offset is accentuated by reports of the higher unit prices found in farmers' markets compared to supermarkets. These "new spaces" and their imaginaries are not accessible to all, inviting charges that organic consumption is a form of "class diet", highly differentiated by income, race, and other attributes. Allen (1999), for example, cites a 1995 survey of California CSA members that found that 71 percent had annual incomes of $40,000 or more, while a 1992 study reported that people of colour represented only 5 percent of the total CSA membership.

The creative, but highly fragmented and partial, nature of efforts to resolve the commercial production – affordable consumption dilemma emphasises the obstacles facing progressive agendas for sustainable agro-food networks. Not surprisingly, these difficulties have stimulated a variety of urban-based agriculture and community gardening projects to enhance food security, generate income in kind, and strengthen community organisation. The Northern California Food Systems Alliance formed by the San Francisco League of Urban Gardeners and other Bay Area organisations exemplifies this focus on gaining greater control over local food supply as a source of community empowerment. In other programs, public resources, notably school district meals funds, are being used to provide markets for organic family farms and enhance their integration with local communities. The "Farmers' Market Salad Bar" program in which nine Santa Monica schools are participating and the Berkeley Food Systems Project are two of many such initiatives in California (Mascarenhas 2000). In their different ways, such projects simply side-step the dilemma presented by market-based approaches to sustainable food consumption and food security. Instead, they create allocative schemes less strongly disciplined by market values and the conflation of consumption and citizenship.

These experiences reveal the contradiction between the social reproduction of commercial organic farmers and equitable access to affordable organic food. Under present rules of the game, in other words, the rural-urban bridges of progressive imaginaries are too fragile. This recommends, in turn, that sustainable agriculture and urban food movements build coalitions that can engage with the politics of the State to secure public resources for locally-based sustainable agro-food networks. The need for non-market support is the crucial lesson of projects to connect farmers' markets and CSAs with low-income groups.

The imaginative use of cost and price subsidies would not place producers and consumers outside the market economy, but it would give viability to agro-food networks where access to safe, healthy food does not depend on the ability to pay. Hegemonic conventional networks have enjoyed such institutional arrangements for decades! The redirection of public agro-food subsidies to advance the symmetrical construction of sustainability as both agroecological praxis and social justice would represent a powerful societal project. It may not transform capitalist instrumental rationality *tout court*, but it holds far greater promise of changing the world for present and future generations than inequitable technocentric readings of sustainable food consumption.

The issue of symmetry, of a truly "socio-ecological" ordering of sustainable consumption, also arises in the extended networks of international organic foodstuffs. In the case studies presented below, however, the parallel perhaps is better drawn between the organic as ecocentric, as represented by the ecolabelling narrative of biodiversity conservation, and the organic as social justice through fair trade. Both networks are built upon codified agro-ecological practices, but fair trade stands in more ambivalent relation to the objectified logic of capitalist markets.

3. Consuming 'Green' in an International Context: The Cases of Organic Ecolabelling and Fair Trade

The international networks of organic food production and consumption have experienced remarkable expansion (ITC 1999), but not all organic commodities are created equal. Indeed, the marketplace is seemingly awash with a diversity of products, each anchored in its own organic "nature", yet often purveying very different socio-ecological imaginaries. In this section, we explore the imaginaries deployed in the provisioning of two important categories of organic products emerging within the international organic marketplace: those sold through ecolabelling schemes and those that are associated with the "fair trade" pathway.

The purpose of these case studies is to begin to evaluate and offer critical reflections on the transformative potentials of these particular ways of consuming "green". How are these commodities and their networks produced and discursively constructed as "different" from those of conventional products, other organic commodities, and each other? This task requires a broad investigation of the co-produced social and material relations imprinted on ecolabelled and fair trade products and the processes by which these relations become embedded. Equally important, we wish to evaluate the "agency" of these commodities; as we will show, these foods are about "doing" more than just producing and consuming organic products. This agential dimension is considered on two related levels. First, on a practical/normative level, what is it, through the specificity of their co-production relations, that these products are purported to do and how do they go about doing it? And, second, on a theoretical level, how is capitalism theorised in the functioning of ecolabelled and fair trade organic foods? We begin with a discussion of the general processes of the construction of ecolabelled and fair trade products.

"Eating Green" for Tropical Conservation: The Ecolabelling of International Organic Foods

The organising principles of the ecolabelling of international organic foods very often require the specific creation of networks devoted to the conservation of tropical nature. In generalising across a diversity of products, labelling practices, and tropical "natures," organic ecolabelling displays a dual "constructive" strategy. First and foremost, this strategy requires that the material production relations be recognised as organic, in accordance with a set of internationally codified production techniques, which are legitimated by the system of organic certification. Yet, it is here that ecolabelled products seek to go beyond this codified organic "nature" to actively distinguish themselves from other more "generically" marketed organic foods. This differentiation is performed by making explicit and additional claims about the synergistic links between the production of organic commodities and tropical biodiversity conservation. These claims, found predominantly in the networks that provision organic chocolate and coffee, are made through textual and visual cues imprinted on the label. For example, one manufacturer states:

> Your purchase of this product helps support sustainable organic farming of cacao beans in the tropics. Ten percent of our profits on our chocolate bar go to conserving tropical rainforest lands. (Wild Oats, n.d.)

Another puts it this way:

> Hot, humid, and chemical-free. Tropical Source, searching worldwide for local growers committed to leaving nature on its own ... nothing but heat, earth, and cocoa beans ... roasting all day under the intense equatorial sun ... at the Tropical Source ... We donate ten percent of our profits to conserve tropical rainforests where cocoa beans are grown. Please join us in this conservation effort. Your purchase makes a difference. Thank you. (Cloud Nine Chocolate Company, n.d.)

One of the fastest growing segments of this market includes a host of "bird-friendly" products, whose production and consumption, it is claimed, promote tropical biodiversity and shade trees as migratory bird habitat.

The second strand of the organic ecolabelling strategy, as demonstrated in the above examples, involves the participation of manufacturers and importers in donation schemes. Here a portion of the profits from the sale of a commodity, often upwards of ten percent, is given to organisations involved in tropical conservation programs. Very often, these two strategies are combined in one product, as in the case of marketing the "Tropical Source" bars from the Cloud Nine Chocolate Company (www.cloudninecandy.com) that sells organic products and donates money to the Rainforest Alliance, an NGO involved in tropical forest conservation.

There are two striking characteristics of ecolabelled organic products. First, organic foods generally attempt to make the ecological relations of their production transparent within the commodity form (D. Goodman 1999; Raynolds 2000). Yet as demonstrated in the case of ecolabelled international organics, the transparency between organic farming and tropical nature is given a greater specificity and "connectedness" in the entangled network of organic agroecology, consumers, tropical conservation, and conservation schemes. Arguably, the discursive, economic, and geo-material specificity of these links through ecolabelling is carving out another niche within that of the organic marketplace. The second distinguishing characteristic of this form of green consumerism is the role it affords consumers. Couched in the moral discourse of "helping", consumers are implored to "join in conservation efforts" to "make a difference" through their purchases that support organic farming and fund conservation. Thus consumption and tropical conservation are joined in this imaginary and green "agency" is made real through the neo-liberal mechanisms of consumer sovereignty and choice "for change".

Opening the Boundaries of Organic Consumption: Fair Trade Networks and the Re-emergence of Productive Labour

A fascinating development in the international organic food trade has been the production of organic commodities under the auspices of the fair trade movement.[4] Much of this expansion is the result of the continuing dialogue between the organic agriculture and fair trade movements in recent years and the actions of individual companies (refer to IFOAM 1997). These "fair trade" products, typically cacao, coffee and teas,[5] are "bearers" of consumers' commitments not only to more environmentally-friendly production methods, but also to socially-responsible trade, which creates more equitable and favourable conditions for increasingly marginalised small-scale producers in the global South. These involve, but are not limited to, trading relationships defined by a bundle of characteristics: long-term contracts, direct trading routes, democratically-run producer groups and co-ops, advanced credit, and a guaranteed minimum price. The regulation of fair trade labelling is still somewhat in flux. The Fair Trade Labelling Organisation (FLO) is offering a more codified set of criteria for burgeoning European markets and fledgling North American and Japanese markets (Raynolds 2000; Robins *et al.*, 1999:54) while some companies have established their own criteria or voluntarily comply with those of the fair trade movement. As the movement and its institutionalisation continue to grow, compliance with FLO guidelines presumably will become mandatory. In actor-network terms, the fair trade movement at this point would begin to take on the characteristics of a "translation regime"; that is, a durable, strongly coordinated network, "heavy with norms" that gradually "tends to shed its history" and become taken for granted (Callon 1991).

The discursive armoury marshalled by fair trade foods not only lends transparency to their material relations in the ecological organic, but also attempts to re-embed the social relations of production in the fair trade "portion" of the commodity form. In other words, growers and their labour are made visible and tangible to consumers. This visibility is "performed" through the discursive tactics of label text and images and the concerted marketing efforts of those non-governmental organizations (NGOs) that have spearheaded fair trade.[6] This "laying out and viewing" of who is producing these commodities and the social and material conditions under which they are produced is altogether absent from other conventional, organic and ecolabelled-organic products as they sit on store shelves. For example, on one fair trade coffee, known as Café Mam®,[7] consumers learn that:

---

[4]Links between organic and fair trade have not been without considerable discussion (see IFOAM 1995 and 1997) and constraints and barriers, many of which still exist. See Browne *et al.* (2000), Sams (1997) and Robins *et al.* (1999) for a discussion of these and related issues.

[5]The markets for fair-trade bananas and orange juice are expanding rapidly (see ITC 1999; Raynolds 2000; Murray and Raynolds 2000).

[6]While this is clearly changing with the Internet, many manufacturers offer brochures full of rich textual and visual material in conjunction with their products to explain the principles of fair trade and/or organic production and give more detail of producer communities.

[7]For interesting work focusing directly on the community of ISMAM, see Hernández Castillo and Nigh (1998) and Nigh (1997). See also www.cafemam.com.

Café Mam is grown by ISMAM (Indigenous peoples of the Sierra Madre of Motozintla), a social solidarity cooperative of native Mayan farmers living in the highlands of Chiapas, Mexico. The growers are primarily from the Mam, Tzetzal, and Mochó peoples. ISMAM is organised on egalitarian and democratic ideals that stress responsibility to the co-op, hard work, and high standards of quality. Their programs help the communities in many positive ways … ISMAM's mission is equally one of conserving and rebuilding the natural environment and one of working towards a higher quality of life for the indigenous campesinos and their families. Each purchase of ISMAM coffee helps support goals of:

- Direct Marketing (no intermediaries or coyotes);
- Self-sufficiency and political independence;
- Democratic decision making among communities;
- Sustainable Development of rural infrastructure;
- Child Welfare, including education and nutrition;
- Defense of indigenous cultural identity;
- Protection of forests, rivers, and tropical fauna;
- Justice for indigenous peoples;
- Promotion of women and women's rights … (Royal Blue Organics, n.d.).

Often fair trade products thus enact the life histories of producers. In this sense, many of these foods carry the imprint of their workers' place-based, economic and social livelihoods.

Thus, at a discursive level, both organic ecolabelling and fair trade seek to establish what Whatmore and Thorne (1997) call a novel "mode of ordering of connectivity" among the actors and intermediaries enrolled in these networks: producers, organic nature, consumers, product labels, organic, conservation and fair trade NGOs, regulatory texts, certifiers, traders and importers. Such "modes of ordering" (Law 1994) operate in ecological, geographic, and economic spaces relatively marginal to the larger conventional agrofood system, but also in ideological and discursive spaces at the boundaries of the neoliberal logic of commodity production and world trade. On this ideological terrain, a "relational ethic" (Whatmore 1997) forges links of eco-social "right" action across ecolabel and fair trade networks.

Yet, there are important differences in this regard between the two networks. For ecolabelled commodities, the mode of ordering creates a relational ethic between consumers and tropical nature. In the fair-trade network, a more expansive ethic is constructed to connect consumers, nature, and, now, producer groups. For producers, this ethic finds material expression in the fair trade price premium that is available for investments in local social and economic development, and in the textual discourses of "helping", "support", and "difference making". Thus, in fair trade commodities and their "nourishing networks" (Whatmore and Thorne 1997), consumption and the relational ethic it creates is tied not only to the support of organic farming and tropical conservation, but explicitly to the very livelihoods of the producers themselves, no longer occluded by the commodity form's objectification of work, nature and place.

Two 'Moments' of Construction: Networks, Text and Acting at a Distance

Since ecolabelled and fair trade organic products are abstracted from conventional food-stuffs and then re-embedded with sets of alternative and more ethical eco-social relations, we need to look at the processes through which this occurs. The embedding processes are located at two co-production "moments" of network construction: at the moment of their socio-ecological production and the moment of discursive or narrative production through label text.

At the point of production, it is the specific co-production of agroecological nature and social labour, which is encoded as "organic" and endowed with ethical content. Implicit in this organic moment, however, is a rather tightly disciplined sense of how organic "nature" is to be produced. Organic nature is policed through an international system of organic regulation, the core of which is based around the production standards of the International Federation of Organic Agriculture Movements (IFOAM). Thus, the organic moment is not only defined by specific production practices grounded in agroecology, but also by the history and struggles of actors and their intermediaries to determine what the organic is and should be. For fair trade commodities, not surprisingly, this first moment compre-hends both organic production processes and the bundle of ethical labour and commercial practices that encode alternative eco-social production relations into the constitution of these products.

The second co-production moment in the construction of these alternative networks occurs through the narrative strategies of label texts. These readings of eco-social relations construct the meaning and identity of ecolabelled and fair trade foods. This discursive moment clearly is necessary and complementary to the organic production moment as it is through these narratives that consumers come to understand and perceive the relations imprinted on these foods: ecolabelled organics are about conservation and fair trade organic is about conservation of nature, equitable exchange and producer livelihoods. These textual inscriptions also endow the networks with the capacity to "act at a distance" and thereby translate affluent green-consumer constituencies and the socio-ecological environments of poor rural communities. The textual moment of production, and the prac-tical and theoretical implications of these discursive tactics and their transformative potential, have received little attention in the literature on organic and fair trade (Barrett-Brown 1993; Browne *et al.*, 2000; Buck *et al.*, 1997; Guthman 1998; Murray and Raynolds 2000; Nigh 1997; Renard 1999; Raynolds 2000; Whatmore and Thorne 1997; but see James 1993).

The function of label text is not only to enable consumers to learn about and interact with the imprinted material and symbolic qualities of these products, but also, not surpris-ingly, to entice consumers into making a purchase. Labels and their discourses, thus act as "immutable mobiles" to enrol human actors as consumers into the respective networks. Through intermediaries, ecolabelled organic and fair trade networks seek to "lengthen" across the spaces of consumption, to work against and translate actors from more conven-tional agrofood networks. Two observations are appropriate here. First, in green consumption networks, the struggles for a sustainable agriculture and society are as much about the competition for the "hearts and minds" (and purchases) of consumers through the discursive tactics of language and symbols as they are about agroecological production methods. Second, enrolment involves not only the literal corporeal consumption of the food, but also the consumption of the label discourse. Consuming is thus both the metabolisation of productive "nature" and the figurative symbolic ingesting of the tropics and producer livelihoods.

Furthermore, the "connecting" and re-embedding discourses of the texts and the messages they contain have a series of implications. Most importantly, because consumers are enrolled as agents of positive eco-social change and thereby given the ability to "make a difference," the act of consumption is infused with novel meanings: consuming becomes a tool of long-distance eco-social development, with consumers as the agents of that development. The encoding of consumption with developmental attributes is the symbolic and material means by which the networks "act at a distance" and affect the conditions of tropical nature and producers' lives. The drawing of overt links between consumption, environmentally sensitive production, and livelihood strategies, which frequently feature as goals of Third World "sustainable" and "green" development (Adams 1990; Redclift 1987), is becoming a common strategy in the provisioning of a multitude of First World consumables, such as shampoos and clothes, in addition to organic food items (e.g., Dove 1993). One of the authors has characterised the growing market-based links between consumption, environment and social development as "developmental consumption" (M. Goodman 1999).

In the ecolabelling and fair trade networks, the notion of developmental consumption conveys not only a geography of Third World production and First World consumption, but also maps out a cartography of network power. Clearly, in the ecolabelling network with its relatively invisible producers, the powers of conservation lie in the hands of the "green" First World. The fair trade network, on the other hand, while still mirroring this geography of production and consumption, cleaves to a less hierarchical set of power relations: it is the actions of both farmers and consumers that go into the making of the fair trade network (Whatmore and Thorne 1997). As the movement likes to highlight, "fair trade isn't charity, it's simply good business" (San Francisco Chronicle 1999), with producers portrayed as "partners" and consumers as "activists".

Transformative Foods?

The eco-social relations encoded in ecolabelled and fair trade organic networks assign to these products agential roles distinct from those of their more conventionally produced counterparts. In part, both challenge the objectified relations of conventional international commodities in material terms: ecolabelled in their "organic" status and fair trade products as organic, "fairly produced", and equitably exchanged. Similarly, both seek to reduce the social distance between production and consumption by infusing material and discursive connections between consumption and tropical conservation into ecolabelled items and, for fair trade, between consumption and livelihood protection (in the widest possible material and social sense). Thus material and symbolic use values in ecolabelled and fair trade commodities are reconfigured: these products are tools of natural and human development, in addition to offering the (rather dubious) nutritional/metabolic food values of coffee and chocolate.

The growth of the international organic and fair trade markets has been remarkable. International trade in organic foods, including ecolabelled and more "conventional" organic products, has reached an estimated $10 billion (ITC 1999). The market for fair trade products is estimated to be $400 million per year and expanding rapidly (Raynolds 2000). These figures are minuscule when compared to the international trade of conventional goods and, since ecolabelled and fair trade organic are a subset of their respective markets, their market presence is even smaller. Rather, as Raynolds (2000) observes, it is the political and institutional challenge that ecolabelled and fair trade products posit to the conventional agro-food system that is most compelling about these commodities. With this challenge comes the creation of "spaces of transformative potential" in the imaginaries of eco-social sustainability encoded into these commodities. We turn now to assess the transformative content of ecolabelling and fair trade in their claims to make consumption more sustainable.

The form and processes of ecolabelling contain a relatively simplistic reformist imaginary of sustainability anchored in conventional trading relations and the social relations of an exploitative agrofood system. Indeed, the imaginary transmitted through the "minimalist" ecolabelled pathway relies solely on the organic, with the implication that sustainability and conservation are technological matters resolvable through the promotion and spread of organic farming practices. Ecolabelled products are constructed within the relational and ideological spaces of the current capitalist system and seek little fundamental change in the social and economic pathways of food production and trade, which would be a part of a wider, more progressive agenda of sustainable consumption. The novel relational ethic created by the connection of consumption to tropical nature only becomes operational through the realisation of profits and changing consumer choices mediated through market sales. Ecolabelling is more about bringing organic production, tropical conservation, and thus sustainable consumption, within the purview of capitalism than an operationalisation of substantive eco-social change in the provisioning of international commodities. It is perfectly consistent with the "universalist" perspective of green consumption discussed in the introduction to this paper.

Several further limitations to the transformative potential of organic ecolabelling require brief mention. First, while organic production methods are presumably better for worker health and safety, ecolabelling standards neglect the social conditions of production and trade, particularly for labourers on large organic farms and plantations, nor is there any commitment to ensuring that the premium price for organic reaches those producing the commodities or labouring in the fields. Furthermore, ecolabelling is bounded by a very lax regulatory structure, with little or no effort to evaluate and monitor the validity of claims made on ecolabelled commodities. Transparency, in short, stops with agroecology. Yet, even here problems are evident, particularly in the acceptable definitions of "shade-grown" peppering the multitude of bird-friendly products on the market. As one researcher has found, shade-grown can, in reality, mean anything from being grown under a full, complex tropical understory to production under a veritable monocrop of trees spaced widely apart (Perfecto, 2000).[8] As such, bird-friendly might quickly become a race to the

---

[8]Indeed, the reputation of Rainforest Alliance and the ECO-OK label it has developed in conjunction with Dole has been tarnished by their minimalist attempts at tropical conservation (Raynolds 2000). Partially as a result, ECO-OK labeled products are not available in the European market.

agroecological bottom, similar to the prospect facing organic agriculture in California, as competition and the market for these products expands. A second concern is that ecolabelling schemes and developmental consumption represent a form of what Sachs (1993) refers to as "eco-colonialism". This places the control of the state of nature, albeit in a green organic guise, in the hands of First World NGOs, standards-creating institutions, consumers, and organic companies to the exclusion of local producers. Finally, for small-scale producers, many of whom are "organic" by default, the costs of organic certification are prohibitive and they receive little or no economic or agronomic help in making the transition to organic methods (Hamm 1997; Porritt 1997; Raynolds 2000).

The fair trade network's eco-social imaginaries offer a deeper, richer and more radical promise of transformation. Based on the stories and relations of sustainable environments, livelihoods, and exchange, this moral ecology and, now, economy, reconfigures the neoliberal logics of price and efficiency into ethical-relational structures defined by Third World social and environmental development. Fair trade links recontextualise everyday practice in both the worlds of consumers and producers in the local contexts of "place" and, at the same time, seek to transcend the social, economic and spatial distances between growing food and eating it. The project of organic fair trade presents a dual challenge to the conventional agro-food system by seeking to reposition larger North-South relations both through notions of eco-social transparency and equity in production, consumption and trade.

However, two compelling sets of questions remain for the fair trade movement and purveyors of these products. The first set revolves around the ability of the fair trade-organic market to shed its alternative status and make substantial economic and ideological inroads into the conventional global food system. In this respect, the alternative trade movement must find ways of incorporating low-income consumers into its networks, while maintaining its commitment to price premiums and long-term contracts for producers. Moreover, fair trade organic must extend its reach beyond the nutritionally insignificant commodities of coffee and chocolate, and enrol large-scale retailers and socially excluded consumers into a more broadly based coalition that prioritises its political commitments.

A second set of questions surrounds the ambivalent nature of the fair trade organic network that in some ways operates in spaces marginal to capitalist rationality, but simultaneously is situated in the larger agrofood market and subject to its characteristics and discipline (see Whatmore and Thorne 1997). Three brief points deserve more attention here. First, it is arguable that fair trade labels, their texts, and the processes of developmental consumption actually may deepen rather than subvert the processes of commodification by objectifying and commoditising the very things they are trying to save. Indeed, in some way, small-scale producers, their livelihoods, farming knowledge, and natural surroundings become commodified, reduced to the price of fair trade products.[9] Second, it is worth

---

[9]From a contradictory view, small-scale and indigenous producers and the other actors in the fair trade organic network have been able to heed Michael Taussig's suggestion to engage with and "seize" the commoditising fetish of capitalist markets and turn it more explicitly towards economic and social development (Taussig 1992, cited in Cook and Crang 1996; see also Cook and Crang 1996:147–148). Possibly, the commodification of environmental conservation, indigenity, livelihoods and difference can make a difference (e.g., Nigh 1997; Hernández Castillo and Nigh 1998).

considering the meaning of "fair" in fair trade and the asymmetries of power at work in deciding what is "fair". The fair trade networks offer selected Third World producers a set of market-based incentives — premium prices, guaranteed-minimum prices and long-term contracts — but are these inducements an adequate representation of "equal exchange" or "fairness" in relation to the rich consuming North? Finally, while fair trade organic has opened up "spaces of inclusion" for small-scale producers, the dictates of "quality" act as an exclusionary force at odds with the relational ethic of the movement. Many producers, typically the poorest in both resources and natural endowments, even if they can meet the costs of organic certification, may be excluded from the network because of the strict quality standards imposed by importers and suppliers. One author experienced this first hand in the exclusion of cacao growers looking to enrol in a fair trade organic cooperative in Costa Rica.[10]

These spaces of exclusion also are located in Northern sites of consumption as the premium attached to fair trade organic makes them high-priced luxury items, out of reach of the everyday purchases of lower-income consumers. Nor is there much consumption of these products in either the local or regional Southern contexts of their production (M. Goodman 1998). Fairness in the network does not extend to the sites of consumption, which suggests that explicit discussion is needed about the place of these food items in the universe of sustainable *and* just consumption. If the fair trade project is to make progress towards its declared aim of displacing the conventional agrofood trading system, new institutional mechanisms will be needed to promote more socially inclusive patterns of sustainable consumption.

4. Conclusion

This paper has argued in favour of symmetrical socio-ecological conceptualisations of sustainable consumption and against technocentric and ecocentric approaches, exemplified here by minimalist "standards" oriented organic food production and international ecolabelled organic products. In our view, these approaches reinforce, rather than attempt to bridge, the fault lines of social exclusion in both local and international communities. This truncated green imaginary fosters niche production for those consumers who can afford to pay premium organic prices and are knowledgeable about the health risks of conventionally produced foods. In Andrew Szasz's insightful phrase, technocentric green consumerism represents an "inverted quarantine", permitting privileged bodies to avoid harmful substances that potentially contaminate the metabolic relations of the less fortunate (Szasz, forthcoming). In these risk politics, green consumerism becomes a dimension of technological competition based on market segmentation rather than a societal project open to all.

The technocentric imaginary is curiously "place-less" since actual production conditions, other than being codified organic, are secondary to the nutritional and symbolic

---

[10]In this respect, recent recommendations to expand the participatory assessment of fair trade networks are especially pertinent (see Robins *et al.*, 1999).

properties of the product at the point of sale and in consumption. This abstraction of social production relations in particular localities fits easily with the instrumental rationality of multinational agrofood sourcing from "a global everywhere". Sustainable consumption in this form would create an international patchwork of production zones, differentiated by cost-price criteria, supplying high-income consumers in distant markets.[11]

In discussing more socially inclusive imaginaries of sustainable consumption, we drew attention to the difficulties presented by the commercial production-affordable consumption dilemma. Efforts to link market-based yet socially progressive forms of organic production with equitable food access for consumers are compromised by dependence on charitable sources of cross-subsidy to offset premium prices. This experience indicates that robust state institutional initiatives are needed to rupture and reconfigure the present market-embedded identity between agroecologically sustainable production and the ability to pay to consume sustainably. In market economies, publicly funded programs could create the necessary room for manoeuvre to develop socio-ecological projects that comprehensively address issues of sustainability, social justice and food poverty at the sites of both production and consumption. This vision is no more "political" than techno-centric elitist green consumerism; it simply advocates a more progressive integration of the ecology and politics of organic food consumption.

References

Adams, W. (1990), *Green Development: Environment and Sustainability in the Third World.* London: Routledge.

Allen, P. (1993), "Connecting the social and the ecological in sustainable agriculture." In P. Allen (ed.) *Food for the Future: Conditions and Contradictions of Sustainability* (pp. 1–16). New York: John Wiley.

Allen, P. (1999), "Reweaving the food security safety net: mediating entitlement and entrepreneurship." *Agriculture and Human Values 16* (2), 117–129.

Allen, P., & Sachs, C. (1991), "The social side of sustainability: Class, gender, and race." *Science as Culture 2* (4), 569–590.

Altieri, M. (1995), *Agroecology: The Science of Sustainable Agriculture.* Boulder: Westview Press.

Altieri, M., & Rossett, P. (1997), "Agroecology versus input substitution: A fundamental contradiction of sustainable agriculture." *Society and Natural Resources 10* (4), 283–295.

Barrett-Brown, M. (1993), *Fair Trade: Reform and Realities in the International Trading System.* London: Zed Books.

Belasco, W. (1989), *Appetite for Change.* New York: Pantheon Books.

Browne, A., Harris, P., Hofny-Collins, A., Pasiecznik, N., & Wallace, R. (2000), "Organic production and ethical trade: Definition, practice and links." *Food Policy 25*, 69–89.

Buck, D., Getz, C., & Guthman, J. (1997), "From farm to table: The organic vegetable commodity chain of northern California." *Sociologia Ruralis 37* (1), 3–20.

[11]International out-sourcing of organic cotton by multinational clothing corporations in India and other Third World areas, where organic methods often are used by default, apparently is undermining the market for organic cotton produced in California's Central Valley (Bunin 2001).

Bunin, L. (2001), Organic Cotton: The Fabric of Change. Unpublished Dissertation, University of California, Santa Cruz, Sociology Department.

Buttel, F. (1993), "The production of agricultural sustainability: Observations from the sociology of science and technology." In P. Allen (ed.) *Food for the Future: Conditions and Contradictions of Sustainability* (pp. 19–45). New York, NY: John Wiley.

Buttel, F. (1997), "Some observations on agrofood change and the future of agricultural sustainability movements." In D. Goodman & M. Watts (eds) *Globalising Food: Agrarian Questions and Global Restructuring* (pp. 334–365). London: Routledge.

CAFF (Community Alliance with Family Farmers). (1998), *Agrarian Advocate 20* (3), Summer.

Callon, M. (1986), "Some elements of a sociology of translation: Domestication of the scallops and the fishermen of St. Brieuc Bay." In J. Law (ed.) *Power, Action and Belief: A New Sociology of Knowledge* (pp. 196–229). London: Routledge and Kegan Paul.

Callon, M. (1991), "Techno-economic networks and irreversibility." In J. Law (ed.) *A Sociology of Monsters: Essays on Power, Technology and Domination* (pp. 132–161). London: Routledge.

Cloud Nine Chocolate Company. (n.d.), *Tropical Source® Organic Java Roast Dark Chocolate.*

Cook, & Crang (1996), The World on a Plate: Culinary Culture. Displacement and Geographical Knowledges. *Journal of Material Culture 1* (2): 131–153.

Dove, M. (1993), "A revisionist view of tropical deforestation and development." *Environmental Conservation 20* (1), 17–24.

DuPuis, E. (2000), "Not in my body: BGH and the rise of organic milk." *Agriculture and Human Values 17* (3), 285–295.

FitzSimmons, M., & Goodman, D. (1998), "Incorporating nature: Environmental narratives and the reproduction of food." In B. Braun & N. Castree (eds) *Remaking Reality: Nature at the Millennium* (pp. 194–220). London: Routledge.

Goodman, D. (1999), "Agro-food studies in the 'Age of Ecology': Nature, corporeality, bio-politics." *Sociologia Ruralis 39* (1), 17–38.

Goodman, D. (2000a), "Organic and conventional agriculture: Materializing discourse and agroecological managerialism." *Agriculture and Human Values 17* (3), 215–219.

Goodman, D. (2000b), "Regulating organic: A victory of sorts" (Guest Editorial). *Agriculture and Human Values 17* (3), 212–213.

Goodman, D., Sorj, B., & Wilkinson, J. (1987), *From Farming to Biotechnology.* Oxford: Blackwell.

Goodman, M. (1998), The Internationalization of the Organic Food Trade. Unpublished MA Thesis. University of Oregon, Department of Geography.

Goodman, M. (1999), *Developmental Consumption: Embedding Relationships in International Organic Foods.* Paper presented at the Agro-Food Studies Workshop, Conventional and Organic Agriculture: Encounters at the Interface, University of California, Santa Cruz, 7–8 May 1999.

Gottlieb, R., & Mascarenhas, M. (1997), *Building Community Food Systems for All: Learning From the Market Basket Program.* Occidental, CA: Community Food Security Project.

Guthman, J. (1998), "Regulating meaning, appropriating nature: The codification of California organic agriculture." *Antipode 30* (2), 135–154.

Guthman, J. (2000), "Raising organic: An agro-ecological assessment of grower practices in California." *Agriculture and Human Values 17* (3), 257–266.

Habermas, J. (1987), *The Theory of Communicative Action (Volume 2): The Critique of Functional Reason.* Cambridge: Polity Press.

Hamm, U. (1997), "Organic trade: The potential for growth." In T. Maxted-Frost (ed.) *The Future Agenda for Organic Trade.* Proceedings of the Fifth International IFOAM Conference in Oxford, September 24–27 (pp. 18–21). Tholey-Theley: IFOAM.

Hernández Castillo, R., & Nigh, R. (1998), "Global processes and local identity: Indians in the Sierra Madre of Chiapas and the international organic market." In V. Napolitano & X. Solano (eds)

Encuentros Antropologicos: Politics, Identity and Mobility in Mexican Society (pp. 110–29). London: Institute of Latin American Studies.

IFOAM. (1997), *The Future Agenda for Organic Trade*. Proceedings of the Fifth International IFOAM Conference in Oxford, September 24–27, T. Maxted-Frost (ed.). Tholey-Theley: IFOAM.

IFOAM. (1995), *Trade in Organic Products: Producer Countries, Target Markets — Growing Together, Joining the Markets*. Proceedings of the Fourth International IFOAM Conference, Frankfurt, February 28–March 2, M. Haccius, A. Bernd & B. Geier (eds). Tholey-Theley: IFOAM.

ITC (International Trade Centre). (1999), *Organic Food and Beverages: World Supply and Major European Markets*. Geneva: International Trade Centre.

James, A. (1993), "Eating green(s): Discourses of organic food." In K. Milton (ed.) *Environmentalism: The View from Anthropology* (pp. 205–218). London: Routledge.

Jessop, B. (1997), "Capitalism and its future: Remarks on regulation, government and governance." *Review of International Political Economy 4* (3), 561–581.

Klonsky, K. (2000), "Forces impacting the production of organic foods." *Agriculture and Human Values 17* (3), 233–243.

Klonsky, K., & Tourte, L. (1998), *Statistical Review of California's Organic Agriculture 1992–1995*. Davis: Agricultural Issues Center, University of California.

Kloppenburg, J., Henrickson, J., & Stevenson, G. (1996), "Coming into the foodshed." *Agriculture and Human Values 13* (3), 33–42.

Latour, B. (1987), *Science in Action*. Milton Keynes: Open University Press.

Latour, B. (1993), *We Have Never Been Modern*. Brighton: Harvester Wheatsheaf

Law, J. (1986), "On the methods of long-distance control: Vessels, navigation and the Portuguese route to India." *Sociological Review Monograph 32*, 234–263.

Law, J. (1992), "Notes on the theory of actor-network: Ordering, strategy and heterogeneity." *Systems Practice 5*, 379–393.

Law, J. (1994), *Organising Modernity*. Oxford: Blackwell.

Mascarenhas, Michelle (2000), pers. comm.

Miller, D. (1995), "Consumption as the vanguard of history: A polemic by way of an introduction." In D. Miller (ed.) *Acknowledging Consumption* (pp. 1–57). London: Routledge.

Murray, D., & Raynolds, L. (2000), "Alternative trade in bananas: Obstacles and opportunities for progressive social change in the global economy." *Agriculture and Human Values 17*, 65–74.

Nigh, R. (1997), "Organic agriculture and globalization: A Maya associative corporation in Chiapas, Mexico." *Human Organization 56* (4), 427–436.

Perfecto, Ivette (2000), pers comm.

Perry, Kristina (2000), pers comm.

Porritt, J. (1997), "Organic and fair trade: The need for integration." In T. Maxted-Frost (ed.) *The Future Agenda for Organic Trade*. Proceedings of the Fifth International IFOAM Conference in Oxford, September 24–27, (pp. 35–37). Tholey-Theley: IFOAM.

Raynolds, L. (2000), "Re-embedding global agriculture: The international organic and fair trade movements." *Agriculture and Human Values 17* (3), 297–309.

Redclift, M. (1987), *Sustainable Development: Exploring the Contradictions*. London: Routledge.

Renard, M. (1999), "The interstices of globalization: The example of fair coffee." *Sociologia Ruralis 39* (4), 484–500.

Robins, N., Roberts, S., & Abbot, J. (1999), *Who Benefits?: A Social Assessment of Environmentally-Driven Trade*. London: International Institute for Environment and Development (www.iied.org/scati).

Royal Blue Organics. (n.d.), *Café Mam®: Organically Grown, Socially Responsible Coffee*. Product Brochure.

Sachs, W. (1993), "Global ecology and the shadow of 'Development' ". In W. Sachs (ed.) *Global Ecology: A New Arena of Political Conflict* (pp. 3–21). London: Zed Books.

Sams, C. (1997), "Integrating the social agenda — benefits to business." In T. Maxted-Frost (ed.) *The Future Agenda for Organic Trade*. Proceedings of the Fifth International IFOAM Conference in Oxford, September 24–27, (pp. 38–41). Tholey-Theley: IFOAM.

San Francisco Chronicle. (1999), *Support Brewing for Cooperatives' Coffee Beans*. Oct. 14.

Szasz, A. (forthcoming), *Inverted Quarantine/Imagined Refuge*. Minneapolis: Minneapolis Press.

Vos, T. (2000), "Visions of the middle landscape: Organic farming and the politics of nature." *Agriculture and Human Values 17* (3), 245–256.

Whatmore, S. (1997), Dissecting the autonomous self: Hybrid cartographies for a relational ethics. *Environment and Planning D: Society and Space 15* (1), 37–53.

Whatmore, S., & Thorne, L. (1997), "Nourishing networks: Alternative geographies of food." In D. Goodman & M. Watts (eds) *Globalising Food: Agrarian Restructuring and Global Restructuring* (pp. 287–304). London: Routledge.

Wild Oats. (n.d.), *Organic Imported Belgian Milk Chocolate*.

Chapter 7

"Changing Nature": The Consumption of Space and the Construction of Nature on the "Mayan Riviera"

Michael Redclift

1. Introduction

The concept of sustainability is increasingly used in a variety of different ways, and for a variety of different purposes. This chapter examines this apparent adaptability, and some of the ambivalence to which it gives rise in the context of recent eco-tourist development on the Yucatan Peninsula of Mexico. Tourism — including its "environmental" variants — is an important aspect of consumption, and points to some key questions for sustainability. Tourism involves both the "consumption of space" and, by representing nature as a consumption good, the "consumption of place".

The discussion of the environmental impact of tourism, and the search for more "sustainable" forms of tourism, really began with publication of the Brundtland Report (WCED 1987; Croall 1995), but the term *eco-tourism* did not gain currency until some years later. The World Wide Fund for Nature has defined eco-tourism as "tourism to protected natural areas, as a means of economic gain through natural resource preservation. A merger of recreation and responsibility" (Kallen 1990:37). In the course of time, however, the epithet "eco" has been applied, with something approaching abandon, to almost any form of tourist development which claims "ecological" objectives (Mowforth 1993; France 1997; Wahab and Pigram 1997).

I suggest in this chapter that terms such as "eco-tourism", and "sustainable tourism", are more than merely cases of semantic diplomacy, designed to present a favourable image of tourist development. Rather, these terms have come to constitute significantly different discourses for public policy, enabling diverse political interests to advance their commercial, or environmental, objectives (Darier 1999). What may have begun as a packaging of tourist operations, has developed into a major recreational activity, with many variants, and distinctive forms of self-justification.

In manifold ways these discourses reflect both lifestyles and livelihoods: the sets of consumer preferences and labels to which different groups — hosts and tourists — become attached, and the economic constraints and opportunities that eco-tourism introduces for the labour force and entrepreneurs in the area. Perhaps of even more significance, however, are the environmental implications of these discourses for the protection of particular places, for example the natural marine environment of Yucatan, and for management of the waste

Exploring Sustainable Consumption: Evironmental Policy and the Social Sciences, Volume 1, pages 121–133.
Copyright © 2001 by Elsevier Science Ltd.
All rights of reproduction in any form reserved.
ISBN: 0-08-043920-9

and pollution that accompanies tourist development. In some respects "eco-tourism" represents, then, a phenomenon with implications for consumption at both the level of tourist "inputs", including the way in which tourist destinations are represented, and that of "outputs" in the form of pollution, environmental depletion and the consequent 'revaluation' of nature.

2. The Concept of Nature

Environmental struggles, and tourist development, both make much use of "Nature", as a symbolic and cultural category. Usually resort is made to "nature" (particularly in upper case) in contemporary discourse, when a distinction is being made with human society and culture. Thus, as the German philosopher Mittelstrasse has put it, Nature is "the great other", that which lies beyond and apart from the work of Man (Mittelstrasse 1999). In practice, of course, nature is always adulterated or transformed by human hands; it is seldom, if ever, *natural*. We view nature, then, in translation, as it were, without acknowledging that we are the translator — a process of dissembling that works partly because a variety of different human cultures have had a hand in altering, and interpreting, the text.

Our view of "nature", however, is historically contingent. Up until the late-seventeenth century Nature was seen as a wise being with intelligence, created by God, so that humans should gradually come to understand and unlock her powers. Man was the observer of a Nature created by God. Even in the writing of Galileo we find the remark that "she [nature] ... teaches us every one of her works: our task is to understand and interpret." This early "Enlightenment view" of nature persisted, in various forms, until the scientific revolution of the nineteenth century. Such approaches are very different from the late twentieth-century perspectives reviewed below, in which nature becomes a work of *our* imagination, even "a leisure-time scenario filled with the colourful dreams of the tourist industry", as Mittelstrasse (1999) observes. At the same time, I suggest that the different interpretations of nature since Aristotle are still used, albeit unconsciously, in defence of distinct cultural and political interests, and bear heavily on the language and discourses of eco-tourism.

The concept of nature changed during the Enlightenment with the rise of science and scientific thinking. Drawing on the much earlier writing of Aristotle, nature was increasingly seen as "poetics", as produced by the hand of Man. Thus Nature came to take on a paradigm function, for work itself, rather than for passivity and abandon. Nature became a paradigm of 'poetic Nature', with a building, productive essence that could serve as a model for the industry of humans and a warning against inactivity.

However, even in Aristotle we can detect the distinction between crea*tive* nature and crea*ted* nature, which resonates today in the battles around conservation and the ecological movement. Gradually, the understanding of nature became part of the wider hermeneutic tradition — the view that we can *only* understand that which we have produced. This emphasis on our transformative powers (rather than those of Nature) has served to reinforce a dualism between "nature" and "culture", and one that has deepened during most of the twentieth century.

For most of the twentieth century the concept of Nature, as part of the Western philosophical tradition, has been subservient to the guiding epistemological conventions of modern science. If a philosophy of nature had any purpose it was as the handmaiden of scientists whose confidence, and social prestige, earned through the examination of nature in the laboratory, enabled them to produce accurate pictures of the world. These pictures though are partial and only accessible to those versed in specialist scientific method. Nature was no longer simply observed for its infinite wonder. Rather it was to be deconstructed and dissected, divided into fragments and atoms.

Instead of the great eighteenth-century model of Nature as "order", science seemed to depict nature as "disorder". This view might have originated with Newton, for whom matter withstood the effects of forces or principles. In other words, Nature was a "non-material other" most clearly represented in the work of the greatest discoveries of nineteenth- and twentieth-century science. For Darwin, for example, the organic realm of nature became part of cultural nature — a "natural" selection undertaken by humans. In Einstein's hands, the Newtonian version of the non-material ether that acted upon us, was transformed into the idea of relative space in which gravitational forces were bound up with matter itself.

By the end of the twentieth century the stance adopted by most of the natural sciences towards nature was one of modernist "agnosticism". Discovery lay less in the realisation of the whole than in professional application to the parts. Nature was no longer the "Great Other" that we might hope to approximate, but instead the building blocks in each of us and of which we were composed. Nature was less "a world to live in", as conceived by Aristotle, and more an abstract world in which, as Einstein depicted it, "we" are indistinguishable from other forms of matter. This, in turn, has left as a legacy the central problem that confronts a realist analysis today. Is there any way of understanding nature that is not bound up with scientific understanding that does not take as its starting point, the human experience of nature *through science*, and through the categories of the natural scientist?

The moral dilemmas of a "produced" nature have informed current debate to a considerable degree. On the one hand, there is a growing, and vigorous literature in the social sciences on the ambiguities and ethical inconsistencies of our approach to nature (Braun and Castree 1998; Darier 1999) and its "privatisation" (Thompson 1997). Within the humanities, too, there are examples of similar concerns. In a recent novel by Julian Barnes (1998), *England! England!*, we find an attempt at "simulated authenticity", through heritage, represented as the clearest example of mass culture. And, today, it is observed that, even before we confronted the moral vacuum of a 'produced' nature, the British observed, uncomfortably, that other cultures could transform nature. This acknowledgment constituted at the time a serious threat to national self-confidence and was most vividly seen in the nineteenth-century march of European imperialism. We find this anxiety profoundly illustrated in a passage from W. G. Sebald's, *The Rings of Saturn*, in which the imperialist armies of Britain and France "discovered", and destroyed, the "man-made" production of nature in China:

> In early October [1860] the allied troops [British and French] happened apparently by chance on the magic garden of Yuan Ming Yuan near Peking, with its countless palaces, pavilions, covered walks, fantastic arbours, temples and towers. On the slopes of man-made mountains, between banks and spinneys, deer with fabulous antlers grazed, and the

whole incomprehensible glory of Nature and of the wonders placed in it by the hand of man was reflected in dark unruffled waters. The destruction that was wrought in these legendary landscaped gardens over the next few days, which made a mockery of military discipline or indeed of all reason, can only be understood as resulting from anger at the continued delay in achieving a resolution. Yet the true reason why Yuan Ming Yuan was laid waste may well have been that this earthly paradise — which immediately annihilated any notion of the Chinese as an inferior and uncivilised race — was an irresistible provocation in the eyes of [the] soldiers (1998:144).

3. Modern Ecological Thinking and "Produced" Nature

In some respects the modern ecological movement has sought to restore the pre-Enlightenment view of nature in which we do not stand apart from it or seek moral justifications for "our" (human) nature through a better understanding of the abstract rules of science. Green thinking can then be seen as an emergent property of the advance of science itself, one in which a "citizen science" emerges to challenge the authority of experts and politicians (Irwin 1997; Yearley 1997).

It has become increasingly clear that "nature" is not made easier to grasp because we produce it, as an artifact. In fact, it is more difficult to grasp "nature" precisely *because* we produce it — whether through biotechnology, genetic engineering or cultural representations of the natural in everyday life. Nature is now one of the most contested domains of human choice, subject to interpretation and invoked as moral justification in a world of rival epistemologies and "epistemic communities", each claiming legitimacy and validity (Braun and Castree 1998). The very plurality of ethical and religious beliefs about nature, strongly reflected in this book, has become an essential element in the hermeneutic tradition which some critics see as leading to relativism, particularly within the work of Martin Heidegger and Hans-Georg Gadamer. The "hermeneutic circle", has been criticised for its insistence that we cannot understand the whole before we understand the parts (Mueller-Vollmer 1985).

These deliberations have led to some serious problems for modern ecological thinking. How do we begin to understand "nature" externally, as it were, without recourse to scientific understanding, when this understanding has often served to undermine our relationship with nature itself? This is the dilemma that a realist approach to the environment presently faces.

We need then to begin by dealing adequately with our own ambivalence toward the idea of sustainability. In viewing the way that we invoke the idea of sustainability to describe both conditions within 'natural' ecological systems and human-made cultural artifacts we may be merely apprehending different ways of "producing" nature. Hotels or theme parks constructed according to "sustainable" principles may be more politically or culturally contentious, but are they qualitatively different from "nature reserves" or "protected areas"?

We might focus on economic, cultural and political processes that serve to transform both *material* nature and our consciousness so that terms such as "sustainability" can be accommodated within rival, and very different, discourses. Later in this chapter the development of global "eco-parks" on the Mexican Caribbean is considered as an example of both the way nature is materially transformed and represented. Before moving to the analysis of this case, however, this chapter considers the potential contribution of a perspective that is not usually linked to these discourses on nature. Sidney Mintz, in his work, has sought to address both the structural conditions behind environmental change and its cultural representations.

4. "Inner" and "Outer" Meanings to Cultural and Environmental Change

In his study of sugar, *Sweetness and Power* (1985), Mintz sought to bring together sugar as a commodity, the product of markets and production processes, and its symbolic dimensions. He distinguishes between what he refers to as the "inside meanings" that people attach to their consumption of food, and the "outside meanings". The inside meanings refer to the conditions of everyday life in which food is consumed. These connotations refer to the way individuals, families and social groups integrate their behaviour through daily or weekly practices, forms of everyday behaviour that provide "familiarity", and cultural meaning to the material world. In this sense the "inside meanings" that individuals attach to goods represent what these goods mean to people themselves through their institutionalised, cultural practices. They constitute the conditions of everyday life and the established practices of consumption.

In contrast, Mintz refers to outside meanings as the structural conditions under which behaviour takes place; in other words, the economic, social and political context of behaviour. The outside meanings establish the outer boundaries for determining, in the case of food and eating, when and how it occurs. This meaning, in this instance, encompasses the hours of work undertaken, places of work, mealtimes, the buying power of households, child-care arrangements and the organisation of leisure time (Mintz 1985). They are the context for consumption. In similar vein, Eric Wolf (1982) has equated these outside meanings with what he calls "structural power". They also parallel roughly with what Anthony Giddens (1984) calls "the organisation of social time-space", part of what he terms "authoritative resources".

Mintz's distinction can be usefully applied to how we view the consumption and production of nature through tourism. At one level, the environment and nature are subject to symbolic interpretation alone, but to appreciate the ambiguity of "eco-tourism" implies considering another dimension, namely that of structural conditions, in which spatial and political systems, and the material conditions under which they function, also acquire cultural significance. The structural binds that determine environmental change and "sustainability" are closely linked to the symbolic representation of "nature". The discussion in the next section of the development of the Mexican Caribbean coast illustrates the need to combine both structural analysis of eco-tourism and the post-structuralist analysis of its representation. Using both approaches can help us to resolve questions about the divergent discourses of sustainability with which the chapter began.

5. Sustainability Discourses on the Mayan Riviera

Interest in sustainability can be linked to two related economic and social processes, or tendencies, that have come to characterise the relationship between human aspirations and the mastery of nature. The first process involves the translation of social behaviour into purely economic values — the "economisation" of society. This current strikes at the legitimacy of one form of "value" (that of the marketplace) over all others. Jurgen Habermas expressed his criticism of this approach in a forceful passage:

> [C]an civilisation afford to surrender itself entirely to the driving force of just one of its sub-systems — namely, the pull of a dynamic ... recursively closed, economic system, which can only function and remain stable by taking all relevant information, translating it into, and processing it in, the language of economic value (1990:43).

The translation of human activities into purely economic terms removes them from both their environmental and cultural contexts — a point to which we return later in this chapter.

The second process is linked to the first, and complements it. This tendency involves the revaluation of nature in another way — by "naturalising" human behaviour — in such a way that human interventions, including environmental planning and management, are regarded as enhancing the *natural* quality, or qualities, of the environment. The paradox is that the use of language to restore "nature" to human-made acts while attempting to give them legitimacy also subjects nature to more human control. In the process, while the rhetoric of public policy and the market becomes naturalised, the environment becomes "socialised", and increasingly divorced from the form that preceded large-scale tourist development. Both these processes — the economisation of society and the socialisation of the environment, are evident in how eco-tourism has developed in Yucatan, Mexico.

The coastal stretch of the Mexican Yucatan Peninsula, south of Cancun, is increasingly referred to as the "Mayan Riviera". To the north lie the resorts of Cancun and Isla Mujeres, both of which have been extensively developed since the 1960s. As Simon (1997:181) points out:

> [O]ne of the great selling points [of Cancun] was that it was considered environmentally friendly ... [I]t was often described as "an industry without smoke-stacks" ... [P]rotecting the environment meant avoiding pollution — industrial waste, smog, the garbage and sewage of the poor. Altering or destroying the natural habitat was not a concern.

The collapse of oil prices in 1981 forced a massive devaluation of the Mexican currency the following year and, as a consequence, heightened efforts were pursued throughout the 1980s and 1990s to earn additional foreign exchange from tourism. Environmental concerns, although frequently voiced, did little to hold back the pace of tourism on the Yucatan coast or the gradual destruction of the coastal habitat. Pollution became a growing problem. Cancun spawned slums that spread northward and sewage turned the lagoon on which the city was constructed into a diseased sewer, alive with algal blooms and exuding a terrible stench. Ecological problems were mirrored by a growth in criminal activity, including the large-scale laundering of drug money through inflated resort development. Drug barons moved into Cancun in the late 1980s and one of them, Rafael Aguilar Guajardo, was gunned down in Cancun in April 1993.

By the early 1990s Cancun had lost much of its initial appeal, even to tourists. It had developed too quickly, and at too much cost. The developers feared that despite considerable lip service to the environment it was evident that mass tourism, especially from the United States and Europe (which was increasingly the market for Cancun's resort owners), was moving elsewhere. As Cancun lost its glitter, so the tourists began moving south in a quest for the unspoiled beach and the living reef. Cancun had been the principal example of what has been described as an "archipelago of artificial paradises" in tropical Mexico (Loreto and Cabo San Lucas in Baja California, Ixtapa near Acapulco, Puerto Escondido on the coast of Oaxaca). It had always been the jewel in the Mexican tourist crown (Simon 1997).

Gradually, foreign tourists began to follow the Mexican tourists, the back-packers and the beachcombers south of Cancun to the coastal area opposite Cozumel. One town on this coast grew particularly rapidly, Playa del Carmen, which in the 1960s had been a small fishing village, but soon became an area of rapid urban expansion — with a rate of urban growth among the fastest in the whole of Latin America. Playa's ascendancy on the world-tourist stage has given rise to a veritable mythology of its own, encapsulated in this extract from the tourist literature:

> [Playa] was *discovered* by a sixteen year-old boy in the summer of 1966 ... a momentous event which changed forever the face of history for this here-tofore small fishing village ... [I]n 1966 Fernando Barbachano Herrero, born of a *family of pioneers*, arrived there and found it inhabited by about eighty people, with a single pier made of the local zapote wood. Fernando befriended landowner Roman Kian Lopez ... and spent the next two years trying to talk him into relinquishing some of his land (Playa 1999, emphasis added).

In January 1968, Barbachano bought twenty-seven hectares of land for just over US$13,000 or six cents a square metre. Tourist development has been so rapid that this land now constitutes just ten per cent of Playa's development and was recently sold for US$325 a square metre. As Playa developed, piers were built for boats, hotels were constructed on the virgin beach and the list of Playa's celebrated "pioneers" grew longer. However, expansion of the resort of Playa Del Carmen was only the first stage in an even more ambitious process of coastal development.

Simon (1997) describes Xcaret, the first of the global "eco-parks" as "a nature-oriented theme park, an hour south of Cancun "... its billboards exhorting visitors to save the planet, conserve water, and put trash in its place" (Simon 1997:190). Xcaret was followed by Xell-Ha, and then Xpu-Ha, as the recently dubbed "Mayan Riviera" resorts blossomed in imitation of each other, and by turns on an even larger scale, down the coast towards the Biosphere Reserve of Sian-Ka-an on the border with Belize.

On its website Xell-Ha is described as:

> [A] magical place ... This *natural wonder creates the feel of the Caribbean* by inviting you to discover the deep underwater world of the crystal blue seas, the true examples of the *natural* underground rivers produced by this land, the exotic plants and flowers from the botanical garden, a farm with the *original creatures* that inhabit this extraordinary location, and the ancient ruins of the *lost mayan civilisation* (emphasis added).

According to the tourist literature, the eco-parks of Xcaret, Xell-Ha and Xpu-Ha are "legitimate manifestations of the growing concern for the welfare of the planet". It is claimed that they exhibit many of the features of sustainable development in the marine environment: "ecologically-planned" hotels, collaboration with "authentic" environmental organisations, such as the Planetary Coral Reef Foundation (PCRF) and local waste-recycling systems (Playa 1999). However, to its critics such parks have

> no more to do with eco-development than the Bronx Zoo ... [their] success does not increase the value of nature, because all the animals are in cages ... [and] the Mayan village in Xcaret features thatch huts, dugout canoes, and hemp hammocks, but not a single living Maya (Simon 1997:190).

What is clear from rival accounts of the development of the coast, is that the epithets "natural" and "sustainable" carry very positive connotations and, as a consequence, are utilised at every opportunity. Take the following account, again from a tourist magazine, of the activities of one of the coastal "pioneers":

> Ted Rhodes is a local developer and pioneer for ecologically sound technologies, who is attempting to combine state-of-the-art technology, while enjoying the benefits of eco-tourism. He's only been in the Playa area since 1995, but is in the process of planning and developing six major projects ... carrying disdain for the use of the word "eco", which he feels has been an over-abused term for a less than fully-understood concept. Ted describes his ventures as "raw jungle converted with the hand of Mother Nature, to create a positive impact, using Mother Nature's rules ... He works with the *natural* elements of the land, employing natural building materials from agriculture to culture, including water treatment which respects the composition and inhabitants of the land (Playa 1999, emphasis added).

These accounts of eco-tourist development suggest that words such as "nature", "natural" and "sustainable" can be used, to good effect, in a number of ways. By throwing a cordon around part of the coast and enclosing a salt-water lagoon the developers of Xell-Ha were able to brand "nature" with a company name, to privatise it (Thompson 1997). Each of these "parks" provides a variety of tourist facilities — such as restaurants and shops — that help to sell a product which is, in part, "natural", such as the underground wells (*cenotes*) that tourists descend into, caves and shoals of fish with which they swim. The line between the "natural" and the "human-made" is also blurred in other ways. Some of the local staff are doubtless ethnically Mayan, but the restaurants and cafes that sell "Mayan" cuisine and the bands that play "Mayan" music are an embellishment, if not a counterfeit, of Mayan culture. At one level it appears to work. For instance, people signing the visitors' book thank the resort for offering them the chance "to live among the Mayan people". The reality and the allusion are indistinguishable at this point. The *ethnic* label "Maya" is the exact complement of the *eco* labels such as "nature", "natural" and "sustainable" describing almost every activity that visitors are invited to undertake.

In contrast to the global eco-parks, the Yucatan peninsula also boasts a major UNESCO designated Biosphere Reserve, called Sian Ka'an, to the south of the major resorts. The Mexican Government created this reserve in 1986 with an extension of 1.3 million acres. The following year it was designated as a World Heritage Site and ten years later another 200,000 acres were added. Today the reserve accounts for ten percent of the land area of the state of Quintana Roo and contains over 100 kilometres of coast within its boundaries. It includes over 1,000 local Mayan people and 27 archaeological ruins.

However, before declaring this reserve a more "authentic" example of environmental protection than the global eco-parks it is worth reflecting on a number of questions. The Sian Ka'an Reserve is as much an artificial creation as that of Xcaret or Xell-Ha and plays an important role as a sanctuary free from large-scale development. However, most tourists who come to Yucatan and want to experience the natural environment never visit Sian-Ka'an, nor could it withstand mass tourism. To fully appreciate the contribution of reserves like Sian-Ka'an one needs to consider them together with the objects of mass appeal such as Xcaret, Xell-Ha and Xpu-Ha.

These observations suggest that like the descriptions of "eco-friendly" hotels in Playa what we are seeing represented as a manifestation of environmental consciousness on the part of the tourist developers, in the form of eco-parks, is a pre-emptive environmentalism. It is designed to disarm environmental critics and to demonstrate that coastal developers have learned hard lessons from the bad publicity over Cancun. At the same time, these parks absorb increasing numbers of global tourists, many of whom would visit the Yucatan peninsula whether or not the parks existed. Given these circumstances it can be argued that the eco-parks have produced their "own" natural heritage sites, ones capable of withstanding saturation tourism without repelling prospective visitors.

Behind the rhetoric of eco-tourism lie other conflicts of interest over the environment about which most tourists remain oblivious. One example is the opposition being mounted by local peasant families (*ejidatarios*) to the Mexican electricity utility (CFE) that they claim has deforested their land. During the summer of 1999 rallies to condemn these activities were an almost daily occurrence in the region. Similarly, there has been much public criticism of the dangers and risks inherent in speculative development, notably in the construction of sub-standard hotels. In some of these hotels electric cables run dangerously through hotel swimming pools, and visitors are exposed to numerous avoidable hazards denounced in the local newspaper, *!Por Esto!*. These "ecological scandals" now form part of the daily currency of political discussion on the Yucatan coast and serve to fuel the even greater insistence on the part of some tourist entrepreneurs that their products are free from the taint of ecological risk and damage.

Following Mintz's distinction the realities of tourism on the Yucatan coast cannot be adequately represented without uncovering the various "inside meanings" which different groups ascribe to their environment. These groups include: local Mayan people working as "hosts" inside resorts and in coastal villages, migrants to the area from other parts of Mexico (e.g., indigenous women from Chiapas who sell crafts on the beaches) and, of course, tourists and developers themselves.

For an example we need look no further than the name for the zone that was, until 1999, *Solidaridad* (solidarity), a name more suggestive of the Mexican Revolution's imagery and mythology than that of global tourism. On the coast of Yucatan now developed for tourism there were relatively few historical examples of social solidarity, such as those in the *henequen* (sisal) zone to the north (Escalante 1988) or the interior villages that figured largely in the so-called Caste War fought between the Maya armies and those of the Mexican state from the mid-nineteenth century onwards (Brannon and Joseph 1991). However, the evidence of nineteenth-century Yucatecan opposition to outsiders, supported for cynical reasons by the British, prompted messianic movements of great vitality, particularly those of the so-called 'talking crosses" (Reina 1980:385). One view of the "Mayan renaissance" places these historical oppositions firmly within the camp of contemporary protest over environmental/ethnic abuses in the region, while others caution that both ethnic and environmental struggles in contemporary Latin America have failed to deliver a viable political platform (Ellner 1993). The "inside meanings" attached to the contested discourses of eco-tourism are clearly related to how different groups of people seek to integrate these activities with the performance of everyday life.

Mintz's other analytical category, "outside meanings", can also help us to understand the environmental discourses in Yucatan. Throughout the coastal zone developed for tourism, we find evidence of structural power or the "organisation of time-space" (Giddens 1984) in the way the tourist economy has structurally transformed the environment. This is apparent from the changing "life chances" of individuals and the pivotal economic role that nature affords for tourism. The relatively buoyant labour market in Playa Del Carmen has attracted people looking for work towards the coast and served to reduce local peoples' cyclical dependence on subsistence agriculture in the *milpa* (maize) zone. Tourism has created what is in effect a parallel tourist economy based on the tourist dollar and the vicissitudes of the North American vacation season. In terms of the natural environment, the extraordinary invasive capacity of eco-tourism — through dive centres, cruise ships and off-shore facilities — has served to "privatise" the ocean itself by giving differential access to marine resources usually described in the environmental literature as "open access" (Hanna and Munasinghe 1995; Magrath 1989).

6. Conclusion: Discourses of "Nature" and the Objects of Consumption

This discussion of the Yucatan coast and the emergence of global resorts and eco-parks claiming to be concerned with environmental protection leads to an examination of some of the fundamental ideas discussed earlier in this paper.

First, it is unclear whether a clear distinction can be made between "produced" nature in forms such as eco-parks and protected natural areas. To the south of the "Mayan Riviera" lies the large Sian Ka'an Biosphere Reserve. There are only two ways of visiting this area: by a poor quality dirt road (that very few people take) or via a guided tour. These guided tours, though of restricted size, provide the same activities as those available in the eco-parks: snorkeling, floating down the *cenotes* and night observation of marine turtles. There is also considerable "development" within the reserve and few effective planning controls. Although the environment of the Biosphere Reserve has not been so thoroughly transformed as that of Xell-Ha and the other parks, it can be argued that it is better able to repel further development because of their existence.

Second, it is difficult to specify a "correct" use for terms such as "sustainability" when their application is entirely dependent on context. Much of the impetus for environmental protection on the coast comes from the perceived need to internalise environmental costs along the lines of "ecological modernisation" (Giorgi and Redclift 2000). The interest of a minority of tourist entrepreneurs in cleaner, "greener" tourist facilities is distinguishable — although related — to the wider questions of nature protection in the region. We do not know — and it is a research question well worth pursuing — whether the tourists who visit the coast and express an interest in the environment are more concerned, on the one hand, with the environmental standards in their hotels and swimming pools or, on the other hand, with the welfare of the colonies of dolphins and marine turtles. Clearly "sustainability" discourses are used to make claims for both. In addition, the way in which Mayan culture is invoked is beginning to lead to a "third" sustainability discourse, one that seeks to identify "traditional" forms of sustainable living practiced by the eponymous "Maya".

Third, the different temporal dimensions in which sustainability discourses are employed are paralleled by spatial dimensions. The domain of human choice and consumption is heavily contested, and "eco-tourism", however rhetorical, is a convenient label on which to hang contrary messages. "Nature" is used by some groups to suggest something worth preserving by means of market mechanisms — this is, after all, the logic of global eco-parks. Others seek to regulate and "manage" the environment in such ways that access to "natural" areas can be socially controlled. This is the logic of the Biosphere Reserve and of restricted access. In practice, of course, the two currents often converge. The only person patrolling the principal beach on which marine turtles lay their eggs is an employee of the tourist company developing Xpu-Ha, a development just a few hundred metres down the coast. The "naturalisation" and "socialisation" of nature actually serve to reinforce each other.

This chapter has argued that we cannot easily draw a line under "produced" nature that separates it from the "natural" in the face of global eco-tourist development designed to blur this very distinction. Discourses of the "natural" and "sustainability" increasingly incorporate human concern with public access and recreation as well as conservation goals and need to be understood in terms of the structural processes that affect individual choice and lifestyles. Rather than supporting objective accounts from an "ecological" perspective these concerns from the "demand" side, including the ambiguously defined "eco-tourism", have served to underline the importance of different spatial and temporal perspectives.

Clearly the challenge for research is considerable. We need to develop conceptual tools that address the central problems of how we understand "nature", as well as how we consume it, and that provide adequate accounts of the plural epistemologies with which "nature" and its transformation are understood. At the same time we should not ignore the structural features at work in eco-tourist developments, such as those on the Yucatan coast, although these are themselves subject to semiotics. The meanings of "Mayan" and "nature" are no longer, if they ever were, of local or parochial significance. They also carry messages across time — from the Caste Wars and the era of "talking crosses" — and across space — from the United States and Europe, the sources of most tourism in Mexico. The search for "discovery" in the era of global tourism, it might be argued, should not be confined to wilderness areas or wildlife expeditions, but should also take the form of new types of consumption. For instance, tourist recreation is an experience that, in the process of transforming nature, transforms the meaning nature has in our lives. Examinations of the different discourses of "nature" on the "Mayan Riviera" as examples of how nature is consumed suggests that by changing nature we may be widening access to it, as well as adding new meanings to "nature" itself.

References

Barnes, J. (1998), *England! England!* London: Cape.

Brannon, J., & Joseph, G. (eds). (1991), *Land, Labour and Capital in Modern Yucatan*. Tuscaloosa: University of Alabama Press.

Braun, B., & Castree, N. (eds). (1998), *Remaking Reality: Nature at the Millennium*. London: Routledge.

Croall, J. (1995), *Preserve or Destroy: Tourism and the Environment*. London: Calouste Gulbenkian Foundation.

Darier, E. (ed.). (1999), *Discourses of the Environment*. Oxford: Blackwell.

Ellner, S. (1993), "Introduction: The changing status of the Latin American Left in the recent past." In B. Carr & S. Ellner (eds) *The Latin American Left*. Boulder, CO: Westview.

Escalante, R. (1988), *The State and Henequen Production in Yucatan 1955–1980*, Occasional Paper No. 18. London: Institute of Latin American Studies, University of London.

France, L. (ed.). (1997), *The Earthscan Reader in Sustainable Tourism*. London: Earthscan.

Giddens, A. (1984), *The Constitution of Society*. Cambridge: Polity Press.

Giorgi, L., & Redclift, M. (2000), "European environmental research in the social sciences: Research into ecological modernisation as a 'boundary object'." *European Environment 10* (1), 12–23

Habermas, J. (1989), *The Structural Transformation of the Public Sphere*. Cambridge, MA: MIT Press.

Hanna, S., & Munasinghe, M. (1995), *Property Rights and the Environment: Social and Ecological Issues*. Washington, DC: The World Bank.

Irwin, A. (1998), "Risk, the environment and environmental knowledge." In M. Redclift & G. Woodgate (eds) *The International Handbook of Environmental Sociology* (218–226). Aldershot: Edward Elgar.

Kallen, C. (1990), "Eco-tourism: The light at the end of the terminal." *E Magazine*, July–August.

Magrath, W. (1989), *The Challenge of the Commons: The Allocation of Non-Exclusive Resources*. Environment Department Working Paper No. 14. Washington, DC: The World Bank.

Mintz, S. (1985), *Sweetness and Power: The Place of Sugar in Modern Society*. New York: Viking.

Mittelstrasse, J. (1999), *The Concept of Nature: Historical and Epistemological Aspects*. Paper presented at the conference Environment Across Cultures, European Academy, Bonn.

Mowforth, M. (1993), "In search of an eco-tourist." *Focus 9*, 13–27.

Mueller-Vollmer, K. (1985), *The Hermeneutics Reader: Texts of the German Tradition from the Enlightenment to the Present*. Oxford: Basil Blackwell.

Playa! Magazine (1999), "Playa del Carmen, Quintana Roo." Mexico, No. 3.

!Por Esto! (1999), "Playa del Carmen." Mexico, July 9.

Reina, L. (1980), *Las Rebeliones Campesinas en Mexico (1819–1906)*. Mexico City: Siglo Veintiuno.

Sebald, W. G. (1998), *The Rings of Saturn*, trans. Michael Hulse. London: Harvill Press.

Simon, J. (1997), *Endangered Mexico*. London: Latin American Books.

Thompson, M. (1997), "Style and scale: Two sources of institutional inappropriateness." In M. Goldman (ed.) *Privatizing Nature: Political Struggles for the Global Commons*. London: Pluto Press.

Yearley, S. (1994), "Social movements and environmental change." In M. Redclift & T. Benton (eds) *Social Theory and the Global Environment*. London: Routledge.

Wahab, S., & Pigram, J. (1997), *Tourism, Development and Growth: The Challenge of Sustainability*. London: Routledge.

Wolfe, E. (1982), *Europe and the People Without History*. Berkeley: University of California Press.

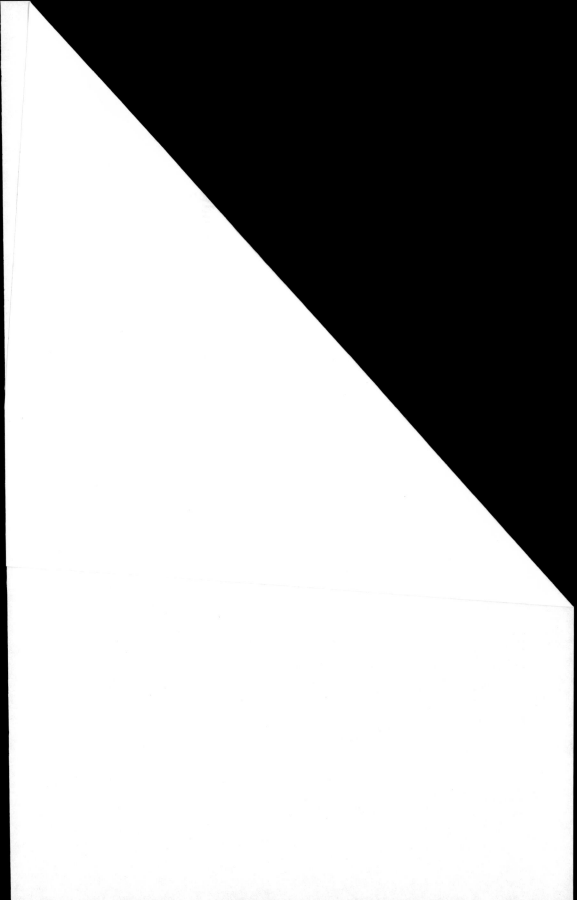

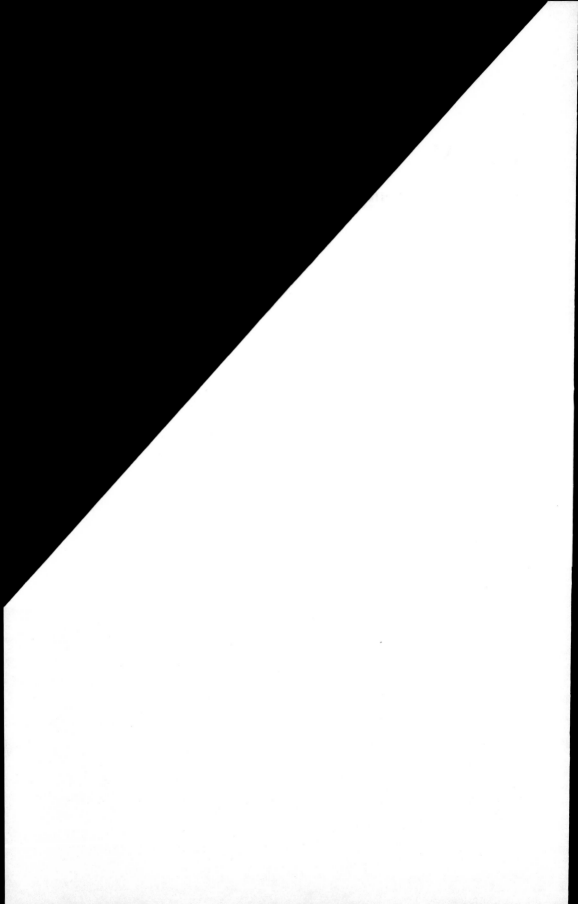

Chapter 8

Working for Beans and Refrigerators: Learning about Environmental Policy from Mexican Northern-Border Consumers

Josiah McC. Heyman

1. Why Learn from Consumers in Industrialising Societies: Aren't They Just Adopting our Bad Habits?[1]

Increasing consumption by "modern" (Miller 1994) households in developing societies worries environmental activists and policymakers, even those, such as Durning (1992), who recognise that most environmentally-deleterious consumption still takes place in over-developed societies (see Heyman n.d. for an overview of consumption in developing societies). Most attention is paid to aggregated phenomena, such as population growth and how gross economic development affects disposable incomes. They determine the number of potential consumers, but not how and why they consume. To address the latter requires learning from people themselves about their ideas and practical behaviours.

The people who shall teach us, albeit through my mediation, are working-class families in Agua Prieta, Sonora, a booming manufacturing city on Mexico's northern border. They present a prototypical case of new consumers whose incomes come from low-wage, world market-oriented industrialisation (in this region, export-assembly plants called *maquiladoras* — see Fernández-Kelly 1983; Kopinak 1996; Peña 1997; Sklair 1993) and whose proximity to the United States exposes them to contemporary global consumer goods and lifestyles (Heyman 1991). Systematic anthropological fieldwork (Heyman 1994a, 1994b) has documented the regional material-culture and how it has changed over time. A sense of culture and history enables us to situate contemporary consumer choices in the available options of material goods and knowledge.

Two observations about consumption in Agua Prieta seem particularly telling for environmental policy. Increasing electricity prices and decreasing real incomes during the mid-1980s did not reduce household reliance on electricity. Price incentives were ineffective, at

[1] I thank my informants in Agua Prieta; I hope that my small efforts to tell the world of their lives provides indirect repayment for their help in my work. I also thank Maurie Cohen and Joseph Murphy for their thoughtful comments on this chapter. The research was generously supported by the National Science Foundation, the Wenner-Gren Foundation for Anthropological Research, and the Henry L. and Grace Doherty Foundation. All responsibility for errors of fact and interpretation remains my own.

Exploring Sustainable Consumption: Evironmental Policy and the Social Sciences, Volume 1, pages 137–155.
Copyright © 2001 by Elsevier Science Ltd.
All rights of reproduction in any form reserved.
ISBN: 0-08-043920-9

least in a simple way; electricity was a necessity more than an option or a want. Meanwhile, a popular Catholic parish was unable to attract factory-labouring youth to their mostly preparatory-school "teen groups" that emphasised, among other issues, the critique of consumerism. Moral suasion against desire and wastefulness had little hold on its intended audience. Why were these two common modes of environmental policy so limited? Their flaws reside in widely shared ideas about consumerism (for overviews, see Goodwin *et al*., 1997; Miller 1995a; Stern *et al*., 1997), chief among them the notion that obtaining and possessing goods are rooted in wants or desires, and that such wants reside in the individual person. While seemingly drawing on opposite impulses in the human psyche, both moral suasion and price incentives assume a simple input to/response by an isolated decision-making unit, be it person or household. To seek alternatives, we need a more social and cultural notion of consumption than that allowed in the tiny space between individual desire and possession (Carrier and Heyman 1997; Lutzenhiser 1997).

We should first question the primacy of desire and possession, without denying the relevance of either factor. Artifacts are not just passive objects of longing or holding; they are actively utilised in both practical and meaningful ways (e.g., Wilk 1999). They are cultural equipment for living. Likewise, we should widen the relevant units of consumption beyond individuals or other isolated entities. Many consumer goods are purchased on behalf of households, after much collective debate. Nor are households neatly bounded and privileged domains of consumption. Internally, they are riven by interpersonal divisions and alliances. Members consume not only in household contexts but also with reference to friendship networks, especially among peers. Externally, they exist in a tremendous matrix of inequality, of both resources and social status (Carrier and Heyman 1997). Consumer actions, whether collective or individual, must be understood with reference to highly unequal contexts and meanings (e.g., Chin 1998). Finally, households and individuals face entities of an entirely different sort, firms and parastatals that supply and market goods and services (see Fine and Leopold 1993; Miller 1997).

The first section of this chapter unveils the scene, the United States–Mexico border, and peoples its stage with urban, consuming households facing serious financial and logistical problems. The next section addresses one of their dilemmas, the need to maintain access to utilities even as real incomes declined, and asks why people did not simply turn the electricity off. From that observation, it explores the historically recent commitment of working and middle-class urban households to consumer durables and external resource inputs. Although that section directs attention toward families and firms and away from personal tastes and desires, such issues remain informative, so the third section addresses the cultural and social development of consumerism on the border, examining blue jeans and other youthful fashions and the changed role of meat in the Sonoran diet. If the second section may be said to ask "why refrigerators?," the third section addresses what Sonorans put in them, their wish for meat and their sense that they just "work for beans." The conclusion draws out the implications of the preceding parts for making an environmental policy that ameliorates the impact of consumption. Without dismissing either price incentives or moral suasion, it argues for a more ample involvement of the public in environmental science and collective-supply systems as a way to tap the manifest concern people have with their consuming lives.

2. "The Money Isn't Even Enough for a Beer": The United States–Mexico Border in a Time of Boom and Crisis

I visited a family I had never met before while surveying changes in the household economy from 1982 to 1986 (discussed below). They patiently trudged through a standard interview. At the end, however, the husband of the family, a lorry driver at a large *maquiladora*, was eager to continue our visit. As I recognised, he sought a certain format of conversation, typical in Mexican culture, in which two people exchange their emotions and anxieties, let forth their worries and concerns. Perhaps he was encouraged to do so by my stated objective of documenting how the Mexican consumer had been hurt by bad times following the debt crisis after 1982. At any rate, he talked about his frustration with having to stop his addition to the house because he ran out of money for building materials. He disclosed his anxiety about having the money to pay the recent electric bill and buy petrol for his ancient car. And, most emotionally of all, he revealed his feeling of duty toward his family. "I bring home every *peso*," he said. "There isn't a *centavito* (one tiny little cent) left over. If I take care of my family, the money isn't even enough for a beer." Beer, of course, sipped among friends, offers an occasion for exactly this unburdening so important to the creation and reinforcement of relations among men. Torn between two compelling kinds of consumption, between household logistics and culturally appropriate desires, worry over money gnawed at Aguapretense.[2]

We shall pay attention to the income problems that confronted these people, but beyond that, we will examine why lost purchasing power hurt them so much, by delving into commodity consumption in and of itself. That is to say, we shall use the difficulties of consumption not to emphasise people's sacrifices on behalf of international banks (see Heyman 1991:176–78), but rather what made purchased goods and services a vital worry to them in the first place. In turn, to understand how these people became consumers, we need to explore briefly the historical formation of Mexico's urban northern-border region (concerning the border generally, see Fernandez 1977; Herzog 1990; Heyman 1991; Martínez 1994; Ruiz 1998; Lorey 1999).

Although some of the United States–Mexico border follows the Rio Grande river and has long sustained small settlements, most of the frontier, including the entire western half that cuts across open desert, urbanised during the twentieth century because of economic interchanges between Mexico and the United States. Most border residents live in these newly formed cities, so their consumer culture, as well as other aspects of their lives, was created in a unavoidably transnational context. For example, Agua Prieta, which abuts on Douglas, Arizona (at about the mid-point of the western half of the border) obtained its water and electricity from that American municipality until the early 1980s. Also, it had free-trade zone status in Mexican customs law, so that locals could shop in the United States and return to Agua Prieta without paying tariffs. This peculiar status was accorded Mexican municipalities on the northwest border because of their great distance from the centre of that nation and proximity to the United States. While, with the advent of the North American Free Trade Agreement (NAFTA), all of Mexico now enjoys open shopping in

---

[2]Aguapretense is the Spanish collective noun for the inhabitants of the city of Agua Prieta.

the United States and the border zone is thus no longer unique, it is also the case that the remainder of Mexico has gravitated toward the borderland pattern rather than the other way around.

Initially, the cities of Mexico's northern border were small and specialised in either tourism or commercial transfers at the boundary port of entry. Mexico as a whole urbanised rapidly during the 1950s–1970s, because of population growth, increased inequality and the decline of the peasantry, and the growth of the state and national industry. The border cities shared in this expansion, receiving migrants from the interior zones of northern states. New households quickly took advantage of access to American goods, especially inexpensive used ones, to equip themselves; in this period, United States banks in border towns gave small consumer loans to Mexican residents, even working-class ones. Many families received income and material culture from the neighbouring side, whether by migrant labour under a variety of legal and extra-legal arrangements or from close relatives who lived across the boundary. (This binational region sustains a remarkable web of cross-border kinship and friendships.) In 1965, Mexico launched the *maquiladora* program to attract labour-intensive manufacturers (i.e., electronics, garments, auto parts, toys, household furnishings, etc.) to its northern border. The *maquiladoras* have grown from a few thousand workers in 1965 to well over a million today, constituting one of the key zones in the global economy. Although hiring patterns have diversified somewhat, it remains the case that most factory operatives are young people, above all women, often living with their parents. *Maquiladoras* provide important income, but few households rely solely on their paychecks. Not only do other household members labour in the city or operate tiny enterprises in the informal sector, but also older generations, above all women, conduct elaborate transactions in consumer durables and provisions to assist the household economy.

The *maquiladora* economy has grown in direct relationship to the stagnation of wages, because that trend maintains Mexico as a pre-eminent source of "cheap" labour. Since 1976, the nation has laboured under the constant drain of foreign exchange caused by its enormous external debt. Its currency, the peso, has devalued repeatedly, which together with inflation has eroded real purchasing power for most households. A radical reorganisation of its economy, blandly called "structural adjustment," has increased its production of exports, which earn foreign exchange to pay the debt. It has also liberalised its importation of consumer and capital goods. Mexico's private economy is strikingly more advanced than in 1982, but its public services are not, and furthermore its households have not shared in this progress, so that we may speak of the nation as undergoing economic, but not societal development (although it *has* moved toward effective democracy).

As an indication of this growth without development, the real minimum wage in Mexico has declined continuously since 1976, today holding less than a third of that year's value. Wages as a share of gross domestic product (GDP) declined from 37 percent to 27 percent from the late 1970s to the late 1980s, and have stagnated or periodically declined (e.g., during 1994–1995) since then. In the *maquiladoras*, real wages of low-skilled workers declined over 40 percent from 1976 to 1993 (Galhardi 1998; ILO 1999). In 1986, when I conducted my study, the Agua Prieta factory base-wage converted to about US$23 for a forty-eight hour week, while at the time I write this, it is worth just about the same (Ibarra 2000).[3] To survive, households often used multiple sources of income, so that in the 1986 survey the median Agua Prieta household income was US$55. Although the cost of living in Mexican-border cities was lower than in the United States, making comparisons to dollar incomes somewhat tricky, the median Agua Prieta household spent about two thirds of its income on food (Heyman 1988:369), suggesting that their budgets were tight by any measure. There is little reason to suppose that conditions for such households differ greatly today; the sharpest wage decline took place from 1982 to 1986, and then flattened out, while the key elements of urbanisation, growing employment, and depressed incomes continue to the present. This welter of economic numbers adds up to one essential point: border householders are fully modern consumers, but impoverished ones. Their consumption in aggregate is probably environmentally significant (e.g., demanding electricity and fresh water), but their immediate household concerns are daily provisioning and obtaining inexpensive clothing, house-construction materials, and cheap or used consumer durables, not discretionary goods. Because of their proximity to the United States, because of the long-established pattern of free trade on that border, and because of the international importance of the *maquiladora* industry, Mexico's northern borderlanders once seemingly exceptional now indicate the fate of many regions of the globe.

3. Increasing Electric Service During a Time of Scarcity: A Curious Paradox with Revealing Answers

Let us examine more closely how border consumers, well established in their material needs, coped with this rapid loss in purchasing power. In late 1981 and early 1982, James Greenberg interviewed 93 Agua Prieta households in two working-class neighbourhoods concerning their family economies, and in early 1986 I reinterviewed 63 of them.[4] The real household income of the 63 families had fallen by about one third (34.3 percent) using conservative assumptions. As a consequence, utility bills, which always posed a financial challenge on their due date, took on crisis proportions. Particularly pressing was the electric bill, received every two months, more costly than piped water and less flexible in scheduling its payment than bottled gas, the two other important resource expenses. A typical electric bill of 6,000 pesos[5] was roughly one half a full week's wages from a *maquiladora*. Thirty-nine percent of families reported reducing their food expenditures during the week electric bills came due. Yet no one went so far in defending their household economy as to drop their electric service.

[3]Ibarra (2000) reports that in Agua Prieta a possible weekly take-home pay with bonuses and incentive- or piece-work-payments was the equivalent of US$50 per week, which is higher than the $22.80 base rate. This was also the case in 1986, though I think bonuses are relatively higher now than then. The general pattern of low pay and little improvement from when I did my study remains true.

[4]The people I was unable to recontact tended to be renters rather than homeowners, so the process biased the information toward mature, better established, and more prosperous households; see Heyman 1991 and 1994b for details on the methodology and the results of these interviews. I have not updated this survey, as my research has turned toward issues of border control, smuggling, and immigration policy, and most recently globalizing elites; but as the text explains, there is solid reason to suppose that the 1982–1986 data remain relevant.

[5]Throughout this essay, I use "old pesos," which in early 1986 were valued at 500 to the U.S. dollar. Mexico later eliminated three zeros from the pesos, thus creating a "new peso."

Indeed, during these same four years of economic travail seven households added electric service (their streets were newly wired), and only three of 63 remained without power. A similar pattern held for bottled gas, used for cooking and heating: in this period thirteen households adopted gas over firewood, an industrial over a regional energy source, again nearly saturating the available households.[6] Meanwhile, Aguapretense strived energetically to obtain water main connections into their homes rather than hauling water from central faucets or delivery lorries. Street by street, people petitioned city hall for water mains and contributed in-kind labour of digging the trenches for their blocks, as well as installing their own connection and domestic plumbing. The pattern is clear: people sought for their homes industrially supplied inputs of power and other resources. Once connected, people were sensitive to prices — for example, they used electric lighting conservatively, dwelling in darkened rooms that felt uncomfortable to this North American anthropologist. The key is the phrase "once connected." Linking to commoditised-resource systems, like the electric grid, was obligatory, no matter the sacrifices entailed, but why?

The surveyed households had by and large settled in cities and joined the working class, in either the formal or informal sectors, during the late nineteenth and throughout the twentieth centuries. In the process, they also became consumers of manufactured goods.[7] The first appliance acquired typically was a kitchen stove, a cast-iron firewood burner through the 1960s and after that a gas range. By 1986, virtually every household had a range. Starting in the 1960s, they bought refrigerators — often from American relatives or dealers in used appliances from the United States — and at the same time blenders and electric crockpots. Less common, but still popular with housewives, were washing machines. These five appliances — and others can be recited — link houses to the utility grid, whether for fuel, motive power, or piped and drained water (see Heyman 1994b for specific household appliance histories, as well as coverage of parallel developments in cars, lorries, and furniture).

Each appliance helps resolve a pressing dilemma for the newly urbanised and proletarianised household, as I learned from many hours of conversations with Angelita Aguirre, an experienced manager of household affairs.[8] Gas ranges cook quickly compared to

---

[6]Unlike electricity, in this case the decision was partly based on price — heating and cooking with subsidised butane gas was much less expensive than purchased firewood. Even so, the effect was the same: dependence on external resources and related technologies.

[7]I have elsewhere delineated a more complex model of the changes described in the text, which the reader may wish to consult (Heyman 1994b:179–83). In a nutshell, it involves two different kinds of household involvement with consumer markets, one conserving of external expenses and resource flows, and the other more deeply committed to flows of money, goods and utilities. For research, this suggests paying more attention to family flows of money, time and resources than rates of purchase and possession of goods; for policy, the perhaps irreversible historical transformation from flow-conserving to flow-through household organisation suggests altering the environmental effects of household inputs (e.g., by the decarbonization of energy services; see Allen 1997; Goldemberg 1996; Goldemberg *et al.*, 1988) rather than exhorting the consuming family to conserve in ways it can no longer afford to do.

[8]Much of this work is done by unpaid housewives, many of whom also work in factories or, like Angelita Aguirre, run cooking and sewing businesses out of their homes. I do not blindly assume a gendered division of household labour; indeed, attention to the roles, interests and actions of mature women is an important part of this analysis. It is also worth commenting that this passage in the text, though spoken in my scholarly language, is derived quite directly from an extensive discussion with Doña Angelita about appliances in her house, as well as constant visiting there.

cast-iron stoves, and they require less effort from the cook to fuel and start. The use of gas also eliminates the need to gather firewood, which was impossible because of urban settlement and lack of proximity to wood sources, immensely time-consuming (for children) even had it been available for free, and otherwise fairly expensive when bought from professional firewood cutters. The refrigerator enables the storage of cooked food as well as frozen meat and tamales, not precisely reducing the housewife's culinary labours but enabling her greater flexibility in scheduling its production and delivery. The blender is an important time- and effort-saver for Sonoran housewives, using the motive power of a small electric engine to replace the arm and hand toil of crushing refried beans, a complement of most meals. Crockpots utilise the electric heating element to facilitate cooking the ubiquitous soups and stews and softening dried beans. (Another time and drudgery saver is purchasing tortillas from the neighbourhood factory, rather than grinding flour and making tortillas by hand.) The washing machine was, by women's own accounts, their most valued device, since washing laundry by hand is achingly hard on the back, shoulders and forearm. Water for washing machines, like other household uses, can be carried in buckets and containers from outside the home, but piped water was strongly preferred because it reduced the time and toil of housewives and children. In summary, each commoditised resource — water, fire, and electricity — in some way added to the production speed, volume, and time-management capabilities of unpaid household labourers.

Such devices do not reduce the total time spent on housework (Simonelli 1986; in general, see Cowan 1983). Agua Prieta housewives do, however, appreciate the reduction in physical effort, according to Doña Angelita. Most importantly, appliances and commoditised inputs facilitate the coping of Mexican households with profound transformations of time. These households had shifted from "freely"[9] allocating among farming and household tasks the full set of adult males, females, and children of both sexes, toward a more rigid model in which adult males devoted a considerable amount of time to paid labour and children many hours to school. Migrant labour in both Mexico and the United States took away some young women and many boys and men. After 1965 households had given over many teenage and unmarried young adult women and men to work in *maquiladoras*. The result was, of course, greater cash income, but also less time available to devote to unpaid household tasks. The use of that income to replace some unpaid work is evident. The burden grew on adult female "housewives," especially when they replaced children's labour. Also highly troublesome to home managers has been the bureaucratic rigidification of time schedules for those who depart the house, both factory workers (Thompson 1967) and school children, as the years of school attendance increase. Rigid time means not only difficulties in scheduling unpaid household work by husbands and children — who, of course, still do many tasks in afternoons, evenings, and Sundays — but requires that the housewife perform key duties like providing hot meals at strictly-determined hours. Bureaucratic regimens (e.g., school) also demand greater attention to the neatness and

---

[9]That is, without being subject to external scheduling constraints; it was, of course, shaped by gender and age roles.

cleanliness of clothing than did older patterns of agrarian life. Domestic productive capacity and rapidity then comes to the fore.

Although the transformation of time is crucial, changes in space are also important, insofar as they alter access to manufactures and natural resources. In the course of the late nineteenth and the twentieth centuries, collective commons came under private or governmental ownership, reducing Sonoran access to the clays, skins, fibres and wood from which they made their traditional material culture; meanwhile, the high pine and oak forest were substantially clear-cut for smelter fuel, mine timbers and commercial lumber. Urban concentration also altered the household's relation to material inputs, as it became increasingly difficult for the 100,000-plus inhabitants of Agua Prieta to walk to and carry back adequate supplies of free, naturally available items like rushes and firewood. If such resources withstood urban demand, they were commoditised and became increasingly expensive relative to industrial alternatives (see note 5). In this process, older skills such as basketry were abandoned and manufactured goods such as glass bottles and plastic containers replaced them. This change also happened when craft practitioners left the social-cultural settings in which they were learned; for example, Sonoran women departed villages where, working in kin groups, they plaited baskets in cool, damp underground shelters, in favour of mine-company towns and border cities. Once a craft is not taught to the next generation, it is dead, gone, useless, no matter if later economic or environmental demands might favour its revival. The loss of skills and resources needed for non-manufactured goods constitutes "consumer proletarianisation," and in my opinion it is as central in making modern consumers as its more famous sibling is in making working classes.

Although consumer proletarianisation involves a taking away, it also brings — for border Mexico, and urban Mexico more generally — an opening up to goods either imported from the United States or manufactured in Mexico by transnational corporations using American, Japanese, and European designs and technologies. As Ruth Schwarz Cowan (1983) demonstrates, such goods were designed for consuming households in the United States in response to a reorganisation of household time and money, gender and generation that is analogous to that described above. So the appeal of such consumer goods in newly industrialising countries such as Mexico should hardly surprise us. While many distinctive goods, like foodstuffs, are produced for the Mexican market, I know of no common appliance in Agua Prieta that differs from those in American kitchens, just that sometimes the items are intriguingly archaic because they are purchased second-hand and strenuously kept alive with repairs.[10] There is in the notion of consumerism as desire an implication of volition or choice, a possibility of acting differently, albeit not grasped. But the "Cowan globalised" phenomenon hardly smacks of choice, either in terms of imperative problems or possible solutions. As I have written elsewhere, "People are not tricked into desiring western consumer goods, nor are they subject to blind imitation, but rather they undergo transformations analogous to western households, generating similar needs, with viable responses limited to those technologies currently marketed" (Heyman, n.d.).

---

[10]Tortilla factories are distinctive to Mexico, because of the fundamental role this flat bread plays in the Mexican diet, and although located outside the home, purchasing tortillas from such factories responds to and causes transformations in Mexican women's lives parallel to those described in the text.

Agua Prieta houses embody the preceding points. Houses are, of course, a vital consumer good, the most valuable item that almost any working-class Mexican will ever own. Relatively few houses are purchased as such; rather, they are mostly self-constructed with the major acts of consumption being renting or purchasing lots, buying materials and making utility connections. Comparing urban to rural Sonoran houses (Heyman 1994a versus Owen 1959 and Sheridan 1988), how might we understand the heightened cost in economic and environmental terms of the former? Typical house size has increased, though homes remain small by American standards; a humble rural house has one or two bedroom/storage areas and a roofed, but open-walled cooking area to the back, while a comparably simple urban house has a front room (often used as a bedroom at night), another bedroom, and a fully enclosed kitchen. Larger and more internally differentiated homes are commonly owned by the more prosperous and well-established families of working-class neighbourhoods. Along with size, the nature of construction materials has changed, with interesting environmental implications. The older house style utilised adobe (unfired, sun-dried mud) bricks for walls, a packed dirt floor, and a cane and mud roof; the current house style, more frequent in town than in the countryside — but present in both places — uses fired bricks, a concrete slab floor, a sheet metal roof, and in some instances reinforced concrete framing. The latter obviously are manufactured inputs and several of them, such as locally fired bricks and industrially kilned cement, require considerable energy to manufacture. They are also poorer insulators than traditional building materials, but far more enduring. Also, houses increasingly come equipped with electrical wiring and interior plumbing, again purchased from the industrial economy and serving as delivery systems for commoditised-resource inputs to the household.

House forms and materials change for many reasons (see Colloredo-Mansfeld 1994; Fletcher 1997; Grimes 1998; Heyman 1994a; Pader 1993; Thomas 1998; Wilk 1989). I find it helpful to follow Richard Wilk's argument that investing in houses is a collective good that unifies households made up of multiple genders and generations with diverse interests and sources of income. As people move to cities from the countryside, they leave behind the inheritance of land, animals and rights to commons as a collective-household good and means of property transmission. The collective interest instead is invested in houses. The aspiration to build houses for children to inherit, typically multiple small ones on a collective lot, is widely shared among Aguapretense, and often fulfilled. Using hard, enduring materials like fired brick fits this new concept of providing a lasting family good. In tandem, the agrarian prestige system drew on public knowledge of land and animal holdings. Amid the rapidly expanding neighbourhoods of the border city, the reputation of the family is not so easily communicated, with households of very different income levels living side-by-side in working-class districts. The family's honour is, however, indicated by the exterior of the house, most clearly in the proud display of family-name plaques (e.g., "Familia Valenzuela" as burnt lettering in wood). The front room offers a public space where outside friends and relatives are received in suitable fashion and collective-family life is enacted, social interactions facilitated by the characteristic sofa and television. Again, in a change from the countryside, guests and family alike eat and socialise indoors, around a kitchen table, rather than in the yard, except for specific occasions like barbecues. In some regards, the newer houses draw on upper-class Mexican or American styles, while in other aspects humble vernacular styles suit the skills and aesthetics of innumerable Mexican men who build their own homes. Status emulation is, at any rate, a by-product of more profound alterations, in that people have additional cash incomes to purchase manufactured inputs and that the social role of the common person's house has changed in such a way as to encourage greater investment and elaboration.

Together with the increased use of the house as a place for visiting, the new time regimen favours interior lighting. The day no longer necessarily begins before dawn, as in the countryside, but the solid blocks of time devoted to factory work, school and house-work during prime daylight hours heighten the pleasure of collective time spent during evening hours with family and friends, visiting or watching television, itself a significant reinforcer of new time patterns. Likewise, the reorganisation of housework, combined (not coincidently) with ideologies of modern bodily hygiene and comportment, promotes the shift from dirt to cement floors and the piping of water into interior washing and plumbing spaces. For houses, as for appliances, the technologies available to northern-border Mexicans are precisely the same as those in the United States, especially since North American discount-hardware centres and used-building materials are important resources for Mexican homebuilders. Exteriors, layouts and colours offer more space for local aesthetics, and thus choice than do house components, but the process by which houses are made larger and more elaborate seems unconscious and thus not amenable to environmentalist exhortation. The same appears to be true of appliances and water and energy inputs. Is there, hence, no hope of a policy that would address the energy and resource-intensive features of houses and households in contemporary societies, rich and poor? I will argue in the conclusion that there *are* appropriate policies, but they must work with people's needs and decisions, and not against them.

4. Barbecue and Blue Jeans: Consumers' Tastes and Desires, From Whence Do They Come and Where Might They Go?

The consumer goods surveyed so far — houses, refrigerators, water mains and the like — are enduring and expensive. This emphasis was deliberate. Such items loom large in the household economy, and they also involve extensive environmental inputs and resource flows. Yet in the study of materialism and global consumer ideology (Sklair 1994), such goods receive far less scrutiny than they deserve (Carrier and Heyman 1997), while attention is heaped on less expensive items of adornment and style, such as clothing or recreation, that are meant precisely to be visible rather than functional. The point, in terms of study and policy, has been made sufficiently by now, however, and it would be a mistake to neglect altogether small and stylish items, not least because people themselves contemplate consumption through such goods (Foster 1991; Wilk 1999). An important scholarly development, meanwhile, has been to view this sort of item as not simply foisted on people by mass marketeers, but as part of various social projects of defining oneself and communicating these identities with others (see Carrier 1994; Miller 1995b). In the case we shall first take up, designer jeans among factory workers, a notion of active consumers is necessary to understand desire, possession and display. Yet it begs another historical question, namely how such consumers are made in the first place.

With the advent of waged and schooled life, the intergenerational bonds involved in the inheritance of fixed property crack and give way. Disputes between older and younger generations worsen and a self-conscious youth culture emerges, aided by alert marketers (Heyman 1990). In the Mexican-border case, we have already noted the *maquiladoras'* summoning together a million-plus army of teenage and twenty-some-odd operatives. Their work is intense, meticulous and repetitious, partaking of the universal character of assembly lines. Typical of time-disciplined labour throughout the contemporary world, the border-factory experience promotes in working youth alternation between intensive duties, subject to external authority, and release during the hours of leisure, celebrating not only pleasure but also autonomy. As María Patricia Fernández-Kelly (1983) narrates in her impressive ethnography of these factories, young people gain their temporary liberation with groups of their peers — in her experience, groups of young women going to night-clubs to dance. At the same time, factory wages give these young people a little money to spend on their small wishes.

Little money it is indeed. As I have mentioned, the 1986 standard factory wage equated to US$23 weekly. Most of the paycheck went home, but not all, at least for unmarried family members; working children hold a portion of their income for their own uses (Heyman 1991:185; also see Baer 1998). The amount varied (it averaged 31 percent in my survey) according to the personal relationships and negotiating situation of that individual within the household. Hence, the goods they bought with their portion of the earnings represent a bit of freedom not only from the factory routine, but also parental demands. The most common, as well as largest expenditure of this sort was low-price "designer" blue jeans, bought on credit from clothing stores or home-based dealers. A pair of jeans might be taken home after four or five instalments at a downtown retailer. For example, in one relatively poor family, a working daughter from her monthly 46,000 peso pay covered a 8,000 peso per month household debt payment (about US$16) and paid 2,500 per month (about US$5) for her own clothing-instalment plan, as well as general family expenses. Obviously, children's spending replaces the family buying the clothes, but this practical interpretation, while not wrong, misses the personal importance of such items to young adults (also see Mills 1997).

In anthropological fieldwork, insight often comes from witnessing conflicts, when the normal performance of cooperative daily life breaks down and contradictory ideas and prac-tices are revealed. While working children usually contribute generously to their parents' budgets, they are also tugged by desires for consumer goods of their own. To my embarrass-ment, I witnessed such a conflict while visiting a friend's home. The mother vociferously criticised her daughter for spending too much money on clothes and snacks with her friends at the factory where she worked. She stressed the family's need for money to buy heating gas and pay the electric bill. The young woman was less articulate, even sullen, except to say that it was money she earned with hard work. One sensed in her non-verbal language, however, pulling back into herself and away from her mother, her conflicted feelings of personal autonomy and yet reluctance to attack her mother and her family obligation. Of course, the stressful economy is the context of this argument, and even more fundamentally, the dual role of consumption as household logistics and personal, meaningful activity.

Discretionary spending certainly does not turn Mexican working people into uncon-trolled materialists. But, to my understanding, it does produce and reproduce desires and needs for consumer goods, which in short we might call consumerism. First, it provides an inducement to utilise consumer credit. Second, it links youth-peer culture with the styles seen on television variety shows and *novelas* (the Latin American form of soap opera, which is shown in evenings as well as during the day). And television is certainly the most potent contemporary medium for marketing specific goods and general lifestyles.[11] The debate on whether people are coerced by or are creative with style and marketing is, for present purposes, beside the point (see Miller 1995a for a review, and also Miller 1997's ethnography). The key is that such consumption is willful and pleasurable, especially when understood in its social and cultural contexts. Hence, a puritanical approach to environmental-consumption policy is unlikely to succeed. A successful policy, especially one that mobilises participation, will partake of the conviviality and hopeful sentiments that enable such hard-working and hemmed-in people to persist and thrive.

Lest it be thought that in emphasising either personal meaning or household logistics I rationalise developing society consumption growth and underestimate its potential impact, allow me to examine the environmentally significant topic of dietary meat. Cattle ranching for domestic-meat production is the largest cause of deforestation in Latin America, although the latter's causes are complex and vary considerably (see Moran 1993). In Sonora, beef cattle raising for local and United States markets promotes overgrazing of sensitive arid pastureland, mediated by complicated property arrangements (Sheridan 1988). Domestic-meat consumption in Mexico also diverts land and water from the production of corn for tortillas, the foodstuff of the common man, to the raising of sorghum for animal feed (Barkin and DeWalt 1988). It is not possible, within my data, to tell if Aguapretense have increased their total beef, pork, goat or chicken consumption over time, but there is reason described below to suspect they have, and likewise that if their income was to increase with Mexico's industrial development rather than stagnate, they would demand even more meat.

It is probable that human beings crave high-energy, fat-bearing foods, including meat (Eaton *et al.*, 1988). Even if this biocultural generalisation proves not always true, it certainly is the case that northern Mexicans, rooted in a cattle-ranching culture, value meat. In the rural setting, however, beef and other meat meals were rather sparse. They mostly occurred at times of family or community-wide celebrations, the baptism of a child or the visit of a state governor. At such times, meat was distributed to a wider set of people than just the household (Sheridan 1988:33, 212). Historically, lack of refrigeration meant that slaughtered animals had to be consumed quickly or dried. In the border city, families have more access to refrigeration, both on their own and via stores. Their sociality increasingly focuses on the immediate family, as explained above, though by no means have collective celebrations disappeared. And they have a different relationship to animals: rather than meat animals being a moderate to large investment which is completely liquidated when slaughtered — favouring a intermittent style of meat-eating — they purchase via a steady cash income small pieces of meat to be consumed on a regular basis,

---

[11]Some Aguapretense started to watch American television broadcasts in the 1960s and 1970s, but the placement of a retransmission tower by the Mexican government in 1981 increased interest in television, because it was now in the Spanish language. Popular programming was Mexican, not American in origin. There is not enough room here to elaborate on the role of television, but what I found resonates with the Brazilian ethnography by Conrad Kottak (1990).

facilitated by refrigerators. In my 1986 survey, I conducted a previous 24-hour recall of meals; 48 percent of households reported eating at least one meat meal, roughly an even mix of chicken and beef with pork, goat and fish also included. And while I gathered this dry data, I spent time conversing with people. Amid the tremendous economic crunch of the mid-1980s, they emphatically remarked on having to cut out meat and replace it with more beans and potatoes (to wit, a catch-phrase they often repeated: "the poor never lack for beans and potatoes"). Beans and potatoes might have kept them nourished, but meat was what they wanted. It reminded them of the ranch life, it reminded them of happy times with family and visitors, and like sugar in Sidney Mintz's (1985) analysis of the British industrial revolution, it was a deeply-satisfying reward achieved when they spent their hard-won earnings. I therefore consider it highly likely that meat consumption in Mexico will rise as that nation urbanises, industrialises, and if that country sustains real increases in income for common people. It hardly begrudges Mexicans fair earnings and simple pleasures to note the difficult environmental dynamic entailed by meat production and consumption. An honest social and cultural view of consumption reveals intractable phenomena as often as it discloses novel policy approaches and suggests potentially optimistic outcomes.

5. The Environment–Consumption Nexus: Possibilities and Problems in Public Participation

Given the dispersion of households, any meaningful effort to affect their environmentally significant practices will require popular involvement, commitment and enactment. Yet in view of the Agua Prieta experience, I am sceptical about moral suasion and price incentives, the two most common and least politicised approaches to inducing widespread consumer participation in environmental amelioration. A moralistic environmental policy, following a long tradition of asceticism about material life (Shi 1985) — admittedly here serving as a straw man, but a relevant one — aspires to dissuade novice consumers in developing societies from leaping into modernity, from radically changing their material tools, needs and desires. It is premised on the notions that global consumers recapitulate the mistakes of the West and that such mistakes were and are made voluntarily, blindly or greedily, rather than for socially- and culturally-systematic reasons. Were such views to inform environmental policy, it might well ignore the actual points of leverage, the reasons why Aguapretense and others like them purchase manufactured goods and use industrial resources, and thus become a cause of resentment and resistance rather than success and its diffusion. Let us take electricity, for example. For housewives needing its motive power for their productive appliances and its evening light for their schoolchildren's work and public sociability, it hardly constitutes a willful lifestyle choice, to be turned off as easily as it is turned on. Value-directed politics are relevant, I shall argue shortly, but we need to go beyond the notion of the individual chooser to frame collective-consumer issues, and hence go beyond the idea of persuading people toward giving them "capabilities" (Sen 1992) to think and act on public alternatives.

Price incentives have some potential, especially for households that watch every peso. Many environmentally deleterious practices are premised on the availability of energy and material resources at inexpensive market or artificially subsidised prices (Roodman 1999:171–74). Mexican working-class consumers are active cost minimisers within a given set of technologies. On the one hand, such people will respond to price incentives within limits (e.g., conserving electricity, but not cutting its service off), and hence some environmental policies may be enacted by anonymous price incentives. On the other hand, such consumers, bereft of a collective commitment to environmentalism, may strenuously resist environmental policy-driven price increases in petrol, natural gas, electricity, water and sewage. Politics may then turn angrily against environmentalism. Also, price incentives alone cannot solve all consumer environmental issues. Householders as dispersed decision-makers often shun more costly but less polluting or more resource-efficient devices. They cannot fully respond to environmental policies unless they wield fundamental capabilities to reorganise their systems of household production/consumption and promote their personal and collective goals. Here I delineate two approaches. The first simply assists poor consumers overcome some practical limitations on their ability to improve their material culture and resource flows. The second asserts a more robust idea of participation, in which people are active participants in policy and are thus motivated to enact it, rather than being resistant recipients of persuasion and price manipulation.

One opportunity for environmental policy is to give the hard-working but poor and highly circumscribed consumers a wider range of realistic options and capabilities. An income-poor household has little hope of making large lump-sum purchases, but they can spread expenses (often at added cost) over time. Most households where I did appliance histories had used-American refrigerators, though older and less energy-efficient models. They saved precious money up front, but paid in electric bills and added carbon to the atmosphere via utilities over the long haul. Analogous observations can be made about other appliances and home heating, cooling and lighting systems. The Mexican researchers Omar Masera, Odón de Buen, and Rafael Friedmann (Tevis 1993; also see Friedmann *et al.*, 1995) are exploring policy options for subsidising and spreading out the costs of new and efficient household- and office-energy technologies. Although necessary to enable consumers to participate in changing their environmental impacts, this kind of adaptive policy perhaps will not prove sufficient to motivate them to care and act, both as householders and as users and masters of collective resources. Participatory strategies seem to be called for.

As the recent florescence of "participation" has shown, however, the word is easy to use but the approach hard to utilise. It might help to begin by inquiring into what common Aguapretense actually did to affect the conditions of their consumption in a collective fashion. In the mid-1980s, there was no widespread environmental activism in Agua Prieta, though this has since changed.[12] But they were not passive, not purely recipients of costs and technologies. Consumption was an explicit public concern, not surprisingly, because of price inflation and loss of purchasing power. For example, I accompanied a march from a large working-class neighbourhood to the offices of the national electrical

---

[12]Environmental participation has focused on toxic releases by *maquiladoras* and on public involvement on planning water supply and sewage treatment systems. The former, of course, involves acting on production entities outside the local sphere of consumption while the latter does involve consumption, but on a collective (municipal) rather than household scale. It is also not clear how deeply such participation has penetrated in the middle to lower income neighbourhoods of the city.

utility that protested sudden and unevenly applied bill increases. The demonstrators did not, however, request a strict return to the old price levels. They sought instead a gradual implementation of the increase, allowing their household budgets to adjust, and a review of what seemed inexplicable inequities among bills. Afterward, standing amid his power tools, Juan Bautista Valenzuela remarked that it seemed unreasonable that his elderly neighbour received higher electric charges than he did for his house and a mechanical workshop that relied heavily on an electric-arc welder. The demonstrators clearly understood the relationship between their own consumption practices and the use of electricity, and held the electric utility publicly responsible for performance of its duties.

The nexus between utility and household as a public concern is vital, because key environmental effects of many consumer goods emanate from the industrial suppliers rather than the household demanders (see Allen 1997 for the United States). Sonorans use electricity generated by a large parastatal utility. Sonorans make houses with bricks fired by minuscule manufacturers in border cities (see Cook 1998). They adopt American plumbing, but its water efficiency is a byproduct of older and cheaper manufacturing standards. This is not the place to explore opportunities and problems in utility and industrial ecology; however, a successful environmentalist reading of consumption will carefully distinguish between final consumers and proximate polluters, and then explore how they might be connected. As I have argued strenuously elsewhere (Heyman n.d.), environmental policy should focus on the linkage between consumers and bureaucratised resource suppliers, governmental and private. Considered just as a matter of prices and private decisions, this nexus will likely frustrate environmental advocates, but as a matter of democratic policy-setting in the collective arena, there is reason to hope that an informed and active public will bring its weight to bear on technology mixes, productive and consumptive efficiencies and cost structures. In the south Indian state of Kerala, for example, vigilant and aggressive social movements have forced public institutions and service providers to function with remarkable efficiency and responsiveness (Franke and Chasin 1994), though this is not specifically reported in the environmental domain. We must insist, however, that this approach to policy assumes a deeply politicised public.

The politicisation of seemingly private environmental issues depends, in substantial part, on widespread understanding of and interest in environmental sciences. Working-class Mexicans with a (typically) junior high-school education cannot be expected to immerse themselves in the subtleties of global climate-change models, but the example of the Kerala popular-science movement shows that relatively uneducated people have a tappable reservoir of interest in nature, science and technology, including environmental issues. Furthermore, in participatory education commitment and motivation are more important than maximising information (Zachariah and Sooryamoorthy 1994:115–22). Hence, popular participatory science would emphasise knowledge capabilities — active control over learning, debating and deciding publicly on options for both households and organisations — rather than passive environmental education, being told (or sold) what is "best" for nature. Often, the latter means simply being given the results, the do's and don'ts of environmental science, and perhaps some terrible perils if they are not obeyed, rather than engaging the thinking chain from fundamental facts and simple models to those final do's and don'ts. At the end, people can develop practices applicable to their own circumstances and capabilities, and informed demands on powerful firms and institutions.

In the thinking process, people come to *own* the conclusions. To do this, however, they will have to engage in hard educational work. Is that a realistic expectation?

The possibility of common Mexicans understanding their effects on the environment exists. When I went to sell a used refrigerator before leaving Agua Prieta, a friend and factory mechanic carefully timed the compressor's cycle to see if it was running efficiently or not, which bears on its electric usage (he had considered buying it for his parents, but it was highly inefficient, something I had suspected, but he was far-better equipped to diagnose). This knowledge of critical technologies and concern with how well they function was not exceptional by local standards. It was, admittedly, aimed at cost minimisation and concerned most with proximate rather than distant effects of the technology on resource use. Also, competing against participatory education are the time pressures of factory and other paid and unpaid work, as well as the obstacle of television's pacifying relaxation. While best viewed with realistic caution, participatory popular science and engineering, with its appreciation for everyday technologies and the life of goods, promises a more welcoming door to environmentalism than anti-materialist exhortation.

In the 1980s and 1990s, border Mexico has indeed been highly politicised. The main focus has been effective democracy and the control of corruption and malfeasance. Also, the popular notion of social justice included the consumer goods on which Aguapretense built their lives (Heyman 1997). Justice, in this instance, meant giving access to consumption to all households. The use of the term justice in the environmental literature as "environmental justice" focuses, instead, on communities controlling and distributing fairly the burden of non-household polluters, such as the *maquiladoras* (e.g., Peña 1997). There is a chasm between the environmental notion of justice and the populist notion of distributive-material justice. Popular movements may have a hard time bridging this chasm other than with rhetoric, so supportive intellectuals have work to do in learning about and thinking through this issue. I close with one suggestion. Greater popular income is sometimes seen as a bad, as giving common people more means to pollute (e.g., Brown 1999). For cases like meat, this will likely prove true. But, when we examine households' irretrievable commitment to resource-gobbling technologies and inputs, and ask what are the alternatives within that scenario, we find that low income precludes use of the most physically-efficient options and that it favours cost-minimising attitudes that have at best mixed environmental effects. Fundamental change will require a radically redistributive social economy that in the face of existing monetised income inequality delivers significant added capabilities to households, perhaps in the form of specific environmentally directed opportunities and motivations. Only this will give the householders of Agua Prieta, and people around the world like them, the options and tools not to harm environments that give them and us sustenance.

References

Allen, D. (1997), "Wastes and emissions in the United States." In P. Stern, T. Dietz, V. Ruttan, R. Socolow & J. Sweeney (eds) *Environmentally Significant Consumption: Research Directions* (pp. 40–49). Washington DC: National Academy of Sciences.

Baer, R. (1998), *Cooking — and Coping — among the Cacti: Diet, Nutrition and Available Income in Northwestern Mexico*. Amsterdam: Gordon and Breach.

Barkin, D., & DeWalt, B. (1988), "Sorghum and the Mexican food crisis." *Latin American Research Review 23* (3), 30–59.

Brown, L. (1999), "Crossing the threshold: Early signs of an environmental awakening." *World Watch 12* (2), 12–23.

Carrier, J. (1994), *Gifts and Commodities: Exchange and Western Capitalism Since 1700*. London: Routledge.

Carrier, J., & Heyman, J. McC. (1997), "Consumption and political economy." *The Journal of the Royal Anthropological Institute N.S. 3*, 355–373.

Chin, E. (1998), "Social inequality and servicescape: Local groceries and downtown stores in New Haven, Connecticut." In J. Sherry, Jr. (ed.) *Servicescapes: The Concept of Place in Contemporary Markets* (pp. 591–617). Chicago: NTC Group.

Colloredo-Mansfeld, R. (1994), "Architectural conspicuous consumption and economic change in the Andes." *American Anthropologist 96*, 845–865.

Cook, S. (1998), *Mexican Brick Culture in the Building of Texas, 1800s–1980s*. College Station: Texas A&M University Press.

Cowan, R. (1983), *More Work for Mother: The Ironies of Household Technology from the Open Hearth to the Microwave*. New York: Basic Books.

Durning, A. (1992), *How Much is Enough?* New York: W. W. Norton.

Eaton, S., Shostak, M., & Konner, M. (1988), *The Paleolithic Prescription: A Program of Diet and Exercise and a Design for Living*. New York: Harper and Row.

Fernandez, R. (1977), *The United States–Mexico Border: A Politico-Economic Profile*. Notre Dame, IN: Notre Dame University Press.

Fernández-Kelly, M. (1983), *For We are Sold, I and My People: Women and Industry in Mexico's Frontier*. Albany: State University of New York Press.

Fine, B., & Leopold, E. (1993), *The World of Consumption*. London: Routledge.

Fletcher, P. (1997), "Building from migration: Imported design and everyday use of migrant houses in Mexico." In B. Orlove (ed.) *The Allure of the Foreign: Post-Colonial Goods in Latin America* (pp. 185–202). Ann Arbor: University of Michigan Press.

Friedmann, R., De Buen, O., Sathaye, J., & Gadgil, A. (1995), "Assessing the residential lighting efficiency opportunities in Guadalajara and Monterrey, Mexico." *Energy 20*, 151–169.

Foster, R. (1991), "Making national cultures in the global ecumene." *Annual Review of Anthropology 20*, 235–260.

Franke, R., & Chasin, B. (1994), *Kerala: Radical Reform as Development in an Indian State*, 2nd Ed. Oakland, CA: Food First Books.

Galhardi, R. (1998), *Maquiladoras as Prospects of Regional Integration and Globalization*. Employment and Training Papers No. 12, International Labour Organization. Geneva: ILO.

Goldemberg, J. (1996), *Energy, Environment, and Development*. London: Earthscan.

Goldemberg, J., Johansson, T., Reddy, A., & Williams, R. (1988), *Energy for a Sustainable World*. New Delhi: John Wiley Eastern.

Goodwin, N., Ackerman, F., & Kiron, D., (eds). (1997), *The Consumer Society*. Washington, DC: Island Press.

Grimes, K. (1998), *Crossing Borders: Changing Social Identities in Southern Mexico*. Tucson: University of Arizona Press.

Herzog, L. (1990), *Where North Meets South: Cities, Space, and Politics on the U.S.–Mexico Border*. Austin: Center for Mexican American Studies, University of Texas.

Heyman, J. McC. (1988), The Working People of the United States–Mexico Border in the Region of Northeastern Sonora, 1886–1986. Unpublished doctoral dissertation, City University of New York, Graduate School.

Heyman, J. McC. (1990), "The emergence of the waged life course on the United States–Mexico border." *American Ethnologist 17*, 348–359.

Heyman, J. McC. (1991), *Life and Labor on the Border: Working People of Northeastern Sonora, Mexico 1886–1986*. Tucson: University of Arizona Press.

Heyman, J. McC. (1994a), "Changes in house construction materials in border Mexico: Four research propositions about commoditization." *Human Organization 53*, 132–142.

Heyman, J. McC. (1994b), "The organizational logic of capitalist consumption on the Mexico–United States Border." *Research in Economic Anthropology 15*, 175–238.

Heyman, J. McC. (1997), "Imports and standards of justice on the Mexico–United States border." In B. Orlove (ed.) *The Allure of the Foreign: Post-Colonial Goods in Latin America* (pp. 151–184). Ann Arbor: University of Michigan Press.

Heyman, J. McC. (n.d.), *Consumption in Developing Societies*. Forthcoming in Encyclopedia of Life Support Systems. Geneva: UNESCO; available on the Internet at <http://dizzy.library.arizona.edu/ej/jpe/consumpt.htm>

Ibarra, I. (2000), "Mexico's minimum wage unlivable." *Arizona Daily Star*, July 23, 2000, A1.

ILO (1999), *Minimum Wage Fixing in Mexico*. Briefing Note No. 13, Labour Law and Labour Relations Branch, International Labour Organization. Geneva: ILO.

Kopinak, K. (1996), *Desert Capitalism: Maquiladoras in North America's Western Industrial Corridor*. Tucson: University of Arizona Press.

Kottak, C. (1990), *Prime-Time Society*. Belmont, CA: Wadsworth Publishing.

Lorey, D. (1999), *The U.S.–Mexican Border in the Twentieth Century*. Wilmington, DE: Scholarly Resources.

Lutzenhiser, L. (1997), "Social structure, culture, and technology: Modeling the driving forces of household energy consumption." In P. Stern, T. Dietz, V. Ruttan, R. Socolow & J. Sweeney (eds) *Environmentally Significant Consumption: Research Directions* (pp. 77–91). Washington, DC: National Academy of Sciences.

Martínez, O. J. (1994), *Border People: Life and Society in the U.S.–Mexico Borderlands*. Tucson: University of Arizona Press.

Miller, D. (1994), *Modernity: An Ethnographic Approach*. Oxford: Berg.

Miller, D. (ed.). (1995a), *Acknowledging Consumption: A Review of New Studies*. London: Routledge.

Miller, D. (1995b), "Consumption and commodities." *Annual Review of Anthropology 24*, 141–161.

Miller, D. (1997), *Capitalism: An Ethnographic Account*. Oxford: Berg.

Mills, M. (1997), "Contesting the margins of modernity: Women, migration, and consumption in Thailand." *American Ethnologist 24*, 37–61.

Mintz, S. (1985), *Sweetness and Power: The Place of Sugar in Modern History*. New York: Viking Penguin.

Moran, E. (1993), *Through Amazonian Eyes: The Human Ecology of Amazonian Populations*. Iowa City: University of Iowa Press.

Owen, R. (1959), *Marobavi: A Study of an Assimilated Group in Northern Sonora*. Anthropological Papers of the University of Arizona No. 3. Tucson: University of Arizona Press.

Pader, E. (1993), "Spatiality and social change: Domestic space use in Mexico and the United States." *American Ethnologist 20*, 114–137.

Peña, D. (1997), *The Terror of the Machine: Technology, Work, Gender, and Ecology on the U.S.–Mexico Border*. Austin: Center for Mexican-American Studies, University of Texas.

Roodman, D. (1999), "Building a sustainable society." In L. Brown (ed.) *State of the World 1999* (pp. 169–188). New York: W. W. Norton.

Ruiz, R. (1998), *On the Rim of Mexico: Encounters of the Rich and Poor*. Boulder, CO: Westview.

Sen, A. (1992 [1983]), "Development: Which way now?" In C. Wilber & K. Jameson (eds) *The Political Economy of Development and Underdevelopment*, 5th Ed., pp. 5–26. New York: McGraw-Hill.

Sheridan, T. E. (1988), *Where the Dove Calls: The Political Ecology of a Peasant Corporate Community in Northwestern Mexico*. Tucson: University of Arizona Press.

Shi, D. (1985), *The Simple Life: Plain Living and High Thinking in American Culture*. New York: Oxford University Press.

Simonelli, J. (1986), *Two Boys, a Girl, and Enough!: Reproductive and Economic Decisionmaking on the Mexican Periphery*. Boulder, CO: Westview Press.

Sklair, L. (1993), *Assembling for Development: The Maquila Industry in Mexico and the United States*, Rev. Ed. La Jolla, CA: Center for U.S.–Mexican Studies, University of California, San Diego.

Sklair, L. (1994), "The culture-ideology of consumerism in urban China." *Research in Consumer Behavior 7*, 259–292.

Stern, P., Dietz, T., Ruttan, V., Socolow, R., & Sweeney, J. (eds). (1997), *Environmentally Significant Consumption: Research Directions*. Washington, DC: National Academy of Sciences.

Tevis, Y. (1993), "Cookstoves to air conditioners: Improving energy efficiency in Mexican homes." *UC MEXUS News 30, 1*, 5–10.

Thomas, P. (1998), "Conspicuous construction: Houses, consumption, and 'relocalization' in Manambondro, southeast Madagascar." *Journal of the Royal Anthropological Institute N.S. 4*, 425–446.

Thompson, E. (1967), "Time, work-discipline, and industrial capitalism." *Past and Present 38*, 56–97.

Wilk, R. (1989), "Houses as consumer goods: Social processes and allocation decisions." In H. Rutz & B. Orlove (eds) *The Social Economy of Consumption* (pp. 297–322). Lanham, MD: University Press of America.

Wilk, R. (1999). " 'Real Belizean food': Building local identity in the transnational Caribbean." *American Anthropologist 101*, 244–255.

Zachariah, M., & Sooryamoorthy, R. (1994), *Science in Participatory Development: The Achievements and Dilemmas of a Development Movement: The Case of Kerala*. London: Zed Books.

Chapter 9

Control and Flow: Rethinking the Sociology, Technology and Politics of Water Consumption

Heather Chappells, Jan Selby and Elizabeth Shove

1. Introduction

There is no doubt about it, water is an essential ingredient of everyday life. It is also a subject of increasing environmental and political concern, albeit for very different reasons in different parts of the world. In this chapter we switch back and forth between two contrasting contexts, the West Bank and the United Kingdom, in an effort to extract, compare and sometimes criticise theories and understandings of water that dominate environmental discourse. Water crises are generally conceptualised in terms of resource scarcity. When problems arise it is because there is not enough water to go around: demand exceeds supply. Rather than treating water as an unproblematically homogenous resource, we argue that it is highly malleable and that the details of its organisation, management and meaning are central to an understanding of sustainable consumption.

Environmental commentators are more ready than most to recognise the diversity of water and to acknowledge the inter-linking of shortage and quality. Hence situations of scarcity are not just those in which water consumption exceeds supply, but those in which the balance between useful, clean, dirty and dangerous water is out of kilter. It is sometimes, but not always, possible to respond to shortage by substituting between types of water, hence initiatives to replace clean with grey water or to manage demand through re-use and recycling. In practice, the prospects for reconfiguring water and managing water supplies depend upon a still submerged social and institutional infrastructure of control and flow. As we argue here, systems both of supply and of demand are anchored in an already existing landscape of technologies. They are also embedded in (and constitutive of) attendant regimes of power. Through our focus on the routine structuring of choice and the social meanings of water, we tacitly challenge taken-for-granted assumptions about the nature of choice and the beliefs and actions of individual consumers.

Our broadly sociological orientation allows us to generate new ways of thinking about water shortages and water quality, prompting us to re-open fundamental questions about what water is and how it is channelled, contained and constituted. Resource economists and natural scientists tend to have their own ready-made answers to such questions. Whether referring to the water crisis of the West Bank, or discussing leakage control and new initiatives in demand-side management in England, the reference point is similar:

Exploring Sustainable Consumption: Evironmental Policy and the Social Sciences, Volume 1, pages 157–170.
Copyright © 2001 by Elsevier Science Ltd.
All rights of reproduction in any form reserved.
ISBN: 0-08-043920-9

water is defined as a resource and described by means of chemical equations. It is H_2O. These definitions are supplemented by a technical language of water management, including baseline flows, distribution losses, and measured or unmeasured consumption. We consider such understandings of water in the first part of this chapter, and suggest that definitions of this kind overlook, or at least under-emphasise, the critical point that water is part of the social fabric and political order of everyday life. The importance of this observation is explored in the remainder of the chapter.

Developing a "sociology" of water is no easy task given the immeasurable variety of social situations through which it flows, is ordered and is in some sense constituted. To simplify our task, we concentrate on three genres of water technology, considering the "barriers", "containers" and "purifiers" which are used to separate wet from dry; to store water; and to create and distinguish between different types. We take these moments and technologies of management as a means of organising our discussion and exploring the social relations of water in two hugely different contexts. As well as using technologies of water management as narrative tools through which to develop accounts of water flow and control, we suggest that such technologies play a fundamental role in "making" water and defining how and when it can be used and consumed. In short, we argue that the systems and devices of control and flow have the central — and often understated — effects of simultaneously constructing the many identities of water as well as all those practices, social relations and human identities associated with its constitution, management and use. In this respect our ambitions are wide ranging.

We nonetheless recognise that such relations are embedded and formed by specific political and institutional histories. In the sections that follow we tread a fine line, examining differences and complementarities in the technological, political and institutional ordering of water in the UK and Palestine[1] as a means of articulating what we believe to be a generally-relevant approach.

2. Conceptualising Water

All expert discourse involves and is founded upon a range of assumptions, and this is as true of discourse on water as on any other subject (Foucault 1970, 1972). We begin by elucidating some of the conceptual foundations on which water-policy discussions are typically based, and then develop our own re-conceptualisation, one that stresses the role of technologies in constituting waters and human subjects.

Peter Gleick's thorough and much-cited compendium on global water issues, *Water in Crisis* (1993), makes a good starting point, not because it is remarkable, but on the contrary, because it is quite typical in its representation of water problems and policies. This is not to suggest that the book presents a single, unified and coherent picture of global

---

[1]The paper draws on material generated in the course of two quite different research projects. Heather Chappells and Elizabeth Shove have recently completed water-related research as part of a European Union (DGXII) funded study of domestic utilities and consumers titled DOMUS. Jan Selby has just finished doctoral research on the Palestinian water situation in the occupied West Bank. The cases and examples referred to in this chapter are taken from one or another of these two studies.

water issues, but rather that, despite the various disagreements and differences in emphasis between them, the contributors share some basic assumptions about their subject matter. Among these are the following: first, the assumption that water is a pure and purely-physical substance; second, that water is a static "resource"; and third, that social practices and social relations are of marginal importance in understanding water problems and policies.

First, Gleick's volume implicitly conceives of water as H_2O. Nowhere is water explicitly defined in these molecular terms — everyone knows what water is, after all — but it is clear that water is being thought of as something which has self-evident and absolute physical properties. Yet water need not necessarily be thought of in this way. Water could be thought of, even in wholly physical terms, as an essentially *impure* substance, as one that, except within the confines of the laboratory, is always mixed with other chemicals (i.e., irons, chlorides, etc.), and with bits of organic and inorganic matter (i.e., plankton, silt, etc.). Water could also be thought of as having an identity that, far from being purely physical, is intimately bound up with social (and socio-technical) relations, practices and values. From a perspective informed by these two points, we can view water as essentially impure and heterogeneous. From such a perspective, there is not one substance called "water", but many different "waters": sweet water, grey water, soft water, rain water, commodified water and so on.

A second point is highlighted by Gleick's claim, made at the very opening of *Water In Crisis*, that "fresh water is a fundamental *resource*, integral to all environmental and societal processes" (1993:3, our italics). This understanding of water as a "resource" is significant in two regards. First, the designation "resource" carries with it the claim that water is an economic good. Second and more interestingly, this designation implies that the water in question is fixed and finite, that water comes in the form of a "stock" or "body" that is just waiting to be exploited. The word "resource" implies a relatively stable and static conception of water, yet water need not be pictured in such terms. Water could instead be characterised as being in a state of continual instability, as ceaselessly flowing and cycling through natural and social systems, and as constantly changing between gaseous, liquid and solid forms. This is not to suggest that water experts are ignorant of the highly mobile and fluid nature of water, but rather that expert texts, especially those concerned with policy, tend to represent water primarily through the language of "stocks" and "resources", and only secondarily through the language of "flows". Our suggestion is simply that water could be thought of in much more dynamic terms.

Finally, Gleick's volume says very little about social practices, relations or values, seemingly implying that these are of marginal importance in understanding water problems and policies. People do of course appear, but only in the roles of "consumer" or "expert manager" of water resources. Setting experts aside for the moment, nothing is said about the actual practices of consumption, or about how acts of consumption affect and are affected by the fabric of daily life, or about how waters are perceived and valued in different contexts. Yet such sociological issues could be seen as crucial to an understanding of water problems and policies.

Partly because water is viewed as an innocent resource, the technologies of its management are similarly invisible. Like so much expert work on water issues, Gleick's text devotes plenty of space to discussion of economics, but barely any to technologies. Yet material technologies need not be thought of as either peripheral or innocuous. If we view water not as a stable resource waiting to be exploited, but as an unstable and dynamic fluid, then the central management problem is not one of exploiting available resources, but of controlling chaotic flows. From such a perspective, the key tools of water policy are not, or not simply, the management of economic incentives or institutional arrangements. They also include manipulation of those material systems and devices — the reservoirs, pipes and taps — that do the work of controlling distribution, storage, access and flow.

Technologies are important in one further way, namely that they have productive effects. They control waters, but more than that, they also *constitute* them, transforming both their physical and social identities. And they have similarly productive effects on social practices and relations, transforming people into particular types of subject. In both these senses, technologies are key to understanding water issues: technologies constitute waters and subjects. This is not to suggest that technologies are intentional agents (which have "aims" or "goals"), but merely to highlight the fact that, once in place, technologies have durable productive effects on nature and society. As such, we are not concerned with *intentions*, but with *effects* (and we are not interested in whether these effects are intended or unintended). Neither are we trying to invoke a form of "technological determinism", but simply to observe that expert discourse on water, in common with so much social-scientific discourse, tends to ignore or understate the enormous effects of material things within and upon social and natural systems (Latour 1988; Pfaffenberger 1988). To adopt Winner's (1986) terms, expert discourse on water is, like most sociology, perhaps guilty of "technological somnambulism".

3. Water and the Technologies of Control and Flow

In what follows, we discuss the constitutive effects of three broad genres of technology: "barriers", "containers" and "purifiers". By considering their deployment and operation we are able to say something about the dynamics of constitution and what this means for the production and politics of water. Our opening comments on "barriers" raise questions about how water is "made" and how the generation of wetness is bound up in a pervading culture of staying dry. Discussion of the technological family of "containers" offers most scope for exploring the control and flow of "useful" water. Finally, focusing on "purifiers" reminds us of the social and technical potential for differentiating between and so multiplying types of water. This is important given the potential for managing demand for "pure" water by means of recycling and substitution.

Concentrating on these three classes of technology, we use examples from the UK and the West Bank to show how even simple technological devices and systems regulate social relationships including those of access and control, just as they regulate the flow of water and its abundance, scarcity and quality. Such technologies do not literally determine the terms on which people interact (as our UK examples show, new institutional arrangements can modify the deployment of technologies designed in another era), but they nonetheless embody more or less resistible messages about relations between water consumers and those who influence the details of provision and supply.

By concentrating on these three classes of technology we are able to reveal something of the different political, environmental and institutional logics configuring the social organisation of water systems in the UK and the West Bank. In the final section we review the implications of these insights for the framing of environmental debates about water and sustainable consumption.

Barriers: Making Water

Roofs, damp-proofing systems, dehumidifiers, sandbags, anoraks, umbrellas and Wellington boots: all of these technologies, and many more besides, have the effect of keeping unwanted waters outside and away from the human environment. These exclusionary technologies define and defend us against the wet. Moreover, they have effects both on social norms and values, and on the physical and social identities of water.

To begin with, they produce and reproduce a "culture of dryness" and an ideal of "comfort" (Shove 1997). They define an essentially modern, urban way of life that is insulated and apart from the volatile whims of nature, and a culture that does its utmost to deter or hide dampness, mud and sweat. In addition, many of these technologies direct and channel water and hence determine its distribution. Roof tiles, gutters, drains and drainage systems have the collective, physical effect of producing "floodwater", and of generating uniquely urban crises as run-off water sweeps across the hard landscapes of modern cities. These barrier technologies confer on water a range of symbolic identities. Our dry culture, and the technologies through which this culture is performed and reproduced, tend to treat ice, rain, dampness and so on as "bads" that must be kept at bay. Such "natural waters", waters which are beyond or which exceed our attempts to control them, are constituted as threats or "risks" to the human environment partly by our obsessive attempts to control them. As Beck (1992) observes, modern society actually produces environmental risks, real physical by-products of our attempts to control nature; or as Lash (1994) argues, slightly differently, our efforts to subdue nature are increasing social *perceptions* of risks. Either way, these and other kinds of barrier technologies embed and engender certain understandings of water.

These observations about bounding and barriers represent the first step in the systematic separation and management of water, and wetness, from dryness. Cultures clearly differ in their valuing of water, being more or less dependent or tolerant in ways that still connect to climatic and seasonal variation. While they make some sense in the UK, grumpy comments about "nice weather for ducks" have no place at all in the vocabulary of those who long for rain of any kind. Wherever they are drawn, lines between welcomed, acceptable, and problematic margins of wet and dry require careful and continuous policing. Taking this analysis a step further, we now focus on the technologies involved in containing and managing a distinctive subset of water that is "useful" water.

Containers: Making Water Useful

Wells, dams, plugs, sinks, swimming baths, buckets, cups and bottles: all these have the effects of collecting, confining and containing waters, and of rendering them accessible for human use. Unlike the genre of barrier technologies, which keep uncontrolled waters outside the human environment, these devices enable the controlled introduction of water into the human environment. The technologies of containment confine water both spatially and temporally while the related technologies of flow and access (pipes, taps, valves and in a different role, buckets) permit the controlled movement of water through space at given times, and allow its retrieval again at particular points in time and space. Moreover, processes of containment also and simultaneously involve the production of particular types of water, and of human subjects and social relations.

In the subsections that follow we consider the social ordering of containment and access first in the West Bank, and then during the last century or so in the UK. In both cases we take note of infrastructural and domestic[2] systems and reflect on the social and political significance of storage and management strategies.

Containment and Access in the West Bank: Politicised Water

The wells pumping into the Eastern basin of the West Bank's mountain aquifer withdraw water from incredible depths of three to four hundred metres, a technologically complex (and also economically-taxing) feat. Before the advent of powerful drilling and pumping technologies, these waters did not exist as a resource: they are only constituted as such by the technological possibility of their exploitation. Such large-scale technologies of access and containment (i.e., wells and reservoirs) have various social effects, as suggested below.

In the West Bank, water is supplied through an Israeli-dominated network of wells, pipes, valves and reservoirs. This technological network channels water to some places and some users at the expense of others, with the effect of limiting Palestinian water consumption while ensuring that Israelis on either side of the Green Line have regular and plentiful supplies.

The West Bank's water network is one that differentiates between Israelis and Palestinians in a number of respects. First, the dearth of wells on the Western and Northern flanks of the West Bank ensures that the greater part of the territory's groundwater flows into (and is exploited within) Israel. Second, hundreds of Palestinian communities are not connected to mains supplies at all. Third, the fine structure of the water network ensures that, in general, Palestinian communities in the West Bank receive lower and less regular water supplies than Israeli settlements. For instance, a reservoir to the south of Hebron stores and provides water for the Palestinian town, as well as for the nearby settlement of Kiryat Arba. The reservoir has two outflow pipes, one feeding Kiryat Arba exiting from the lowest point of the reservoir, the other feeding Palestinian Hebron exiting from a point two meters higher up. The effect of this structure, a structure of both pipework and politics, is that when the reservoir's water level falls below two meters, as it does for long periods during the summer, all of the remaining supplies go to Kiryat Arba. Similar examples of large-scale containment and management technologies are to be found throughout the West Bank.

---

[2]We do not make use of agricultural or industrial examples in this discussion.

The West Bank's water network does not simply differentiate between Israelis and Palestinians, however, but also between and within Palestinian communities. Some Palestinian communities, such as the village of Duwarra, near Hebron, are located by and connected to main distribution lines: they thus receive almost continual supply during the summer months. Other communities, such as the village of Quasiba, just five miles to the north, are much further from main lines and are fed by small-diameter pipes and weak pumping systems. These villages can go without piped water for five or more months a year. On an even more microscopic level, the water network often produces differences from one street or one house to the next. For instance, during the height of summer, piped supplies reach the foot of Dheisheh refugee camp for one week in every three. By contrast, the highest areas of the camp go without water for three months each year; in between the foot and top of the camp, supply conditions vary from street to street.

As a result, and in contrast with the situation in most of the developed world, water in the West Bank is both highly conspicuous and highly politicised. Furthermore, water scarcities, as well as people's quotidian responses to these scarcities, are an arena for the exercise of skills, and for the production and affirmation of social relations and identities. Storage again plays an important part, but this time at the level of individual or household response, as illustrated by this example from Quasiba. On the Eastern side of the village lies an enormous cavern, nine-meters deep and almost twelve-metres square, excavated by members of several water-short households in 1994. The cavern is filled every winter by groundwater flowing down through the mountain that rises sharply above, and now meets the domestic-water needs of the six households who manage it. This storage technology has produced a new resource for these households, and has simultaneously created and embedded a new set of social relations (Selby 1999).

Sharp differences in supply regime have productive effects both upon social relations and identities, and upon the identity and significance of water. First, people are forced to engage in a variety of socio-technical practices: searching for water (at local springs, at the local garage, at the houses of friends and family, etc.), collecting it (in canisters, bottles, buckets, etc.), transporting it (by foot, by donkey, by car, in rubber tubing, etc.), storing it (in roof-top tankers, in underground cisterns, etc.) and conserving it (fitting taps with pieces of sponge, washing clothes only when piped water returns, etc.). Second, these practices involve, and in turn constitute, relations of cooperation (sharing waters, sharing the everyday work of collecting and coping, etc.), relations of conflict (between those who have and those who do not have water, between those who steal and those who are stolen from, etc.), and relations of difference (most noticeably, the solidification of the domestic division of labour). Third, shortages and storage-related practices have effects upon identities, and especially upon the experience and idea of being a Palestinian. In one regard and for some people, shortages are tangible, material affirmations of occupation and dispossession, while in another sense and for others, shortages merely lead to conflict and hence threaten communal identities. To sum this up, water shortages and associated systems and technologies of water storage have a heterogeneous array of social and political effects in the West Bank.

As we have seen, macro-level institutions, politics and technologies of access and containment are countered by micro-level strategies developed in response. In this way, both "levels" are woven into the fabric of daily life in ways that influence the experience and meaning of water. Whatever the precise character of the technical organisation of water and its impact on daily life, one can say that, in the West Bank, water is not simply water, but a conspicuous and politicised form of water, quite different from that which is consumed, so unreflectively, in most of the developed world.

Containment and Access in the UK: Commercialised Water

Although UK water may not be as politicised as its Palestinian counterpart, the history of its containment and supply over the last two centuries nonetheless reveals shifting institutional logics, each of which have produced, confined and constituted water in different ways. In this section we reflect on the commercialisation of water following the privatisation of previously public utilities.

Water consumption in the UK has not always been an unreflective and inconspicuous activity. Rendered redundant by the modern technologies of mains supply (in which private households have private supplies and private taps) the village-water pump once played a central role in the social ordering of everyday life. It was both a powerful symbol of community effort and an important site of local political interaction (Ward 1997).

The transition from local (and locally-variable) water to the standardised, mass-produced form that now issues from the private tap is the result of an heroic effort to tame free-flowing sources and turn them into an ordered, well-managed system of public supply (Guy and Marvin 1996; Porter 1998). Several decades of public investment from the end of the nineteenth century turned British water into an homogenous, relatively well behaved and domesticated resource. The scale of the technological challenge involved in constructing a comprehensive and reliable infrastructure should not be underestimated. All year round, water is pumped from the massive containment systems we know as reservoirs into a vast network of underground pipes, travelling incredible distances before finally emerging in kitchens and bathrooms around the country. This invisible, inaudible, almost incomprehensible system of provision has arguably de-politicised both water and the practice of its consumption (Foucault 1977).

Over the last two decades the once-unifying institutions of UK water supply have been subject to a mixture of social, organisational and technical strains. Concerns over decaying infrastructures, environmental degradation from over-abstraction and drought, and (most significant of all) the privatisation of public utilities have undoubtedly changed perceptions and practices and have, in the process, created a more differentiated landscape of water, water management and water consumption (Cryer 1995). Previously invisible aspects of the water system ("fat-cat" managers, shrinking reservoir capacities, leaking pipes and water-poor consumers) have become the focus of public and private scrutiny. As with the West Bank, a discussion of the technologies of containment illuminates (some of) the social relations assumed and constituted by the contemporary organisation of water supply.

In the summer of 1995, water shortages hit the headlines in the UK bringing scarcity and storage to the top of the public agenda (Durham 1995). The sight of tankers being used to transfer water from the Kielder reservoir in Northumbria to water-short villages in neighbouring Yorkshire revealed the centrality of storage technology in the newly commercialised landscape of water supply (Bannister and Wainwright 1995). As the "owner" of the 200,000 million litres of water contained in the Kielder reservoir, Northumbria Water was in a powerful position. As well as extracting water for its own customers, Northumbria was able to trade and negotiate with other less fortunate regions.[3] Throughout this "dry" period, Yorkshire Water found itself in the embarrassing situation of having nothing to sell. Water was suddenly and dramatically conspicuous by its absence, a fact that severely damaged the company's commercial credibility and challenged the public's long-standing perception of water as a tamed and reliably available resource. Moral appeals to the collective good — that had underpinned previous (public) campaigns for water conservation — echoed hollowly when repeated in this straightforwardly commercial environment. Why should consumers use less of what they had paid for? It made no sense.

As this episode revealed, privatisation has changed the constitution of water. No longer something to be saved and managed for the benefit of all, it is explicitly and evidently a commodity, bought, sold, stored and distributed, like any other. This re-orientation transforms the perception and the management of the infrastructure itself. Reservoirs are not simply locations in which water lingers in its circulating journey, nor should they be seen as triumphs of engineering over nature in the cause of public health and welfare. They have become the warehouses of an industry and are now subject to appropriately commercial management.

The 1995 drought momentarily laid bare the bones of commercial and technical interdependence that constitute the UK water system. It showed, with instant clarity, that water had been thoroughly commodified. Supply chains of provision were thrown into sharp relief, as were the stores, stockpiles and strategies of competing corporate enterprises. Relationships between householders and water suppliers were those of captive customer and dominant provider, no more than that.

While reservoirs are significant and revealing storage technologies, there are other smaller scale but still important points at which water is collected, organised and managed. As the following account of an admittedly atypical initiative suggests, UK consumers are not entirely at the mercy of the mass producers of standardised water. Before exploring this case of "off grid" water self-management, we first acknowledge more conventional patterns of infrastructural inter-dependence within the UK system.

A vast amount of the UK's water is stored in peoples' homes. Added together, the capacity of the nation's toilet cisterns, and its hot and cold water-storage tanks is considerable. These localised "reservoirs" form part of the total water system and are integral to its effective operation. Moreover, they too have a part to play in conditioning the use and management of water and the relations and obligations between those involved. To give just one example, gravity-fed plumbing systems protect mains water from accidental contamination. Such arrangements complement and support rather than challenge the commercialised provision of mains supply, but there are exceptions to this general rule.

---

[3]Water distribution depends upon an infrastructure of storage combined with long-distance pipelines. The physical landscape and the arrangement of natural watersheds influence the form of the distribution network. Such features make rather less difference to other infrastructures, for example, the national electricity grid or the telephone system.

Some households have, for instance, sought to break free of standard systems of water provision and their associated regimes of control and access. As in Quasiba, where the villagers developed their own mini-reservoir, a handful of families in the UK have taken it upon themselves to manage their own infrastructure of water supply and containment. Motivations clearly differ from those of their Palestinian counterparts. Nonetheless, the strategies described below also represent a response and a form of resistance to the prevailing social order.

In an effort to "keep everything in their own valley" three Yorkshire households decided to group together in the early 1990s to construct an autonomous water-supply system for their self-built homes. The households collect rainwater for drinking and use recycled grey water for other domestic purposes. Since rainwater is subject to wide seasonal variation the water self-managers have installed large tanks in a specially designed basement area which acts as the heart of the household storage and treatment plant. Rainwater falling on the roof is channelled through a series of pipes into these basement reservoirs. Having been treated and filtered, it is turned into "useful" water for normal consumption. Symbolically at least, these localised arrangements represent a significant challenge to the institutions that provide and police mains water storage and distribution. Perhaps not surprisingly, these "deviantly self-sufficient" householders have faced considerable resistance from water regulators and environmental health officers who have insisted on intensive monitoring of this "risky" form of water management.

At a socio-political level in the UK, as in the West Bank, power over containment, management and flow is the subject of negotiation and conflict between a range of actors. While water in the UK may not be as unstable and unpredictable as it is in the West Bank, in both cases we observe the development of large-scale storage infrastructures linked to sometimes complementary, sometimes contradictory systems of cisterns, butts and buckets. The interface between the two reveals the constant overlapping of the political, institutional and technological and reminds us of the extent to which the histories of these and other societies are quite literally inscribed in their plumbing.

So far we have talked of water as a more or less undifferentiated substance. In what follows we reflect on the heterogeneity of water and on the uses to which it can be put, both of which depend on technologies of purification.

Purifiers: Making Water Different

We now turn our attention to technologies for treating and managing water by means of filters, chemical dosing, biological treatment, desalination[4] and so on. Large-scale treatment and purification plants ensure that water companies produce and deliver a standard

---

[4]Israel has recently decided to embark on the construction of its first major desalination plant. Although the exact details are still unclear, the development of this form of large-scale "purifier" technology promises to reframe the organisation of water control and flow between Israeli and Palestinian territories and to redefine issues of water quality and scarcity. While not pursuing this case here, we acknowledge that exploring the changing organisational and technical arrangements of desalination would provide a useful contrast to the UK initiated grey-water schemes we describe, revealing further differences and similarities in relations of water purification.

grade of water to all their customers. Such systems enable the UK water industry to make the confident claim that mains water is one of the purest and most thoroughly tested products households are ever likely to consume (Essex and Suffolk Water Guide 2000). While the industry is committed to the mass production of (apparently) uniform tap water, the profusion of filtering technologies, not only in water-treatment plants, but also in households, gives some indication of a further, endlessly rich vocabulary of purity, propriety and purpose. For example, specialist companies sell water-softening devices that promise to banish unnecessary levels of scum, scale, and unsightly staining suffered, they claim, by 60 percent of UK households (Aqua Dial 1997). Though "soft" water is good for towels, clothes and hair washing, it is not so good for arteries, hence the advice to keep a separate supply of "hard water" for drinking. There are two points to make here. First, distinctions between hard and soft water are drawn within a regime of uniformly "pure" supply. Second, such distinctions — and those that lie behind rapidly escalating sales of bottled drinking water — do nothing to disturb the established institutions of "normal" water provision.

Other qualitative distinctions present more of a threat to the conceptual uniformity of tap water. Environmentally inspired experiments with grey-water technologies involve treating and recycling contaminated water (e.g., from baths and showers) for use in situations where mains-quality drinking water is not required (e.g., for flushing the toilet or watering the garden). The goal is to use grey water in place of purer varieties and hence conserve the latter. At first sight, this is a simple enough ambition, but as these experiments have shown, the relationship between quantity and quality demands careful management. In addition, the production of new types of water requires close attention to the technologies and practices of purification.

Making "good" grey water involves a process of addition (chemicals, chlorine, bleach and colouring) and subtraction (filtering, cleaning and unblocking) which together contribute to the production of a water which, though grey and "dirty", does not appear to be so and does not smell as if it is. Filters prove to be critical "purifying" technologies throughout this process, since the production of "useful" grey water involves separating potentially problematic waste from that which can be safely retained. Working back towards the plug-hole, households with grey-water systems have found themselves changing showering and bathing routines (to avoid clogging filters or introducing inappropriate additives) and taking other steps to improve the "quality" of their wastewater.

Should grey-water systems take hold, householders, not water companies, would be the makers and producers, as well as the users, of this new grade of water. Likewise, social conventions of grey-water usage would have to become established. As one UK water company discovered when it tried to introduce a communal grey-water tank, households may not mind using their own waste water to flush the toilet, but they are not prepared to use other people's. Social norms regarding the management and sharing of water are deep rooted and, from a cross-cultural perspective, immensely varied. The challenge of injecting parallel types of water into more and less established classificatory systems raises the spectre of localised, household level, technologies of filtration and extraction (from baths and sinks as well as rivers and reservoirs); and of a more conscious appreciation, and perhaps even a new moral order, of water qualities and water uses. In the UK at least, this implies a rather radical reconfiguration of a currently centralised system grounded in an ideology of uniform purity and sustained by an intersecting network of cultural as well as technological arrangements.

This brief discussion of purifying technologies reveals the social and institutional structuring not just of water supply, but also of water quality. Households using grey-water systems still rely on mains supply and, as we saw above, domestic practices of purification and storage have to be understood alongside those of the water industries with which they intersect. Multiple systems can and do co-exist yet the point remains — the effective introduction of parallel systems of grey-water management requires more than a network of appropriate technologies. Such initiatives also imply a reconfiguration of domestic and water-institutional relationships.

4. Water Consumption in Theory and Practice

Having considered the part that the technologies of exclusion, containment and purification play in managing the control and flow of water, we now reflect on the wider implications of the approach we have sought to develop in this exploratory chapter.

Our first move was to challenge representations of water as a uniform resource subject to more or less sustainable consumption. This theoretical manoeuvre had the immediate effect of redefining the agenda: rather than considering depleting stocks of water we turned our attention to the institutions and infrastructures of flow and control. Instead of viewing water as a mono-dimensional substance we took note of its many forms and meanings. This reorientation in turn required us to reconsider consumption. It no longer made sense to view demand as the expression of individual desires and lifestyle choices, or to expect environmental commitment to engender sustainable consumption. Having recognised the extent to which social, political and technical systems configured both water and those who used it, we had to admit that patterns of consumption were significantly shaped by collective practice and sociotechnical possibility.

The definition, organisation and management of water became our central themes. Abstracting examples from the West Bank and the UK, we showed something of the infrastructural politics at play in these two contrasting situations. But it was not enough to outline formal institutional arrangements. Our methodological strategy of following through the technologies of storage, distribution and access gave further insight into the ways in which such pressures are mediated, translated and made real. As we discovered, close inspection of apparently inert entities like reservoirs provided important clues regarding the day-to-day intersection of macro infrastructures and micro practices. Looking through the "lens" of storage and purification systems we saw how they managed and mediated not just water, but also social relations between consumers and between consumers and the institutions of water supply. In the West Bank these relations are bound up with a broader story about Palestine and Israel; in the UK they are shot through with histories of public health, privatisation and commercial competition. In short, barrier technologies, like those of containment and purification are not innocent instruments of engineering: at every level, they reproduce and inscribe social relations.

Technologies also have a role in configuring meanings and practices of consumption, variously positioning water as a commodity, as a symbol of political status or as a substance that is scarce, abundant, clean, dirty, hard, soft, white, black, grey, and so on. Efforts to juggle between quantity and quality (as illustrated by environmentally-inspired attempts to introduce domestic grey-water systems) touch on all these themes. Likewise, calls for restraint and conservation are positioned and rendered meaningful or ridiculous depending on the precise social, political and technological context in which they are uttered. Though we have yet to make the point explicit, it is clear that patterns of consumption are strongly determined by infrastructural arrangements, and by the habits, expectations and practices they engender and sustain. Like it or not, water consumers are positioned within what Rip and Kemp (1998) refer to as sociotechnical regimes, that is inter-connected networks of technology and practice that constitute "normality". From this perspective, the notion that sustainable water consumption depends upon the decisions and actions of more or less environmentally committed individuals is patently implausible. As we have tacitly assumed all along, infrastructures and systems of water supply actively create and structure demand. They do not simply meet it.

To conclude, we have moved from a uniformly resource-based view to one that recognises the multiple meanings of water and the dynamics of its flow and control. This has practical and theoretical implications for the representation and analysis of sustainable consumption. To understand the process of ordering and management we have concentrated on the specific technologies involved in channelling and organising water. This has the further advantage of showing how consumption practices are configured and organised. Though we have considered only a handful of cases, we suggest that such an approach offers a means of understanding the part that social and technical infrastructures play in structuring the macro and micro dynamics of sustainable consumption.

This is a potentially significant advance, but one that also has some costs attached. By implication, policy analyses that consider the institutions of water supply without also taking note of the technological and other infrastructures through which actions and practices have effect are severely limited. Generalising more broadly, studies of environmental policy need some material, if not technological, anchoring if they are to capture consequences and implications at the level of practical action. In addition, our analysis presents important challenges for those who subscribe to individualistic models of choice and change. To put it bluntly, efforts to characterise or promote "green" consumption as an expression of individual environmental commitment fail to see the big picture or appreciate the structuring of "choice" itself. As a result, we have to question the relevance of investigating the habits and characteristics of green consumers despite the fact that this has by now become a respectable line of social-environmental enquiry. But perhaps the biggest loss concerns the concept of water as a resource. In abandoning this way of thinking, we drift away from a perspective that is deeply embedded in vast reaches of established research.

Putting these losses aside, and concentrating on the benefits of a fresh approach, we suggest that similar arguments might be made with reference to other environmentally significant issues such as energy or food. In these cases too, there is much to be said for setting simple resource-based accounts aside; for taking due account of the subtle but pervasive part that technologies play in configuring the normal and the possible; for recognising that institutional arrangements and environmental policies do not simply determine everyday practice, and for acknowledging the social construction of demand.

References

Aqua-Dial Ltd. (1997), *Experience Heaven on Earth: An Advanced Range of Technically Superior Water Softeners* (Promotional Literature). Kingston-upon-Thames: Aqua-Dial Ltd.

Bannister, N., & Wainwright, M. (1995), "Obscene profit fuels water anger." *The Guardian*, 30 November, p. 2.

Beck, U. (1992), *Risk Society: Towards a New Modernity*, trans. M. Ritter. London: Sage.

Cryer, R. (1995), "Changing responses to water resource problems in England and Wales." *Geography 80* (1), 45–57.

Durham, M. (1995), "Yorkshire Water to admit blame for 'droughts'." *The Observer*, 26 November, p. 5.

Essex and Suffolk Water. (2000), *A Guide to Water Services 1999/2000*. Chelmsford: Essex and Suffolk Water.

Foucault, M. (1970), *The Order of Things: An Archaeology of the Human Sciences*, trans. unidentified collective. London: Routledge.

Foucault, M. (1972), *The Archaeology of Knowledge*, trans. A. Sheridan. New York: Pantheon.

Foucault, M. (1977), *Discipline and Punish: The Birth of the Prison*, trans. A. Sheridan. Harmondsworth: Penguin.

Gleick, P. (ed.). (1993), *Water in Crisis: A Guide to the World's Fresh Water Resources*. New York: Oxford University Press.

Guy, S., & Marvin, S. (1996), "Managing water stress: The logic of demand side infrastructure planning." *Journal of Environmental Planning and Management 39* (1), 123–128.

Lash, S. (1994), "Reflexivity and its doubles: Structure, aesthetics, community." In U. Beck, A. Giddens & S. Lash, *Reflexive Modernization: Politics, Tradition and Aesthetics in the Modern Social Order*. Cambridge: Polity Press.

Latour, B. (1988), "Mixing humans and non-humans together: The sociology of a door-closer." *Social Problems 35*, 298–310.

Pfaffenberger, B. (1988), "Fetishised objects and humanised nature: Towards an anthropology of technology." *Man 23*, 236–252.

Porter, D. (1998), *The Thames Embankment: Environment, Technology and Society in Victorian London*. Akron, OH: University of Akron Press.

Rip, A., & Kemp, R. (1998), "Technological change." In S. Rayner & E. Malone (eds) *Human Choice and Climate Change*, Volume 2: Resources and Technology. Columbus, OH: Battelle Press.

Selby, J. (1999), *Water Developments and Docile Bodies: A Question of Ethics*. Presented at conference on The Uncertain State of Palestine: Futures of Research, University of Chicago, 20 February.

Shove, E. (1997), "The science of comfort and the comfort of science." In *Nytenkning omkring effectiv energibruk og baerekraftig forbruk i husholdninger*, Workshop Proceedings, 23–24 May (pp. 18–21). Oslo: Norges Forskningsrad.

Ward, C. (1997), *Reflected in Water: A Crisis of Social Responsibility*. London: Cassell.

Winner, L. (1986), *The Whale and the Reactor: A Search for Limits in an Age of High Technology*. Chicago: Chicago University Press.

Part VI

Identity, Behaviour and Lifestyle: The Social-Psychology of Sustainable Consumption

Chapter 10

Environmental Concern and Anti-consumerism in the Self-Concept: Do They Share the Same Basis?

Stephen Zavestoski

1. Introduction

This chapter examines the relationship between people's conception of themselves and their concern for the environment and for overconsumption. Rather than focusing on barriers to behaviour change with respect to consumption, and thereby approaching environmental impacts, I ask whether some individuals may be motivated to change their consumption and lifestyle patterns due to an existential crisis in their lives. Specifically, as consumption comes to dominate an individual's options for communicating information about the self, feelings of inauthenticity may emerge and compel alternatives to consumption as a means of self-identification. This is a social-psychological approach to understanding the possible forces motivating a societal shift to sustainable forms of consumption. It questions whether concern for the environmental impacts of our consumption habits needs to be instrumental.

In this chapter I use qualitative and quantitative data drawn from participants in voluntary simplicity (VS) classes offered by the Northwest Earth Institute (NWEI) in the Pacific Northwest of the United States. I attended classes in which participants learned strategies for reducing their reliance on material consumption as a source of meaning in their lives. I also observed and interviewed participants, many of whom enrolled in the classes with the hope of alleviating the stress and frustration they were feeling in their consumer lifestyles, although they had little prior knowledge of the VS movement.

These data, as well as data from a national survey of Americans, are used to determine whether interest in VS (i.e., reducing one's level of consumption) is an egoistically motivated interest or one driven by an underlying concern for the environmental impacts of consumption. If it is lack of fulfilment, excessive stress, agitation, malaise and despair that compels many people to explore VS lifestyles, and this is linked to the culture of consumption, then the search for a simpler and less consumptive lifestyle may be primarily a selfishly motivated concern. But if people identify as the source of these feelings concern about their impact on the environment, then the search for a simpler and less consumptive lifestyle may be more appropriately attributed to environmental considerations.

Exploring Sustainable Consumption: Evironmental Policy and the Social Sciences, Volume 1, pages 173–189.
Copyright © 2001 by Elsevier Science Ltd.
All rights of reproduction in any form reserved.
ISBN: 0-08-043920-9

Given the current scientific consensus about the growing scale of environmental problems social science has an essential contribution to make (National Academy of Sciences 1991; National Research Council 1986, 1987; Stern *et al.*, 1992; Union of Concerned Scientists 1992). The social-psychological approach I develop here, however, is by no means unique. Already social scientists have conducted research demonstrating that value orientations are significantly correlated with beliefs about the environmental consequences of human activity (Stern *et al.*, 1993), with intentions to perform pro-environmental acts (Stern *et al.*, 1995) and with self-reported pro-environmental behaviour (Karp 1996).

This chapter extends the usefulness of this line of inquiry by introducing the self-concept. Drawing on Gecas and Burke's (1995) definition, I conceptualise the self-concept as the product of a process of reflecting on ourselves, an activity that includes the adoption of other's perspectives to determine how we must appear to other social actors. Based on this definition the self-concept can be said to be composed of the various attitudes, ideas and beliefs we form about ourselves — or, in short, our identities.

Previous research on values, attitudes and beliefs has typically required combining knowledge of an individual's value orientation with knowledge of her/his beliefs about a specific attitude object, and/or to whom the individual ascribes responsibility. This chapter treats the self-concept as the root of individuals' values, attitudes and attributions of moral responsibility, and therefore it is a key concept in understanding consumption and environmental behaviours. Identities, after all, which comprise the self-concept, carry with them implications for action. Stern *et al.*, (1999) in their "Value-Belief-Norm Theory" for predicting environmental-movement activism, acknowledge that identity, and its role in the frame-alignment process leading to movement participation (Snow and Benford 1992), is a missing variable.

An understanding of an individual's self-concept, when combined with knowledge of her/his value orientation, should further enhance our ability to predict environmental concern and pro-environmental behaviours. In addition, if the self-concept is the structure that organises our values, examining the self-concept should prove useful in determining whether environmental concern and anti-consumerist attitudes emerge out of the same value orientation or from deeper within the self.

Furthermore, the self-concept's importance can be seen when considering possible motivators of human behaviour. Most species act largely on the basis of environmental stimuli. *Homo Sapiens*, however, are unique in their ability to generate internal stimuli; a capacity made possible by the self-concept. In fact, Goffman (1974) maintains that the attempt to preserve the self — to protect our conception of ourselves — is the chief motivator of human activity. Powers (1973), Burke (1991, 1997), Stets (1995), and Stets and Burke (1994) similarly maintain that behaviour can be explained as the attempt to maintain our self-conception by manipulating how others perceive us. If much of our behaviour aims at preserving our self-conceptions (such as consuming greater amounts of more and more expensive material goods) and this tends to result in environmentally-detrimental outcomes, then exploring instances in which the self-concept is preserved through alternatives to environmentally detrimental forms of consumption is essential. This may be a way of moving us toward societies based on more sustainable consumption.

2. Anti-consumerism and the Self-Concept

To understand consumption's role with respect to self-concept formation in post-industrial societies we need look no further than the marketing industry. Publications such as the *Journal of Marketing Management, Advances in Consumer Research, Psychology and Marketing* and *The Journal of Consumer Psychology* provide us with research suggesting that: consuming is a process of identity formation (Gentry *et al.*, 1995; Hogg and Michell 1996; Wong 1997); persuasion is possible because the self is malleable (Aaker 1999); marketers can benefit by getting consumers to see their identities as linked to a particular brand (Muniz 1997; Simonson 1997), the symbolic power of a product to confer prestige or increase self-esteem can be harnessed (Burroughs 1996; Noble and Walker 1996) and people's sense of attachment and satisfaction can be manipulated through product acquisition (Sivadas and Venkatesh 1995).

Researchers in other disciplines — sociology, anthropology, and cultural studies, for example — take a more critical view of the manipulation of the self in relation to increased consumption. Post-modern theorists such as Baudrillard (1981, 1983), Bourdieu (1984), Featherstone (1991) and Jameson (1984), see the proliferation of goods in consumer societies as resulting in schizophrenic individuals struggling to create identities in a world of transitory and ephemeral signs and meanings. The instability of the self in a post-modern consumer society, these theorists suggest, facilitates social stratification through consumption as a statement of difference. Miller (1987) also acknowledges the role of consumption in social differentiation, but points to the potential of consumption to create social equality when goods are consumed for the purpose of creating strong social networks.

What is clear is that whether we consume to distinguish ourselves from others or to identify ourselves with a desirable group, consumption has become a fundamental mode of self-formation and self-expression. This is evident in research and theoretical developments from throughout the previous century: in Veblen's (1899) notion of conspicuous consumption; in Simmel's (1957) trickle-down theory of fashion; in Rochberg-Halton's (1986) more contemporary analysis of the meanings of material goods in our lives; or in Gillespie's (1995) study of the attachment of oneself to a community through shared consumption of television programming.

If consumption has become a necessary part of self-formation in the lives of citizens of consumer societies, what compels people with anti-consumerist sentiments to seek alternative ways of creating identities? One explanation is that some people are realising that wealth and material possessions cannot meet all of the needs of the self. When greater or different types of consumption no longer overcome feelings of chronic stress, dissatisfaction and lack of fulfilment, some individuals may begin questioning the dominant marketing messages of consumer society contending that consumption is an effective means of self-formation. A participant in a VS course who I interviewed as part of the research reported here spoke of feeling as if she had been lied to: "I grew up being told that if I had all the right things, I would be happy."[1] It is perhaps this sense of having been deceived, which is accompanied by a loss of trust in consumption's ability to deliver

---

[1]Interviews with participants in the courses were conducted between January and June 1997.

happiness, that allows some individuals to break from the tendency to base one's self-concept almost entirely on what one consumes.

Interviews with participants enrolled in VS courses suggest that the realisation that consuming "things" does not consistently result in self-fulfilment and happiness emerges out of an identity crisis. For some the crisis follows an acute personal or family event (such as divorce, children leaving home or a death). For others, the crisis follows years of over-consuming in an attempt to alleviate the stress, fatigue and unhappiness arising from long hours of work. In all cases, the cause of the crisis seems to be related to the relentless pursuit of wealth for the purpose of consuming material goods.

Based on the above account it would seem that awareness of the environmental impacts of consumption activities is not a motivating factor in reducing one's consumption. For some interviewees, however, awareness that simplifying is also about reducing one's burden on the environment does exist. As one participant in a VS course stated, "I'd always had these deep-seated feelings about protecting the earth, and here I was burning gasoline up and down the freeway and paying someone to clean my huge house. That was my life, and that's not who I am." Many others also exhibited an awareness of the burden of their consumption habits on the environment, but their environmental concern alone was not great enough to motivate them to change those habits. Rather, it was not until they experienced a crisis of being that these individuals began to explore alternatives to consumption.

The above interviewee's statement introduces a useful framework for understanding the growing interest in reducing levels of consumption — whether environmentally motivated or not. What she describes is a feeling of inauthenticity. For existentialist philosophers such as Martin Heidegger (1967), the notion of an authentic or inauthentic being has to do with the control that one exerts over her/his existence. In simplified terms, the greater control we exercise in determining our existence, the more authentic we are. Social psychologists (Gecas 1986, 1991) similarly describe authenticity. For Gecas, authenticity describes the extent to which we are acting according to who we really believe we are. Inauthenticity is the feeling that results from acting in a manner inconsistent with who we believe ourselves to truly be. Inauthenticity is captured in the following extract from another course participant:

> Myths that we tell each other — such as don't wear cruddy shoes to an interview — lead us to believe that something external to who [we are] is going to make [us]. And I had certainly unconsciously bought into that ... I had all the stuff that was supposed to make me successful — my car and my clothes, the house in the right neighbourhood and belonging to the right health club — and all the external framework was excellent and inside I kind of had this pit eating away at me.

In short, the appearance or façade that material things can create failed to provide a deeper awareness of her sense of self. This same interviewee explained three courses of action she believes individuals who come to this realisation can take:

> One is they have everything and just put on a smile to say "I am happy," but inside they are being eaten away. [Another choice] is they can go "oh my god, I collected all the wrong things now I have to get rid of them and get

the right things." A new marriage, little red sports car, a younger companion — this is what we typically frame as the mid-life crisis. But they still believe that stuff will make them happy. Or, and I think this is the case with lots of people who are moving on to find themselves, they have all the stuff and still aren't happy, and they are really open to looking at the key issues that are preventing them [from being happy].

According to social psychologists, along with the desire for self-esteem and self-efficacy, a desire to feel authentic is one of the three primary motivations of the self (Gecas 1986, 1991). In the creation and maintenance of a healthy self we are motivated to: (1) be viewed in a positive light by ourselves and others, (2) feel as if we have control over our lives and our immediate environment, and (3) strive for a feeling that we are being true to ourselves. Most forms of labour in a capitalist economy strip the labourer of feelings of esteem and efficacy, and Hochschild's research (1983) suggests that jobs that force employees to manage their emotions may also strip them of their feelings of authenticity.

The argument can be made, then, that labourers in the capitalist work force have difficulty obtaining through their work the levels of self-esteem, efficacy and authenticity that they desire; consequently they seek these forms of satisfaction through the consumption of material goods. Others have also emphasised the failure of consumption to meet identity needs. Sociologist Don Slater suggests that "[c]onsumerism simultaneously exploits mass identity crisis by proffering its goods as solutions to the problems of identity, and in the process intensifies it by offering ever more plural values and ways of being" (1997:85).

Yet, many individuals continue successfully to meet the needs of the self through consumption. As the extracts above indicate, others struggle in their attempts to achieve feelings of authenticity through consumption.

3. Environmental Concern and the Self-Concept

The centrality of consumption in the creation and maintenance of self-concepts lies in stark contrast to the role of the natural environment. Among environmentalists, especially deep ecologists, it is believed that we need a completely new way of conceiving of ourselves in relation to the environment (Devall 1988, 1993, 1995; Devall and Sessions 1985; Matthews 1995; Naess 1989). More recently educators (Orr 1992; Thomashow 1996), psychologists (Fox 1990; Roszak 1992) and sociologists (Weigert 1997) have made similar arguments. The self-concept serves as the ground-zero, so to speak, of certain aspects of cognitive decision-making. The self-concept organises attitudes and values so that the individual can access them easily and effectively, and is intertwined with the functioning of values inasmuch as the values we hold allow us to evaluate ourselves, thus influencing our self-esteem. Therefore, though the self-concept is seldom directly shaped by our interactions with the natural environment, it is nevertheless important in our understanding of the development of environmental attitudes and related values.

One significant function of the self in relation to attitudes and values is to provide an index of all of the possible outcomes of different attitude-behaviour combinations. While it may be values that provide standards or goals that serve to guide action (Howard 1995;

Rokeach 1973; Schwartz 1994), it is the self-concept that contains the values used to compare the desirability of the outcomes of our possible courses of action. Values specific to the quality of the natural environment, in theory, should compel an individual to consider and compare the environmental impacts of possible courses of action.

Unfortunately, the picture is not quite so simple. First of all, very few individuals have highly developed values specifically related to the quality of the environment (although many do have attitudes about environmental quality and value "a clean environment" or "a beautiful countryside" (Stern and Dietz 1994; Inglehart 1990)). Stern and Dietz (1994), for example, failed to find a separate biospheric-value orientation distinct from the social-altruistic orientation identified by Schwartz (1994). Even if such values existed, very few individuals have developed an awareness of the possible environmental outcomes of their behavioural decisions. In fact, as Weigert (1997) notes, social, cultural and social-structural obstacles often mediate our experience of the natural environment so that the environmental outcomes of actions we take are felt at temporal and geographical distances.

Nevertheless, a number of researchers have examined the possibility of an ecological self — a sense of self that incorporates the natural environment so that self-preserving behaviour is also "environment-preserving" behaviour. Bragg (1996) finds evidence for the presence of ecological identities in the self-concepts of Australian participants in "Council of All Beings" exercises — meetings in which human participants adopt the identities of nonhuman elements of the natural world (animals or objects) and speak on their behalf before a "council" of all the other species and objects represented in the meeting. Among Earth First! activists, Ingalsbee (1996) also finds evidence for the existence of ecological identities. Statham (1995) explores the importance of the self-concept in the formation of a connected and integrated self as postulated by eco-feminism. Drawing on interviews with several different groups in southeast Florida, she examines how her subjects' self-concepts reveal varying degrees of connectedness to others and to the natural environment. Statham concludes "our sense of self becomes heavily entwined with where we are — in physical terms — something many self-theorists have failed to recognise" (1995:216).

Thomashow also uses experiences with environmental activists to explore how an ecological identity can emerge in everyday life. "Memories of childhood places, the perception of disturbed places, the contemplation of wild places," he writes, "are examples of transformational moments in people's lives, when they realise that their personal identity is intrinsically connected to their direct experience of nature" (1995:xvi). Drawing on the philosophy of the deep ecology movement — especially, but not limited to, those aspects that are relevant to the "ecological self,"[2] — Thomashow proposes that the key to ensuring an environmentally-sustainable future rests on introducing to wider audiences the process by which environmentalists, like those interviewed in Statham's study, expand their sense of self and develop an ecological identity.

---

[2]Most deep ecologists acknowledge the concept of an ecological self. For specific attempts to conceptualize the ecological self, see Devall and Sessions (1985), Fox (1990), and Macy (1991). Or, for a more general approach to the philosophy of deep ecology, see the edited volumes by Sessions (1995) and Drengson and Inoue (1995).

Weigert (1991, 1997) proposes a process of role-taking that would incorporate antici-pated responses from "environmental others." Because role-taking requires an individual to come to see and feel about her/himself the way others do, Weigert (1997) acknowledges that role-taking the earth seems impractical; after all, the earth does not have "feelings" toward us — at least not as far as we know.[3] "By role-taking the earth or one of its life-supporting dynamics," Weigert suggests, "we see self anew — as an interactor within the biosphere … Role-taking the earth brings us closer to [a] more adequate self" (1997:133).

But at the same time Weigert (1997) acknowledges that except in the case of very local environmental conditions, individuals are not likely to get direct, immediate and interpret-able feedback from the environment. Consequently, the ecological self acquires a social characteristic inasmuch as our ability to anticipate the environment's responses to actions with impacts that are distant and beyond our senses depends on the various cultural forms that transmit the understandings of these impacts. If "ecological selves" or "ecological identities" of the types described by the above researchers currently exist only in special-ised populations of highly committed environmental activists, it may be more useful to view the relationship between the self-concept and environmental concern in terms of the individual's conception of her/himself as a caring, compassionate or altruistic person. The more compassionate individuals perceive themselves to be, the greater the chance that their compassion extends to the environment.

The previous two sections contrast the function of the self-concept with respect to consumption and the environment. In the case of the former, meeting the needs of the self-concept through consumption, especially the need for authenticity, becomes difficult for some individuals. In other words, consumption creates challenges for the self that for some people results in anti-consumerist sentiments. In the case of the latter, though an ecological self may be unrealistic, it is hypothesised that environmental concern increases relative to an individual's incorporation of compassion and altruism into her/his self-concept. With a conception of oneself as altruistic and compassionate, the self-concept may come to include aspects of the natural world so that pro-environmental behaviour, and in some cases environmental activism, become necessary activities for the maintenance of the self-concept.

4. Linkages Between the Self-Concept and Values

If a person behaves inconsistently with respect to her/his values, and in doing so does not experience diminished esteem or a sense of inauthenticity, then those values must not be central to the individual's self-concept. For instance, a researcher may observe an indi-vidual's values and expect those values to be accompanied by a strong tendency for a particular type of behaviour; but if the values expressed are not central to the self-concept, then the self-discrepancy that would follow from acting otherwise will not result. Values

---

[3]Deep Ecologists (Devall and Sessions 1985; Devall 1988; Macy 1991; Naess 1989, 1995; Seed *et al.*, 1988) and other spiritual environmentalists (LaChapelle 1988) would argue that the Earth does, in fact, have feelings toward us. Coming out of a more scientifically grounded tradition, Abrams (1996) argues phenomenologically that there is a process of communication between humans and the "more-than-human" world.

have to be linked to the self in a substantive way or else they have no bearing on behavioural motivations. As Hoffman (1984:300) states:

> One's moral principles are an integral part of one's conception of what one is or ought to be as a person. People may be powerfully motivated to act in accord with their self-conception, and if moral principles are a significant part of it, actions that depart from the principles may produce tension, a feeling of shame, or guilt.

If concern for the environment or over-consumption are related to values then an understanding of their basis in the self-concept seems essential. Do individuals develop concern for the problem of over-consumption only after their environmental concern has led to an understanding of the relationship between over-consumption and declining environmental quality? Or, does concern for the problem of over-consumption develop independently of environmental concern, having a completely separate basis?

Not only are the answers to these questions vital if we are to find solutions to many environmental problems, but the answers may also be essential if we hope to provide social environments that can nurture and sustain individuals with healthy and functional self-conceptions. In addition, we need to know if the self-concept types associated with particular manifestations of environmental concern or concern for over-consumption appear in unique segments of the population with specific social structural positions. The self-concept, therefore, also provides us with the ability to acknowledge structural-level influences on concern for the environment and for over-consumption. To the extent that individuals' social-structural position influences their ability to meet basic needs and the configuration of their self-concept, some types of environmental concern or anti-consumerism may be more likely than others.

Currently, little research exists examining the correlation between environmental concern and self-concept types. No research has explored the correlation between anti-consumerist sentiments and self-concept types. If environmental concern is a form of social altruism, which is also the assumption behind Stern *et al.*'s (1995) application of Schwartz's (1977) norm-activation theory of altruism to environmental issues, then we would expect altruistic self-concept types to be correlated with environmental concern. Anti-consumerist sentiments, as I earlier asserted, seem to emerge out of a self-interested motivation to assert an authentic self. Therefore, it is proposed that anti-consumerism is more strongly associated with a more narrowly defined self-concept. If environmental concern and concern for over-consumption are conceptually distinct, the following hypotheses should hold: the self-concept types correlated with environmental concern, and their level of correlation, will differ from the self-concept types correlated with anti-consumerist sentiments.

5. Methodology and Measurement Methods

To test these hypotheses I analyse data from three different samples. The first is a random sample of 800 Americans who were surveyed in 1995. These respondents were questioned about their attitudes toward consumption as part of the Merck Family Fund's "Yearning for Balance" study. I refer to this dataset as the Yearning sample. The second sample, termed the Student sample, is a convenience sample of 111 students at two non-traditional college campuses in the Pacific Northwest of the United States. The third sample (Simplicity sample) consists of 179 participants in voluntary simplicity classes offered in the workplace by a non-profit group in a large city in the Pacific Northwest.

All three of the surveys used a single-item measure of environmental concern and asked participants to respond on a scale of one to five to the question: "How concerned are you about the quality of our environment?" The Yearning sample also contained a seven-item scale asking respondents, on a scale of one to ten: "How serious is the problem of [air pollution, water pollution, loss of rain forests, toxic waste, population growth, global warming, garbage]?" The Yearning sample further employed a measure of efficacy with respect to the environment. In this case the survey asked respondents to assess on a scale of one to five the following question: "What difference would it make if we recycled more [or if we passed and enforced tougher anti-pollution laws, if we contributed more money to organisations that advocate for the environment, if companies reduced the amount of packaging on their products]?"

The three studies also shared a three-item measure of concern for over-consumption. Respondents were asked to provide personal assessments ranging from one to five to the questions: "How concerned are you about [the amount of greed and selfishness in our society, our society's focus on material wealth, the effect of advertising and television in our lives]?" The Yearning sample had one additional measure of concern for over-consumption. This particular survey asked respondents for their level of agreement (from one to five) with the following statements: "Most of us buy and consume far more than we need — it's wasteful"; "The amount we buy and consume is a major cause of many environmental problems"; "Many of us buy and consume things as a substitute for what's missing in our lives"; "The 'buy now, pay later' attitude causes many of us to consume more than we need" and "Today's youth are too focused on buying and consuming things."

The Yearning sample contained a set of ten value items that asked respondents to indicate the extent to which each value is a guiding principle in their lives. The ten items, which are rated on a Likert-type scale from one to ten, include: responsibility, prosperity and wealth, friendship, financial security, religious faith, pleasure/having fun, freedom, family life, career success, and generosity.

In a principal components factor analysis using a varimax rotation two factors emerged from the ten values. The factor loadings roughly corresponded to the self-enhancement and self-transcendence value orientations previously identified by Schwartz (1992) and Stern *et al.* (1995). Responsibility, friendship, religious faith, family life and generosity strongly load on the first factor (self-transcendence); while prosperity and wealth, financial security, pleasure/having fun, and career success load more strongly on the second factor (self-enhancement). Freedom and friendship are the only two values that do not load strongly on either factor. To create the self-transcendence and self-enhancement scales, the slightly more conservative approach of requiring a loading greater than 0.5 for an item to be included in a factor was used. In doing this, friendship is placed in the self-transcendence scale, while freedom, which does not have a loading greater than 0.5, is dropped from either scale. Based on the two factors, self-transcendence and self-enhancement value orientation scales were created by summing each respondent's score for the respective factor's items.

In the Student and Simplicity samples, a value orientation scale with greater conceptual complexity was employed. This 15-item scale contained three items each intended to tap biospheric, self-transcendence, self-enhancement, openness and tradition value orientations. To ensure a sample large enough to perform a factor analysis, the Student and Simplicity samples were pooled (N = 290). In this pooled sample, a principal components factor analysis using a varimax rotation revealed four factors: biospheric, self-transcendence, openness and a combination of self-enhancement and tradition. Despite the mixed set of values in the fourth factor, five scales were created representing the five types of value orientations that were built into the measure.

Finally, the surveys used with the Student and Simplicity samples, but not the Yearning sample, contained a self-concept measurement scale. The Twenty Statements Test (TST), modified to ten statements for this study, asked respondents to respond ten times to the question, as if they are asking themselves, "Who am I?" Initially developed by Kuhn and McPartland (1954), this approach allows respondents to express spontaneously how they perceive themselves. Though quantitative analysis can be cumbersome, this approach allows for the expression of the contents of the self-concept, rather than a measure of respondents' attitudes toward various components of their self-concepts. This latter approach requires the researcher to predetermine the most important aspects of respondents' self-concepts. Additionally, such a measure is designed to assess self-esteem — the positive or negative evaluations of parts of the self-concept — rather than the overall content of the self-concept.

Given that an altruistically oriented self-concept is expected to be correlated with environmental concern, the research methodology coded responses to the TST in two different ways. The first coding scheme used Triandis' (1988, 1989) collectivism/individualism distinction to identify respondents whose self-concepts are more "other" oriented. Although not necessarily a reflection of altruism, the more "other" oriented a person is, the more her/his actions are aimed at meeting the needs of others (Triandis 1994). This distinction is similar to the interdependent/independent self-concept types identified by Markus and Kitayama (1991, 1994). The second coding scheme relied on the adaptation of self-concept categories created by Gordon (1968) for the purposes of coding the TST. The category of concern for our purposes is what I refer to as the "compassionate/caring self." Responses ranging from "I am a kind person" to "I am sensitive to other's feelings" are coded in this category. The assumption is that the more often a person conceives of her/his self in these terms, the more likely she/he is to extend that compassion and care to the environment. In both coding schemes, percentages were calculated reflecting the proportion of total responses that were coded as "collectivist" or "compassionate/caring self."

6. Findings and Discussion

Table 10.1 reports the standardised regression coefficients for the regression of the five measures of environmental concern and concern for over-consumption on the self-transcendence and self-enhancement value orientations identified in the Yearning sample. A

Table 10.1: Standardised regression coefficients for the regression of environmental concern and concern for over-consumption on value orientations (Yearning Sample).

	Self-transcendence Values	Self-enhancement Values
Environmental Concern		
ENV CONCERN	0.19***	0.09*
SERIOUSNESS	0.27***	0.25***
EFFICACY	0.18***	0.14***
Concern for Over-consumption		
OCONCERN	0.22***	–0.10**
GENBELIEFS	0.12***	–0.05

ENV CONCERN = one-item environmental concern measure; SERIOUSNESS = seven-item scale of perceived seriousness of environmental problems; EFFICACY = four-item scale of perceived effectiveness of solutions to environmental problems; OCONCERN = three-item concern for over-consumption scale; GENBELIEFS = five-item scale of general beliefs about consumption

(* $p<.05$; ** $p<.01$; *** $p<.001$)

significant relationship exists between the self-transcendence value orientation and all five measures of environmental concern and concern for over-consumption. In other words, the higher a respondent scored on the self-transcendence value orientation scale, the more likely she/he was to express concern for the environment and for over-consumption. At the same time, however, self-enhancement values are *also* positively correlated with all three environmental concern measures. The higher a respondent scored on the self-enhancement scale, the more likely the individual was to express environmental concern.

Self-enhancement values were not, on the other hand, positively correlated with either measure of concern for over-consumption. Though self-transcendence values seem to provide a strong basis for both environmental concern and concern for over-consumption, self-enhancement values do not seem to provide a basis for concern for over-consumption. In this sense, concern for over-consumption could potentially be a more refined form of environmental concern. For example, it may be that among those who have concern for the environment, only those who have self-transcendence values also have concern for over-consumption. This explanation appears unlikely when examining the distribution of self-transcendence and self-enhancement values in the Yearning sample. Many respondents seem to hold both self-transcendence and self-enhancement values, as seen by the positive correlation between the two value orientations ($r = 0.28$; $p < 0.001$). Alternatively, it may be that holding both value orientations simultaneously obstructs one from making the connection between consumption habits and environmental or human-rights implications. The drive to consume as a means of self-creation and maintenance, in other words, is not seen as inconsistent with valuing others' well-being.

Table 10.2: Regression of environmental concern and concern for over-consumption on different self-concept types.

	Environmental Concern		Concern for Over-consumption	
	Student Sample	Simplicity Sample	Student Sample	Simplicity Sample
COLLECTIV	−0.09	0.01	−0.15	−0.06
COMPASSION	0.24*	0.00	0.18	−0.18*

COLLECTIV = percent of TST responses coded "collectivistic/interdependent;"
COMPASSION = frequency of "compassionate/caring self" responses in TST

(* p<.05)

Given the mixed findings with respect to value orientations and the two types of concern, a look at the relationship between self-concept types and the two varieties of concern is necessary. All three samples (Yearning, Simplicity, Student) exhibited virtually identical levels of concern for the environment. The Simplicity and Yearning samples, in contrast, were significantly higher than the Student sample in their concern for over-consumption.

Table 10.2 shows the standardised regression coefficients for the simple regressions of the two concern variables on the two different self-concept types that were measured. The number of collectivistic responses in one's self-concept is not correlated with either type of concern in either sample. The second self-concept measure, which used the frequency of "compassionate/caring self" responses, resulted in a significant positive correlation with environmental concern ($r = 0.24$; $p < 0.05$) in the Student sample, and a significant negative correlation with concern for over-consumption in the simplicity sample ($r = -0.18$; $p < 0.05$). In addition, there is no significant difference between the two samples in the mean number of collectivistic responses per respondent ($F = 0.48$, d.f. = 1, 285; n.s.). There is also no significant difference in the mean frequency of "compassionate/caring self" responses between the two samples ($F = 0.24$, d.f. = 1, 285; n.s.).

In the Yearning sample, self-transcendence and self-enhancement values were both found to be positively correlated with environmental concern. In the case of concern for the problem of over-consumption, this research found a positive correlation with self-transcendence values and a negative correlation with self-enhancement values. Most interestingly, it was found that "compassionate/caring self" responses are negatively correlated with concern for over-consumption — while the exact opposite holds in the case of the Student sample.

Based on these findings, it appears that in some instances concern for over-consumption may be another manifestation of environmental concern. For individuals who hold self-transcendence, but not self-enhancement values, concern for over-consumption is high; most likely, this is explained by the importance of these values in the self-concept and the ability to make connections between these values and the impact of one's consumption habits on the environment and others. Among those who hold self-enhancement *and* self-transcendence values, concern for the environment may derive from an egoistic basis. As Stern *et al.* (1995) have noted, it is completely possible to find egoistically based reasons to care for the environment. Additionally, holding both sets of values simultaneously, though cognitively feasible, may result in an inability to link one's consumption habits to the subsequent impacts on humans and the environment.

This examination of self-concept types, however, suggests that people motivated enough to attend voluntarily a course on reducing consumption are not motivated by self-transcendence values that are anchored in a compassionate and caring self-concept. Though they may hold such values, their sense of themselves as compassionate and caring people is not related to their concern with over-consumption. Rather, such concern has more to do with a crisis of self, perhaps originating from difficulties in using consumption to meet the basic needs for self-esteem, efficacy and authenticity. In terms of the participants in NWEI's VS classes, it may be that these individuals have begun a process of self-examination and have opened themselves up to the idea that there may be non-material ways to meet their self-esteem, self-efficacy and authenticity needs. In short, a compassionate/caring self-concept may be more important in the development of environmental concern than concern for over-consumption.

These findings are limited by a number of factors. Analyses of existing data, such as those performed on the Yearning sample, tend to suffer from inadequate operationalisation. In this case, the absence of a self-concept measure was severely limiting. The other two samples were insufficiently large, and insufficiently representative, to allow for adequate generalisations. One consequence of this may have been too little variation in the environmental concern and concern for over-consumption measures. The Pacific Northwest is known for its progressive environmental thinking, and this may have skewed the levels of environmental concern, especially in the Simplicity sample.

In the future, research using larger samples drawn from international populations should help identify more precisely the relationship between environmental concern and concern for over-consumption. Furthermore, Maslow's (1970) theory of the hierarchy of needs and Inglehart's (1990) post-materialism thesis both suggest that as more and more material needs are met, people's priorities move toward nonmaterial issues like justice and equality. Such a shift, these propositions posit, explains the emergence of new social movements including those focusing on human rights and environmental issues. Yet, Maslow's theory holds that after basic-material needs are met, individuals shift their focus to non-material needs such as love and belongingness, and ultimately self-realisation. Multi-national cross comparative research in the spirit of Inglehart's that approaches concern for over-consumption as an outgrowth of blocked attempts to meet higher order needs such as self-actualisation is needed.

Clearly, the research presented here falls far short of such a goal. My intention instead has been to stimulate new social science perspectives on motivations for changes in consumption habits and not to present empirical evidence in support of a particular view. Hopefully, such new perspectives can build on the notion that among some people concern for over-consumption may be linked to strategies for meeting self needs as opposed to concern for the environmental impacts of consumption. This may make an important contribution to discussions about approaches to policy and social change that will move us toward more sustainable forms of consumption.

7. Conclusion

Interest in voluntary simplicity, for many, has a clear environment-related basis. Ultimately, however, these individuals may constitute a very small portion of the growing number of people interested in voluntary simplicity. If this is the case, we need to know more about the rest of the people who buy "how-to-simplify-your-life" books and visit voluntary simplicity sites on the Internet by the thousands. The potential for massive voluntary changes in consumption practices, not for altruistic or environmentally motivated reasons, but for more inwardly oriented reasons must be explored. Such investigations must consider how culture, gender, social class, wealth and other key variables influence changing consumption habits. However, voluntary changes in consumption levels in response to a crisis of self may not be a feasible way of moving us towards sustainable consumption if such a crisis depends on first achieving unsustainable levels of material wealth. Until we determine whether this is the case we will benefit from linking our understanding of the functioning of human values with what we know about the motivational significance of the self-concept.

References

Aaker, J. (1999), "The malleable self: The role of self-expression in persuasion." *Journal of Marketing Research 36*, 45–57.

Abrams, D. (1996), *The Spell of the Sensuous: Perception and Language in a More-Than-Human World*. New York: Pantheon.

Baudrillard, J. (1981), *For a Critique of the Political Economy of the Sign*. St. Louis, MO: Telos.

Baudrillard, J. (1983), *Simulations*. New York: Semiotext(e).

Bourdieu, P. (1984), *Distinction: A Social Critique of the Judgement of Taste*. Cambridge, MA: Harvard University Press.

Bragg, E. (1996), "Towards ecological self: Deep ecology meets constructionist self-theory." *Journal of Environmental Psychology 16*, 93–108.

Burke, P. (1991), "Identity processes and social stress." *American Sociological Review 56*, 836–849.

Burke, P. (1997), "An identity model for network exchange." *American Sociological Review 62*, 134–150.

Burroughs, J. (1996), "Product symbolism, self meaning and holistic matching: The role of information processing in impulsive buying." *Advances in Consumer Research 23*, 463–464.

Devall, B. (1988), *Simple in Means, Rich in Ends: Practicing Deep Ecology*. Salt Lake City: Gibbs Smith.

Devall, B. (1993), *Living Richly in an Age of Limits*. Salt Lake City: Peregrine Smith.

Devall, B. (1995), "The ecological self." In A. Drengson & Y. Inoue (eds) *The Deep Ecology Movement: An Introductory Anthology*. Berkeley: North Atlantic Books.

Devall, B., & Sessions, G. (1985), *Deep Ecology: Living as if Nature Mattered*. Salt Lake City: Peregrine Smith.

Drengson, A., & Inoue, Y. (eds). (1995), *The Deep Ecology Movement: An Introductory Anthology*. Berkeley: North Atlantic Books.

Featherstone, M. (1991), *Consumer Culture and Postmodernism*. London: Sage.

Fox, W. (1990), *Toward a Transpersonal Ecology: Developing New Foundations for Environmentalism*. Boston: Shambhala.

Gecas, V. (1986), "The motivational significance of self-concept for socialization theory." In E. Lawler (ed.) *Advances in Group Processes Vol. 3* (pp. 131–156). Greenwich, CT: JAI Press.

Gecas, V. (1991), "The self-concept as a basis for a theory of motivation." In J. Howard & P. Callero (eds) *The Self-Society Dynamic: Cognition, Emotion and Action* (pp. 171–187). New York: Cambridge University Press.

Gecas, V., & Burke, P. (1995), "Self and identity." In K. Cook, G. Fine & J. House (eds) *Sociological Perspectives on Social Psychology* (pp. 41–67). Boston: Allyn and Bacon.

Gentry, J., Baker, S., & Kraft, F. (1995), "The role of possessions in creating, maintaining and preserving one's identity: Variation over the life course." *Advances in Consumer Research 22*, 413–415.

Gillespie, M. (1995), *Television, Ethnicity and Cultural Change*. London: Routledge.

Goffman, E. (1974), *Frame Analysis*. Cambridge, MA: Harvard University Press.

Gordon, C. (1968), "Self-conceptions: Configurations of content." In C. Gordon & K. Gergen (eds) *The Self in Social Interaction Vol. 1*. New York: Wiley.

Heidegger, M. (1967), *Being and Time* (Sein und Zeit), trans. J. Macquarrie and E. Robinson. Oxford: Blackwell.

Hochschild, A. (1983), *The Managed Heart: Commercialization of Human Feeling*. Berkeley: University of California Press.

Hoffman, M. (1984), "Empathy, its limitations, and its role in a comprehensive moral theory." In W. Kurtines & J. Gewirtz (eds) *Morality, Moral Behavior, and Moral Development*. New York: Wiley.

Hogg, M., & Michell, P. (1996), "Identity, self and consumption: A conceptual framework." *Journal of Marketing Management 12*, 629–644.

Howard, J. (1995), "Social cognition." In K. Cook, G. Fine & J. House (eds) *Sociological Perspectives on Social Psychology* (pp. 90–117). Boston: Allyn and Bacon.

Ingalsbee, T. (1996), "Earth first! activism: Ecological postmodern praxis in radical environmental identities." *Sociological Perspectives 2*, 263–276.

Inglehart, R. (1990), *Culture Shift in Advanced Industrial Society*. Princeton, NJ: Princeton University Press.

Jameson, F. (1984), "Postmodernism, or the cultural logic of late capitalism." *New Left Review 146*, 52–92.

Karp, D. (1996), "Values and their effect on pro-environmental behavior." *Environment and Behavior 28*, 111–133.

Kuhn, M., & McPartland, T. (1954), "An empirical investigation of self attitudes." *American Sociological Review 19*, 68–76.

LaChapelle, D. (1988), *Sacred Land, Sacred Sex: The Rapture of the Deep*. Silverton, CO: Finn Hill Arts.

Macy, J. (1991), *World as Lover, World as Self*. Berkeley: Parallax Press.

Markus, H., & Kitayama, S. (1991), "Cultural variation in the self-concept." In J. Strauss & G. Goethals (eds) *The Self: Interdisciplinary Approaches* (pp. 18–47). New York: Springer-Verlag.

Markus, H., & Kitayama, S. (1994), "The cultural construction of self and emotion: Implications for social behavior." In S. Kitayama & H. Markus (eds) *Emotion and Culture: Empirical Studies of Mutual Influence* (pp. 89–130). Washington, DC: American Psychological Association.

Maslow, A. (1970), *Motivation and Personality* (2nd ed.). New York: Harper and Row.

Matthews, F. (1995), "Conservation and self-realization: A deep ecology perspective." In A. Drengson & Y. Inoue (eds) *The Deep Ecology Movement: An Introductory Anthology*. Berkeley: North Atlantic Books.

Mead, G. (1934), *Mind, Self and Society*. Chicago: University of Chicago Press.

Miller, D. (1987), *Material Culture and Mass Consumption*. Oxford: Blackwell.

Muniz, A. (1997), "Consumers and brand meaning: Brands, the self and others." *Advances in Consumer Research 24*, 308–310.

Naess, A. (1989), *Ecology, Community and Lifestyle: Outline of an Ecosophy*, trans. D. Rothenberg. New York: Cambridge University Press.

Naess, A. (1995), "Self-realization: An ecological approach to being in the world." In G. Sessions (ed.) *Deep Ecology for the 21st Century: Readings on the Philosophy and Practice of the New Environmentalism*. Boston: Shambhala.

National Academy of Sciences. (1991), *Policy Implications of Greenhouse Warming: Synthesis Panel*. Washington, DC: National Academy Press.

National Research Council. (1986), *Population Growth and Economic Development: Policy Questions*. Committee on Population, Working Group on Population and Development. Washington, DC: National Academy Press.

National Research Council. (1987), *Current Issues in Atmospheric Change*. Washington, DC: National Academy Press.

Noble, C., & Walker, B. (1996), "Exploring the relationships among liminal transitions, symbolic consumption, and the extended self." *Psychology and Marketing 14*, 29–43.

Orr, D. (1992), *Ecological Literacy: Education and the Transition to a Postmodern World*. Albany: State University of New York Press.

Powers, W. (1973), *Behavior: The Control of Perception*. Chicago: Aldine Press.

Rochberg-Halton, E. (1986), *Meaning and Modernity*. Chicago: University of Chicago Press.

Rokeach, M. (1973), *The Nature of Human Values*. New York: Free Press.

Roszak, T. (1992), *The Voice of the Earth*. New York: Simon and Schuster.

Schwartz, S. (1977), "Normative influences on altruism." In L. Berkowitz (ed.) *Advances in Experimental Social Psychology 10* (pp. 221–279). New York: Academic Press.

Schwartz, S. (1992), "Are there universal aspects in the structure and contents of human values?" *Journal of Social Issues 50* (4), 19–45.

Schwartz, S. (1994), "Universals in the content and structure of values: Theoretical advances and empirical tests in 20 countries." In L. Berkowitz (ed.) *Advances in Experimental Social Psychology 25* (pp. 1–65). New York: Academic Press.

Seed, J., Macy, J., Fleming, P., & Naess, A. (1988), *Thinking Like a Mountain: Towards a Council of all Beings*. Philadelphia: New Society.

Sessions, G. (ed.). (1995), *Deep Ecology for the 21st Century: Readings on the Philosophy and Practice of the New Environmentalism*. Boston: Shambhala.

Simmel, G. (1957), "Fashion." *American Journal of Sociology 62*, 541–558.

Simonson, A. (1997), "Affecting consumers through identity and design." *Advances in Consumer Research 24*, 64–66.

Sivadas, E., & Venkatesh, R. (1995), "An examination of individual and object-specific influences on the extended self and its relation to attachment and satisfaction." *Advances in Consumer Research 22*, 406–409.

Slater, D. (1997), *Consumer Culture and Modernity*. Cambridge: Polity Press.

Snow, D., & Benford, R. (1992), "Master frames and cycles of protest." In A. Morris & C. McClurg Mueller (eds) *Frontiers in Social Movement Theory* (pp. 133–155). New Haven, CT: Yale University Press.

Statham, A. (1995), "Environmental identity: Symbols in cultural change." In N. Denzin (ed.) *Studies in Symbolic Interaction Vol. 17* (pp. 207–240). Greenwich, CT: JAI Press.

Stern, P., & Dietz, T. (1994), "The value basis of environmental concern." *Journal of Social Issues 50*, 65–84.

Stern, P., Dietz, T., Abel, T., Guagnano, G., & Kalof, L. (1999), "A value-belief-norm theory of support for social movements: The case of environmentalism." *Human Ecology Review 6* (2), 81–97.

Stern, P., Dietz, T., & Kalof, L. (1993), "Value orientations, gender, and environmental concern." *Environment and Behavior 25,* 322–348.

Stern, P., Dietz, T., Kalof, L., & Guagnano, G. (1995), "Values, beliefs, and proenvironmental action: Attitude formation toward emergent attitude objects." *Journal of Applied Social Psychology 25,* 1611–1623.

Stern, P., Young, O., & Druckman, D. (eds). (1992), *Global Environmental Change: Understanding the Human Dimensions.* Washington, DC: National Academy Press.

Stets, J. (1995), "Role identities and person identities: Gender identity, master identity, and controlling one's partner." *Sociological Perspectives 38,* 129–150.

Stets, J., & Burke, P. (1994), "Inconsistent self-views in the control identity model." *Social Science Research 23,* 236–262.

Thomashow, M. (1995), *Ecological Identity: Becoming a Reflective Environmentalist.* Cambridge, MA: MIT Press.

Triandis, H. (1988), "Collectivism and individualism: A reconceptualization of a basic concept in cross-cultural psychology." In G. Verma & C. Bagley (eds) *Personality, Attitudes and Cognitions* (pp. 60–95). London: Macmillan.

Triandis, H. (1989), "The self and social behavior in differing cultural contexts." *Psychological Review 96,* 506–520.

Triandis, H. (1994), "Major cultural syndromes and emotion." In S. Kitayama & H. Markus (eds) *Emotion and Culture: Empirical Studies of Mutual Influence* (pp. 285–306). Washington, DC: American Psychological Association.

Union of Concerned Scientists. (1992), *Warning to Humanity.* Washington, DC: Union of Concerned Scientists.

Veblen, T. 1967 (1899), *The Theory of the Leisure Class.* New York: Funk and Wagnalls.

Weigert, A. (1991), "Transverse interaction: A pragmatic perspective on environment as other." *Symbolic Interaction 14,* 353–363.

Weigert, A. (1997), *Self, Interaction, and Natural Environment: Refocusing Our Eyesight.* Albany: State University of New York Press.

Wong, N. (1997), "Suppose you own the worm and no one knows? Conspicuous consumption, materialism and self." *Advances in Consumer Research 24,* 197–201.

Chapter 11

Sustainable Lifestyles: Rethinking Barriers and Behaviour Change

Kersty Hobson

1. Introduction[1]

Current global levels of domestic energy consumption and waste production have been acknowledged as important contributors to detrimental environmental change (United Nations 1998). Political and academic interest in this component of sustainable development implementation has stimulated debates in post-industrial nations concerning the social practices of contemporary consumerism (Macnaghten and Urry 1998) and how we will live in the future (De Young 1993). In response there has been a call for the development of "national policies and strategies to encourage changes in consumption patterns" (UNCED 1992:64). One approach has been the promotion of environmentally-friendly lifestyles which often take the form of media or community campaigns (for further analysis see Hobson 2001). These campaigns encourage individuals not only to decrease the amount consumed, but also to alter the nature of goods consumed (IUCN/UNEP/WWF 1991; Librova 1999).

This chapter will examine one such campaign, called *Action at Home*, that is administered by the charity Global Action Plan UK. It will discuss a preliminary analysis of qualitative research carried out with individuals taking part in the *Action at Home* programme, with a view to gaining some understanding of how such a programme is received and acted upon by participants. This analysis is set within continually emergent discussions in the social sciences about public meanings and understandings of the concepts and communications of sustainable development (see Blake 1999; Bulkeley 1997; Burgess *et al.*, 1991; Burgess *et al.*, 1998; Darier and Schule 1999; Harrison *et al.*, 1996; Myers and Macnaghten 1998; Hinchliffe 1996; Finger 1994; Macnaghten and

[1]This research was carried out with a ESRC graduate CASE studentship (S00429737001), as part of a collaborative project between Global Action Plan UK and the Environment and Society Research Unit in the Department of Geography at University College London. This paper contains material first presented at the Open Meeting of the Human Dimensions of Global Environmental Change Research Community, held at the Shonan Village Centre, Kanagawa, Japan, June 24–26 1999. Thanks to the Graduate School at University College London for providing financial support to deliver this paper and also to the conference organisers and colleagues present at the meeting for their useful suggestions and discussions. Thanks also to Jacquie Burgess and Gail Davies for helpful comments and suggestions throughout this research, and to Simon Niemeyer for helping to pull it all together.

Exploring Sustainable Consumption: Evironmental Policy and the Social Sciences, Volume 1, pages 191–209.
Copyright © 2001 by Elsevier Science Ltd.
All rights of reproduction in any form reserved.
ISBN: 0-08-043920-9

Jacobs 1997; Macnaghten and Urry 1998). This chapter does not offer an appraisal of this work, but hopes to build upon some of the theoretical and empirical issues discussed therein, by opening up the concept of sustainable lifestyle for further analysis. I will initially discuss the context of current environmental-communication strategies in the UK and then proceed to offer some observations based on empirical work carried out with Global Action Plan UK. The theoretical implications of these observations for understanding "barriers to action" and behaviour change are then discussed, with a final comment on how these ideas might be mobilised in a policy arena.

2. Promoting Sustainable Lifestyles in the UK

Political attempts to encourage changes in citizens' consumer practices have become prominent in the public arena within the last decade. Tools used to promote sustainable lifestyles have included the widespread communication of sustainable development goals, using social-marketing techniques and educational-information campaigns (United Nations 1998). Examples of the latter include the former Conservative government's "Going for Green" programme, launched in 1996 (Blake and Carter 1997) and the "Helping the Earth Begins at Home" campaign (Hinchliffe 1996). These initiatives provided facts on key global environmental change concepts, such as global warming and/ or highlighted small actions that individuals could take within their households to help alleviate environmental problems (Hinchliffe 1996). In May 1999, the Labour government launched a similar "Are You Doing Your Bit?" campaign. This programme aims to encourage individuals to take ownership of their impact on the environment by providing tips for effective action that will also potentially help save on domestic running costs (DETR 1999).

Despite the popularity of this policy tool, research suggests that it is not effective in promoting the public uptake of sustainable lifestyles (Burgess *et al.*, 1998; van Luttervelt 1998). Social scientists have been examining some of the reasons behind this lack of public penetration. In doing so, the political and epistemological assumptions that environmental information campaigns are based upon have been brought into question (see Blake 1999; Burgess *et al.*, 1998; Hinchliffe 1996; Myers and Macnaghten 1998). These discussions will not be revisited in detail here, but it is necessary to briefly recap some of the main underlying assumptions and attendant criticisms that have emerged to set the context for the current discussion.

3. Sustainable Lifestyles Information: Assumptions and Critiques

The success of implementing sustainable development is believed to be contingent upon the existence of an "informed and accepting public" (Macnaghten and Jacobs 1997:15). Sustainable lifestyle information campaigns aim to create this public consent and acceptance. The feasibility of this project rests on the belief that the "environment" has some intrinsic resonance with individuals (Lanthier and Olivier 1999), which can be appealed to, and which is a cause of widespread public concern. This assessment is supported by numerous national and international polls suggesting that substantial public agreement with sustainable development goals exists, expressed as environmental concern and awareness (Taylor 1997). Why this awareness is not acted upon and how an "attitude-action gap" comes into existence, is due to a lack of specific scientific knowledge and behavioural information in the public arena. This lack of information is believed to be the cause of the low public uptake of the sustainability message. Tapping into this supposed reserve of public support is considered achievable by filling the public "information deficit" surrounding environmental issues (Burgess *et al.*, 1998). By providing facts about environmental problems and potential local/personal solutions, knowledge growth will lead us closer towards achieving sustainable development as individuals utilise new facts to make decisions about consumption choices (Ehrlich *et al.*, 1999).

It is assumed that once this information has been disseminated and read by individuals, behaviour change will follow. Such a direct link between information and behaviour is founded upon positivist linear models of behaviour change. These models suggest that human actions are founded upon rational, cognitive decision-making processes (see Argyle 1992; Billig 1987; Shotter 1993). Computational models such as Ajzen and Fishbein's Theory of Reasoned Action have been used repeatedly as predictors of behaviour change (for example, see Staats and Herenius 1995). They have indeed proved useful in their own bounded academic remits, but their main input in the policy arena has been to form a set of prevailing assumptions about the affective nature of information and the process of human-behaviour change.

Behaviour changes are also considered possible as individual lifestyles are viewed as consisting solely of "patterns of actions that differentiate people" (Chaney 1996:4). These patterns are discrete and functional sets of actions that are open to alteration. Thus, the lifestyle can be subject to rationalisation and reorganisation, moving everyone's behaviour in a more sustainable direction (Smith 1996).

Social scientists have questioned these assumptions by investigating the relationships between the environment, communications and lifestyles from more embedded, qualitative and discursive approaches, thus questioning the methodological, epistemological and political assumptions of the above framework. For example, positivist research tools used to measure and analyse individual responses to the environmental problematique have been criticised as offering an impoverished view of the complexity of human-social engagement (Macnaghten and Urry 1998). Contextual investigations into the construction and meanings of lifestyles have suggested that they are not simply a collection of cognitive thoughts and discrete actions, but instead are networks of recursive physical and discursive practices, replete with personal meaning and histories, that form the individual's 'life-world' (see Giddens 1991, Lunt and Livingstone 1992). Any new information, such as a programme like *Action at Home*, is sought, understood, utilised and assimilated as part of the on-going constitution of the individual's fully-knowledgeable lifeworld (Finger 1994). This critique raises questions about the nature of environmental knowledges (Eden 1998) and the very existence of an "information deficit" in the public sphere.

This chapter aims to add to these debates by examining further the relationship between environmental communications, lifestyles and practices. More specifically, I am looking at the *processes* that take place when individuals engage with environmental communications. To do this, I have focused on *Action at Home*, to allow me to ask questions about how environmental information is created, used and acted upon by lay publics. In the following section I will discuss the contents of the *Action at Home* programme and the empirical work carried out in collaboration with Global Action Plan UK.

4. Global Action Plan UK

Global Action Plan is an environmental behaviour-change model and action programme developed in the United States during the late 1980s (Gershon and Gillman 1992) and presented to the 1992 Earth Summit (Global Action Plan International n.d.). It aims to provide willing individuals with tools to alter their domestic behaviour and adopt more sustainable ways of living, by empowering them to feel that they can make effective and worthwhile changes. The foundations of the model rest upon the concept of EcoTeams. These are groups of neighbours that aim to make collective changes to their household behaviours as set out in a Global Action Plan workbook. The EcoTeams meet regularly to offer support and to feed back progress to each other and the national Global Action Plan office (Harland *et al.*, 1993). Advocates hope that through these groups the sustainable lifestyles message will diffuse outwards through a community, creating more widespread change (see Rogers 1995).

The Global Action Plan idea has now spread to many other countries outside of the US, including the UK. In 1994, the Global Action Plan UK (GAP) environmental charity was founded. GAP has reworked the original Global Action Plan model, aiming for more widespread participation by encouraging and helping "individuals to take effective environmental action in their homes, communities and workplaces" (Global Action Plan UK 1998:1). The *Action at Home* programme is a six-month voluntary scheme that encourages changes in individual's household consumption practices by providing information, support and feedback (Church and McHarry 1992). It is not a nation-wide information campaign, but is instead targeted sequentially at specific local areas to enable the establishment of local support and diffusion networks. *Action at Home* participants receive monthly information packs with step-by-step suggestions for making small behavioural changes, plus "money-off" offers on various environmental products. The packs cover topics of waste, water, transport, shopping and energy, ending with a "Next Steps" pack focussing on additional actions that participants could take. This sustained, concentrated action plan makes *Action at Home* a unique form of environmental communication in the UK today.

To date, over 22,000 households have taken part in *Action at Home* (Global Action Plan UK 1999) and this has led to behaviour changes in many of the participant homes. For example, in one *Action at Home* project the questionnaires administered at the start and again at the end of the programme evinced an 18 percent increase in glass recycling and a nine percent increase in individuals turning lights off after use (Global Action Plan UK 1998). However, due to a low return of questionnaires until recently GAP had no clear indications of what was happening to participants during the programme. Engaging with *Action at Home* and its processes presents a valuable opportunity, both for myself and GAP, to examine the experiences of taking part in a concerted effort to adopt a sustainable lifestyle.

5. Research Outline

The empirical part of this research took place between October 1997 and May 1999 in two separate fieldwork locations. I used qualitative interview techniques throughout this aspect of the project. This is consistent with their current widespread use in the investigation of lay environmental meanings and experiences (see Burgess *et al.*, 1988a; Kvale 1996; Shotter 1993). In 1997–1998 I carried out a total of 41 one-to-one semi-structured interviews with *Action at Home* participants in Bournemouth, Dorset. Interviews took place in the participants' homes, both at the start and end of the six-month programme. Then, during 1998–1999, I conducted an evaluation of *Action at Home* in the workplace. Three companies[2] in the North-West of England purchased *Action at Home* as part of a pilot project to offer the programme to employees and to encourage changes in their resource-use behaviours, both at home and work. As part of assessment of this project, each company allowed me to convene one in-depth discussion group at each workplace. The group interviews were chosen as a methodology to allow the examination of the discursive dynamics evoked (Harrison *et al.*, 1996) and also to capture the "communication context" of the workplace environment (Crabtree *et al.*, 1993). Each discussion group met at the start of the programme, three months into *Action at Home* and finally each group member was interviewed individually at the end of the six months. All interviews were recorded and the following discussion is based upon analysis of the interview transcripts.

6. Reactions to *Action at Home*

Action at Home participants offered up varied, complex, sometimes contradictory, but always well-argued reactions to the programme. Reactions were both positive and negative, ranging from debates about the *Action at Home* material to debates about the institutional and social relationships that the information implied and embodied. I will begin by focusing on some of the key issues that add to the critique of prevailing positivist frameworks, by showing how the concept of sustainable lifestyles is thoroughly contested. These contestations centre round questioning the information in the packs, questioning the concept of the "environment" and also considering the meanings of the practices that make up the individual's lifestyle. By looking closely at these reactions, I will suggest that it is possible to begin to construct an alternate and embedded framing of this subject matter.

Questioning "Facts"

Throughout all the interviews, *Action at Home* participants constantly interrogated not only the information in the packs, but also the validity of the institutions and vested interests that these facts represented (see Irwin and Wynne 1996; Myers and Macnaghten 1998;

---

[2]These companies were Norweb in Preston, Lancashire; North-West Water in Warrington, Cheshire and British Aerospace in Warton, Lancashire.

Szerszynski *et al.*, 1996). The step-by-step guides to action were questioned on the grounds of the pertinence and reliability of the information, with many interviewees being highly skeptical about the merits of the recommended actions. This ranged from the actual energy-saving mechanics of putting shelves above radiators to affect changes in room temperature, to the over-all environmental benefits of acts such as recycling.

> Now is that not a better way of doing it? What is the point in collecting glass bottles when silicon is the most common element available on the surface? It costs more in recycling costs and heating costs and all the rest, for a bit of glass. (Male, Bournemouth, April 1998)

The contradictions inherent in the array of suggested actions were pointed out time and time again, such as driving the car to the recycling point to dispose of household waste; one action harming the environment and the other (allegedly) helping it. Participants recognised the contingent and uncertain nature of the information within the packs and questioned whether it was possible to ever know the "truth" surrounding environmental issues.

> And that's just the sort of information which just no-one knows. One makes all these assumptions and ending up doing things that are either worse or the wrong thing. (Male, Bournemouth, October 1997)

There were also questions about who produced the information, the vested interests involved and the implausibility of any purveyor of information collecting "neutral" data. This evoked debates about institutional and social trust.

> I certainly wouldn't trust a pressure group because they are going to be biased to be honest with you. I wouldn't necessarily trust a government because again they've got to be biased as well. Trust no one I think!! I would trust an independent researcher, for example, if it was an established credible university doing a study! I would trust that more than a government or a pressure group, provided of course you haven't been funded by a pressure group. I would want to see your accounts. (Male, North-West, October 1998)

In terms of environmental information and its attendant practices, my interviews suggest that there is no "information deficit" to be filled by new facts. Instead, engaging with *Action at Home* takes the form of an *active debate*, one that contests the truth and values of the knowledge being presented in the packs and makes use of the knowledge that exists and is mobilised from each individual's own life and experiences.

Questioning the "Environment"

The meanings implied and mobilised by the concept of the 'environment' were also highly contextual and contested. For example, the global environmental issues highlighted in the packs were not meaningful to a great number of interviewees.

> To be honest I don't even think about the hole in the ozone layer. It's not there when I walk outside so you just forget about it. You can't see it. Well I suppose if I was here and you could see this big black hole in the sky, you'd be petrified, wouldn't you. And everybody would be doing what they could to make it better, but because you can't see it you don't think about it. But if you were sat here watching it, you'd be dead scared, wouldn't you? You'd be doing all you could. (Female, North-West, October 1998)

Links between individuals' own actions and their global consequences are so remote in time and space (Clayton 1993) many respondents were left feeling alienated from key concepts. Interviewees knew about these mediated ideas, such as ozone depletion, but the absence of any direct experience of them meant that they were drawing on their own knowledge to make sense, and often debunk, the claims. In fact, the desire to take on board global environmental issues was limited as many interviewees expressed a desire to *not* be seen being too "green".

> Male 1: If you take something like Greenpeace, a lot of people know it's there, but they're not 100 percent sure what it's about. You know, you're either involved, part of it or not at all. Those lunatics are at it again doing such and such a thing, so it depends. It's actually how you put it across, not what information's in there, it's the image.
>
> Facilitator: Do you think that people are put off by the "green image"?
>
> Female: Very often yeah. Well, governments are, aren't they, they try to blow 'em up.
>
> Male 2: They're from the funny farm aren't they? On the basis they wear funny clothes and they have funny haircuts, they do strange things like digging tunnels. (North-West, October 1998)

What resonance, then, does the concept of the "environment" have? Very few interviewees made any direct links with nature and the natural environment. Instead, the meaning of the term "environment" was quickly linked to the realm of the social. Interviewees saw the environment as *their* environment, total and lived, which encompassed concerns about loss of communities, lack of positive social interactions in urban environments, social equity and justice, inter-generational relations, political and personal responsibility and historical changes in society. The environment, as a bounded concept situated in nature, did not appear to offer much as a source of feelings, meanings and motivations (Strauss 1992; Burningham and O'Brien 1994).

The Sanctity of Lifestyles

Despite the prevailing concept of the lifestyle as a set of discrete functional practices whose logic can be re-directed, *Action at Home* participants clearly felt that their patterns of everyday activities were not open to external restylisation. The concept of a "sustainable lifestyle" came across as a restrictive set of practices, which ultimately means having to "go without".

> But that is, we can't deny ourselves these things entirely, we have to live today and not in some other fantasy. (Male, Bournemouth, April 1998)

How individuals' preferred patterns of action and choices had become established and executed were contingent upon many factors, such as time, space, circumstances, money, personal preferences, values and goals. The term lifestyle served as a "catch-all" phrase that respondents used to encompass their physical and moral preferences, plus many things over which they felt they had little control. A "lifestyle" was thus a valiant attempt to manage, often contradictory, influences within one life. As far as adopting a more sustainable approach, it was not the case of opening up lifestyles to change, but instead seeing how the suggested new actions might fit into their current patterns.

> I think if it suits your lifestyle and it's not too much effort then yes you do it. But if it's too much effort then you don't. (Female, North-West, January 1999)

Convenience was a key concept, and trying to take on board a whole range of new practices was deemed by interviewees to be both unfeasible and undesirable.

> You basically want stuff on tap to use, you don't want to give up your car and share with a neighbour as you want the freedom to go on your own. And it's very difficult to say, "I like the environment, I want it nice" and at the same time "I want my lifestyle kept as it is." So yes, I will do that, but don't take this off me. (Female, North-West, October 1998)

Lifestyles were therefore not only containers of the multiple demands of modern living, but also were replete with meanings, habits, preferences, memories and others. New behaviours were often rejected on the grounds of going against interviewees' beliefs about the right way to live.

> I wouldn't bother adjusting the toilet to save water, as I don't believe this stuff, that we use vastly, vastly over the top to flush the loos, it is more important to protect your hygiene than save water in that respect. (Male, Bournemouth, October 1997)

Thus, the locale of the home is the site of the creation of a sense of ontological security (Dupuis and Thorns 1998; see also Giddens 1991). This resulted in strong reactions against external calls for alterations to be made.

7. Why Take *Action at Home*?

The pervasive negativity of the above discussions might lead to the conclusion that an investigation into sustainable lifestyles can only critique and cannot provide any constructive insights. I would suggest, however, that taking a closer look at participants' reasons for becoming involved in *Action at Home* allows the positioning of these debates within a discursive framework of meaning and interpretations of environmental communications. To argue this assertion further, I will begin by asking why interviewees decided to take part in *Action at Home* as a means of examining what drives their involvement.

Financial Incentives

Action at Home packs suggest the main benefits of taking part in the programme are helping the environment and also saving money off domestic bills. Several interviewees did cite making financial savings as one of their main reasons for taking part in *Action at Home*. Amidst the continuing postmodern emphasis on "lifestyles", "choices" and "identity" (Featherstone 1991), it is important not to forget that money is a key motivator in domestic behaviour patterns (Brandon and Lewis 1999).

> You get various things out of this and there is the possibility of saving more money as the months and years go by. But only if it can be done at a fairly cheap cost, so I don't want any expensive measures, like to spend a few hundred pounds to save a few pounds on your heating bills. (Male, Bournemouth, October 1997)

Both the Bournemouth and the North-West projects were offering participants one free energy-saving lightbulb per household, upon completion of the energy pack. This inevitably resulted in some participants signing up to *Action at Home* for this reason alone. However, even those respondents who expressed money as one of their main incentives were quick, within the course of the interviews, to elaborate on environmental and social concerns that they believed the *Action at Home* project would also address. It was also clear that the potential for saving money was considered marginal and would not sustain action in the long term.

> I would say there are a lot of things that can be done at the basic level now. I think to go any further would be incurring quite a cost. So it is quite easy to take the first step and do all these little things, but the next steps are quite difficult. You're talking about double glazing, foam insulation, having bins around the back of your house for segregation. It's quite a big step which you will have difficulty in getting people to do without greater financial benefits. (Male, North-West, January 1999)

Even though money was mentioned frequently as a driver for participation, it rarely surfaced as a key incentive for continuing with the project for six months, or for stimulating change. Instead, it seems that *Action at Home* presented an opportunity for individuals to engage in a process of self, and social, evaluation. Participants were making active and personal use of *Action at Home*, not simply subscribing to it.

A Design for Life

Most *Action at Home* participants were not taking part in a personal project of "greening" their lifestyles. Instead, many suggested that their involvement stemmed from being "curious", "interested", wanting to "learn more" and wanting to see what they "could do".

> I wanted to measure myself against what these people think is the proper
> way for us to run our lives I suppose. (Male, Bournemouth, October 1997)

Other empirical research has found that individuals see more information as a solution to environmental problems (Darier and Schule 1999). This does not, however, automatically endorse the "information deficit" model. Rather than seeking facts, interviewees want to find out about possible ways that they might choose to live. They did not want *Action at Home* to dictate a path to sustainable living, as if it represented an absolute goal to strive towards, but instead they sought it out to act as one source of potential guidance, among the many upon which consumers draw (Warde 1997). *Action at Home* offers one perspective, one frame of meaning and reference with which people can examine their own experiences and life practices (Finger 1994), and presents an opportunity for critical self-evaluation using "objective" information (Wayment and Taylor 1995).

> Yes, I was curious about it and wanted to see what was going, as I said
> before, how I fitted into it and whether I was doing as much as I could, so
> having done that I can't see me going on. (Female, Bournemouth, April
> 1998)

Action at Home is being consumed as a "lifestyle guide" with which the individual can address the "fundamental dilemmas of social identity" (Aldridge 1994:899). This finding is in keeping with social-constructionist theories, such as those of Anthony Giddens (1984, 1991, 1994) and Ulrich Beck (1992, 1996), which relate individual engagement with the environmental problematique to the position of the social actor within the processes and institutional relations of current social conditions. Working independently, Beck and Giddens have suggested that one of the defining features of contemporary post-industrial society is an erosion of old forms of stable social identity, such as class and religion. Instead, there is a move towards individualisation "in which agents become ever more free from the normative expectations of social institutions" (Szerszynski *et al.*, 1996:2). It is argued that individuals are now responsible for their own life trajectories and choices, having to constantly ask themselves questions about how they can, and want, to live. This is because "the narrative of self-identity has to be shaped, altered and reflexively sustained in relation to rapidly changing circumstances of social life, on a local and global scale" (Giddens 1991:215). Thus, with ever-changing contexts, individuals are required to, and able to, examine their own lifestyles, as both a project of self-determination and a moral project. These developments have given rise to the emergence of "life politics" (Giddens 1991) where individuals both attempt to maintain a coherent biographical narrative and to ask questions about the right way to live. Taking *Action at Home* can be viewed as part of this on-going engagement with a project of life politics.

This suggestion is partially tenable (although not fully defendable; see Hobson 2001) because, along with constructing a narrative of self-identity, *Action at Home* participants were asking questions about their own personal and social morality, in keeping with their shifting image of the self. They are seeking to address the social issues that trouble them, the anxieties that they express in the course of the interviews and frame their assessments of contemporary society. In short,

> I think Kersty, it's a fundamental re-valuing of where we are at. (Male, North-West, October 1998)

How does taking part in *Action at Home* do this? Signing up to *Action at Home* is considered an act in itself, not an excuse to avoid actual action (cf. Finger 1994). Taking part and "signing up" to a form of active engagement and debate makes participants feel that they are making a contribution to awakening a public sense of the need for change and a need to think about these issues. This is not about overt campaigning, or even the diffusion of particular ideas through social networks. Instead, engaging with the debates provoked by reading and thinking through the packs is a discursive act in itself, one that hopefully will provoke others to think, debate and help to make the changes needed (Szerszynski 1999).

> And I thought well it's only a start, but people have got to think about it. (Female, Bournemouth, October 1997)

Thus, it is the process of taking part in *Action at Home* that is important, not the endpoint of behaviour change. In fact, many interviewees did not have a vision or expectation of what might result from the programme as a whole. Instead, just taking part was enough in itself.

> So, as I say, I can only say that it is contributing in some respects. Whether one can see that contribution in the end I don't know. (Female, Bourne-mouth, April 1998)

Taking part in *Action at Home* is not signing up to a sustainable lifestyle, but rather entering into a "moral conversation" about how we, as individuals, and as a society, should and could be living. Beck (1998:28) encapsulates this state when he suggests "This 'me-first' generation has been much criticised; but I believe its individualism is moral and political in a new sense". Taking *Action at Home* does not just make participants feel better about themselves and their lifestyles. Rather it is part of a wider social debate and level of anxiety about the erosion of social relations and mutual respect that does not encompass the "right" way to live.

8. Rethinking Sustainable-Lifestyles Concepts and Theoretical Frameworks

From the above findings it is possible to begin to construct a social-theoretical framework to better understand the relationship between environmental communications and lifestyles. To do this, it is necessary to get rid of some of the old concepts and to introduce new approaches in this area of inquiry. In the following section I will make some observations on possible components of such a framework, focusing on information use, barriers to action and behaviour change.

Rethinking Information Use

One important point to reconsider is how individuals make use of environmental information. From the contested reaction of *Action at Home* participants, it is possible to consider "learning" in a rhetorically responsive manner (Shotter 1993). Building upon Macnaghten and Urry's (1998) attention to the work of Billig, it is important to revisit the place that argumentation — that is, debate — has in human thought. Billig, in his 1987 book 'Arguing and Thinking', reawakens the concept of rhetoric to construct a theoretical framework in which human thought is not reducible to isolated logic, but is instead a constantly constructive and discursive act. By paying attention to the argumentative dimensions of social life, rather than lamenting them, we can move away from an approach that considers expressed attitudes as verbalisations of inner beliefs, to an understanding of justifications and criticisms as rhetorical stances, realised in the context of social controversy. Billig (1987:141) states "we can expect private thinking to be modelled upon public argument. In consequence, it should possess a dialogic, rather than a monologic, character." This approach helps us to take a more constructive look at the debates that emerge from research interviews, not simply focusing on their contents and reporting them back as public opinions, but allowing a more active approach to be considered. Such an approach examines how individuals make use of particular arguments, discourses or 'commonplaces' (Myers and Macnaghten 1998). This approach also asks questions about how and why particular debates are mobilised in certain contexts and to what political ends (Burningham and O'Brien 1994).

Rethinking Barriers to Action

Sustainable-lifestyle research frequently focuses on an array of "barriers to action" that exist in individual and institutional contexts (see Tanner 1999). These include deficiency of facilities, time needed to take new actions, feelings of powerlessness and lack of agency. I would not suggest that these issues are not real physical and infrastructural problems, as there are very real limitations placed on action by a wide range of socio-economic factors (Blake 1999). What I am seeking to uncover is the development of a framework to understand why actions and awareness are not always related (Finger 1994).

In considering Billig's approach, the contestations around the material shift from being ultimately barriers to the embodiment of the way that humans deal with social controversy and make sense of information. This would also explain why people seek out lifestyle guides, such as *Action at Home*. Entering into these debates, within ourselves and with others, is the very process by which the total social environment is understood. The wide array of social concerns linked to the concept of the "environment" is not something that can, through policy, be eliminated. Instead, they are part of the rich moral conversations and real concerns in which citizens engage. "Barriers to action" thus become a set of discursive practices that individuals use when discussing the environmental problematique.

Rethinking Behaviour Change

Finally, there is one important theoretical issue that has been neglected in much of the work addressing environmental communications and lay publics. That is, where do actions and physical practices fit into a constructionist, discursive and rhetorical approach? By looking at the processes of behaviour change that some *Action at Home* participants experienced it is possible to suggest that a discursive framework for examining such changes is tenable.

Action at Home participants did make some changes in terms of no or low-cost actions. Those already taking many of the recommended actions had little scope for change, but were pleased to confirm to themselves that they are doing the "right thing".

> The actual project itself I haven't found particularly useful, it has just reaffirmed things really that I have already been doing. (Female, Bournemouth, April 1998)

Those who were new to some of the ideas in the packs felt they had been able to make some changes.

> I think it's made me more conscious and I know I never used to put lids onto saucepans and I do that now. But I think that also it makes it boil quicker. You know, just things I had read in a leaflet, about sticking lids on pans and just little things. Like, I don't leave my TV on. I used to leave my TV on stand-by at night and I just turn if off at the mains now. (Female, North-West, January 1999)

Individuals who did make changes did so by an interesting process. They were not learning new facts and then acting upon them. In fact, it was clear from the interviews that few people could recall anything out of the packs only a matter of weeks after reading them.

> I hadn't thought about it, you read and it's a shock and you look at things differently.

Facilitator: Like what, what's a shock?

Male: I can't remember just now, there was something that I were reading in the last one that we got.

Facilitator: Was that the shopping pack?

Male: I think it was the shopping one yeah. I hadn't realised, you know, and I thought "good idea"! I forgot what it was now.

Female: That's the trouble, I can't remember the questions now.

Male: That's right yeah. It was only last week or the week before we got 'em as well.

Facilitator: Do they go out of your head that fast?

Male: Well, yeah !!! (Mixed group, North-West, January 1999)

Rather it would appear that changes in behaviour occurred as a process of the surfacing and questioning of taken-for-granted habits.

> If it's a simple matter of turning a switch off then yes, I think people will get into the habit of doing that. (Male, North-West, October 1998)

Very few interviewees could explain why they had changed what they had and how they went about it. I would therefore suggest — and I have more fully developed a framework elsewhere (see Hobson 2001) to explain this finding — that we can draw on Giddens' structuration theory to help understand the embedded nature of behaviour change (see Giddens 1984). For example, Giddens' concept of practical consciousness, a form of unsaid knowledge that individuals make use of in going about their everyday lives, neatly encapsulates the habits that *Action at Home* helped to change. What *Action at Home* does is to bring these habits, hidden away in practical consciousness, into discursive consciousness, where they are considered by the individual, and either altered or contested.

> Well, you see what you're doing straight away don't you? There are some things, you think 'well I could do that'. Some things click in your mind, so you do tend to read them. (Female, North-West, January 1999)

Because of the place that these habits have in everyday lives, they are not usually bounded by the argumentative defenses of discursive consciousness, which are the readily accessible debates that interviewees evoked throughout this research, about why they should or could not adopt a particular behaviour. Habits can, however, quickly move "from being one of common sense to one of controversy" (Billig 1987:208) and this is what the *Action at Home* material does, by evoking debate about behaviours that are usually hidden from discursive view. Not only are there already debates around the controversial social issues that *Action at Home* discusses, but also habits become controversial in the light of the sustainable-lifestyles concept. This could help explain why there is so much debate and so little behaviour change. The more socially contentious issues, such as transport, find the *Action at Home* interviewees ready and equipped with debates about meanings and justifications. It is mostly the actions that do not evoke controversy — those that slip through the net of debate — that seem to enter into people's routines and habits. These findings put forward the possibility of taking a more discursive approach to behaviour-change research, one that can include within its parameters both human psychology and social contexts.

9. "Are You Doing Your Bit?": Conclusions and Future Research Questions

I will turn finally to some possible implications for this framework in the policy arena and future research agendas. There is a wide range of potential policy measures that can be mobilised to stimulate behaviour change. This includes a broad sweep of regulations (Hinchliffe 1996), the building of participatory institutions to create better trust (Blake 1999) with more open relationships between citizens and institutions (Burgess *et al.*, 1998), as well as creating a groundswell of people who "actively care" about the environment (Geller 1995). As the goals of sustainable development are so diffuse and uncertain, the use of multiple strategies is vital. Wardle (1996:6) suggests[3] that in the longer term individual effort alone will not be enough, but there will also be need for "social and environmental action on a wider scale to modify an environment which will otherwise continue to promote the problem which individuals are trying to counteract". This chapter, along with other contributions in this area, has detailed the serious problems with current political usage, and emphasis on, environmental communications as a valid behaviour-change strategy. It has been shown that how individuals react to communications, how they think about and address changing their lifestyles, and how they consider the current framing of the environmental problematique, all contrast markedly with the prevailing positivist assumptions underlying policy strategies.

However, it is also clear that tools like social marketing are not going to disappear as a preferred strategy. Therefore, a constructive ending would be to suggest how this research might make a positive contribution. One suggestion is that rather than placing the emphasis on learning about global issues, there needs to be an engagement with issues that have meaning in everyday lives to capture the energy of the rhetoric with which individuals think. For instance, take the "Are You Doing Your Bit?" campaign. There are some individuals with whom this message would strike a chord, or at least strike a note of responsibility. Mostly, though, I would suggest, if my *Action at Home* interviewees are valid examples, that a response to the question would be something like, "Well, I'm doing what I can and what I think I should be doing, even though it's not going to make that much difference and anyway, what are you doing about it all?"

If it was possible to go some way to entering into the contingencies and contestations of taking positive actions for the environment, perhaps environmental communications could

---

[3]Wardle (1996) addresses changing the eating patterns of obese people, but it also resonates with debates about the cognitive/emotional side of sustainable lifestyles.

start down a more positive and two-way route. I agree wholeheartedly that "participation requires effective institutions and mechanisms, but it also requires an effective and common language. That language will ultimately be found in the way people talk, not in policy documents" (Myers and Macnaghten 1998:352). This can refer not only to the *language* of communication, but also to the *form* that these communications take. Pursuing this approach would marry with calls by other scholars for further institutional openness and honesty about the uncertainties of environmental knowledge and the nature of environmental responsibility. How refreshing an environmental campaign called "We Haven't Really Been Doing Our Bit, Have We?" would be! This then turns the discussions to issues of institutional responsibility and transparency. In contemporary society where political institutions are not equipped and ultimately do not have a functional purpose of addressing diffuse, long-term environmental problems (Beck 1992), we have to consider who will rise to the challenge of entering publicly into these moral conversations.

GAP is making interesting headway in these issues by engaging businesses in discussions about bringing behaviour-change programmes into the workplace. Although there have been mixed results because of the number of contingencies involved in making these projects a success, they have shown that creating spaces to engage employers and employees in discussions of concerns and responsibility *does* affect positive change. The question still remains as to how this dialogue could be taken out to a wider community that does not have the bounded and spatially-fixed nature of the workplace. Various potential models for implementation exist, such as the original Global Action Plan EcoTeam model of community workgroups (see Staats and Herenius 1995). Yet, how these models of change actually work is unknown owing to the limitations of previous lifestyle behaviour-change research, especially projects using only quantitative methodologies. To move these debates on, out of the academy and into practice, future research has to take a broader look at means and methods of behaviour change, in consideration of rhetorical approaches of human psychology and the movable positions of environmental debates in contemporary society. Sustainable-lifestyles research must question the implicit assumption that changes in lifestyle practices are individuals' ultimate goals, but are hindered by "barriers to action". Instead, by taking a step back from the narrow conception of the "environment" and a step towards a richer engagement with people's moral conversations, we can at least make a start at reformulating our ideas about the place of "environmental" issues in lay discourses and practices.

References

Aldridge, A. (1994), "The construction of rational consumption in 'Which' magazine: The more blobs the better." *Sociology 28* (4), 899–912.

Argyle, M. (1992), *The Social Psychology of Everyday Life*. London: Routledge.

Baudrillard, J. (1998), *The Consumer Society: Myths and Structures*. London: Sage.

Beck, U. (1992), *Risk Society: Towards a New Modernity*. London: Sage.

Beck, U. (1996), "Risk society and the provident state." In S. Lash, B. Szerszynski & B. Wynne. *Risk, Environment and Modernity* (27–43). London: Sage.

Beck, U. (1998), "The cosmopolitan manifesto." *New Statesman*. 20 March, 28–30.

Billig, M. (1987), *Arguing and Thinking: A Rhetorical Approach to Social Psychology*. Cambridge: Cambridge University Press.

Blake, J. (1999), "Overcoming the 'Value-Action Gap' in environmental policy: Tensions between national policy and local experience." *Local Environment 4* (3), 257–278.

Blake, J., & Carter, C. (1997), *Community and Environmental Attitudes and Actions in Huntingdonshire*. Committee for Interdisciplinary Environmental Studies, University of Cambridge.

Brandon, G., & Lewis, A. (1999), "Reducing household energy consumption: A qualitative and quantitative field study." *Journal of Environmental Psychology*, 75–85.

Bulkeley, H. (1997), "Global risk, local values?: 'Risk society' and the greenhouse issue in Newcastle, Australia." *Local Environment 2* (3), 261–274.

Burgess, J., Limb, M., & Harrison, C. (1988a), "Exploring environmental values through the medium of small groups: 1. Theory and practice." *Environment and Planning A 20*, 309–326.

Burgess, J., Harrison, C., & Filius, P. (1998), "Environmental communication and the cultural politics of environmental citizenship." *Environment and Planning A 30*, 1445–1460.

Burgess, J., Harrison, C., & Maiteny, P. (1991), "Contested meanings: The consumption of news about nature conservation." *Media, Culture and Society 31* (4), 499–520.

Burningham, K., & O'Brien, M. (1994), "Global environmental values and local contexts of action." *Sociology 28* (4), 913–932.

Chaney, D. (1996), *Lifestyles*. London: Routledge.

Church, C., & McHarry, J. (1992), *The Household EcoTeam Workbook*. London: GAP UK/GAP International.

Clayton, A. (1993), "The ethics of sustainability." *Ecos 14* (1), 27–30.

Corral-Verdugo, V. (1997), "Dual 'realities' of conservation behaviour: Self-Reports vs. observation of reuse and recycling behaviour." *Journal of Environmental Psychology 17* (2): 135–145.

Crabtree, B., Yanoshik, M., Miller, W., & O'Connor, P. (1993), "Selecting individual or group interviews." In D. Morgan (ed.) *Successful Focus Groups: Advancing the State of the Art* (137–152). London: Sage.

Darier, E., & Schule, R. (1999), "'Think globally, act locally'? Climate change and public participation in Manchester and Frankfurt." *Local Environment 4* (3), 317–329.

De Young, R. (1993), "Changing behavior and making it stick: The conceptualization and management of conservation behavior." *Environment and Behavior 25* (4), 485–505.

DETR (1999), *Every Little Bit Helps: Are You Doing Your Bit?* London: Department of the Environment, Transport and the Regions.

Dupuis, A., & Thorns, D. (1998), "Home, home ownership and the search for ontological security." *Sociological Review 46* (1), 24–47.

Eden, S. (1993), "Individual environmental responsibility and its role in public environmentalism." *Environment and Planning A 25*, 1743–1758.

Eden, S. (1998), "Environmental issues: Knowledge, uncertainty and the environment." *Progress in Human Geography 22* (3), 425–432.

Ehrlich, P., Wolff, G., Daily, G., Hughes, J., Daily, S. *et al.* (1999), "Knowledge and the environment." *Ecological Economics 30*, 267–284.

Featherstone, M. (1991), *Consumer Culture and Postmodernism*. London: Sage.

Finger, M. (1994), "From knowledge to action? Exploring the relationship between environmental experiences, learning and behavior." *Journal of Social Issues 50* (3), 141–160.

Geller, E. (1995), "Actively caring for the environment: An integration of behaviorism and humanism." *Environment and Behavior 27* (2), 184–195.

Gershon, D., & Gillman, R. (1992), *Household EcoTeam Workbook*. Woodstock, NY: Global Action Plan.

Giddens, A. (1984), *The Constitution of Society*. Cambridge: Polity Press.

Giddens, A. (1991), *Modernity and Self-Identity: Self and Society in the Late Modern Age.* Cambridge: Polity Press.

Giddens, A. (1994), "Living in a post-traditional society." In U. Beck, A. Giddens & S. Lash (eds) *Reflexive Modernization: Politics, Tradition and Aesthetics in the Modern Social Order* (56–109). Cambridge: Polity Press.

Global Action Plan International. (n.d.). *Global Action Plan for the Earth.* Global Action Plan International

Global Action Plan UK. (1998), *Action at Home: A Catalyst for Change.* London: GAP UK.

Global Action Plan UK. (1999), *Results to Date.* London: GAP UK.

Harland, P., Langezaal, S., Staats, H., & Weenig, W. (1993), *The EcoTeam Program in the Netherlands: A Pilot Study of the Backgrounds and Experiences of the Global Action Plan.* Centre for Energy and Environmental Research, Leiden University.

Harrison, C., Burgess, J., & Filius, P. (1996), "Rationalizing environmental responsibilities: A comparison of lay publics in the UK and Netherlands." *Global Environmental Change 6* (3), 215–234.

Hinchliffe, S. (1996), "Helping the earth begins at home: The social construction of socio-environmental responsibilities." *Global Environmental Change 6*, 53–62.

Hobson, K. (2001), Talking Habits into Action: An Investigation into Global Action Plan's "Action at Home" Programme. Unpublished doctoral dissertation, University College London, London.

Irwin, A., & Wynne, B. (1996). "Conclusions." In A. Irwin & B. Wynne (eds) *Misunderstanding Science? The Public Reconstruction of Science and Technology* (213–221). Cambridge: Cambridge University Press.

IUCN/UNEP/WWF. (1991), *Caring for the Earth: A Strategy for Sustainable Living.* Gland, Switzerland.

Kvale, S. (1996), *InterViews: An Introduction to Qualitative Research Interviewing.* London: Sage.

Lanthier, I., & Olivier, L. (1999), "The construction of environmental 'awareness'." In E. Darier (ed.) *Discourses of the Environment* (63–78). Oxford: Blackwell.

Librova, H. (1999), "The disparate roots of voluntary modesty." *Environmental Values 8*, 369–380.

Lunt, P., & Livingtstone, S. (1992), *Mass Consumption and Personal Identity.* Milton Keynes: Open University Press.

Macnaghten, P., & Jacobs, M. (1997). "Public identification with sustainable development: Investigating public barriers to participation." *Global Environmental Change 7* (1), 5–24.

Macnaghten, P., & Urry, J. (1998), *Contested Natures.* London: Sage.

Myers, G., & Macnaghten, P. (1998), "Rhetorics of environmental sustainability: Commonplaces and places." *Environment and Planning A 30*, 333–353.

Rogers, E. (1995), *Diffusion of Innovations.* New York: Free Press.

Shotter, J. (1993), *Cultural Politics of Everyday Life: Social Constructionism, Rhetoric and Knowing of the Third Kind.* Milton Keynes: Open University Press.

Smith, R. (1996), "Sustainability and the rationalisation of the environment." *Environmental Politics 5* (1), 25–47.

Staats, H., & Herenius, S. (1995), *The EcoTeam Program in the Netherlands. Study 3: The Effects of Written Information about the EcoTeam Program on the Attitude and Intention towards Participation.* Centre for Energy and Environmental Research, Leiden University.

Strauss, A. (1987), *Qualitative Analysis for Social Scientists.* Cambridge: Cambridge University Press.

Strauss, C. (1992), "What makes Tony run? Schemas as motives reconsidered." In R. D'Andrade & C. Strauss (eds) *Human Motives and Cultural Models* (191–224). Cambridge: Cambridge University Press.

Szerszynski, B. (1999), "Risk and trust: The performative dimension." *Environmental Values 8* (2), 239–252.

Szerszynski, B., Lash, S., & Wynne, B. (1996), "Introduction: ecology, realism and the social sciences." In S. Lash, B. Szerszynski & B. Wynne (eds) *Risk, Environment and Modernity: Towards a New Ecology* (1–26). London: Sage.

Tanner, C. (1999), "Constraints on environmental behaviour." *Journal of Environmental Psychology 19* (2), 145–157.

Taylor, B. (1997), "Green in word." In R. Jowell, J. Curtice, A. Park, L. Brook, K. Thomson & C. Bryson (eds) *British Social Attitudes: The 14th Report* (111–136). London: SCPR/Ashgate.

UNCED. (1992), *Agenda 21 and the UNCED Proceedings*. New York: Oceana Publications.

United Nations. (1998), *Workshop on Indicators for Changing Consumption and Production Patterns: Measuring Changes in Consumption and Production Patterns*. New York: Department of Economic and Social Affairs.

van Luttervelt, P. (1998), *The EcoTeam Programme: A New Policy Instrument in Perspective*. Amsterdam: Global Action Plan Nederland.

Warde, A. (1994), "Consumption, identity-formation and uncertainty." *Sociology 28* (4), 877–899.

Warde, A. (1997), *Consumption, Food and Taste: Culinary Antinomies and Commodity Culture*. London: Sage.

Wardle, J. (1996), "Obesity and behaviour change." *International Journal of Obesity 20* (Supplement 1), 1–8.

WasteWatch/UK Waste Poll. (1999), *Overwhelming Public Support for Recycling: Leading Environmental Charity Calls on Government to Put 3 "R's" — Reduce, Reuse, Recycle — At the Heart of Waste Policy*. London: NOP Research Ltd.

Wayment, H., & Taylor, S. (1995), "Self-evaluation processes: Motives, information use, and self-esteem." *Journal of Personality 63* (4), 729–757.

Part VII

Conclusion: Working Toward Sustainable Consumption

Chapter 12

Sustainable Consumption by Design

Kate Fletcher, Emma Dewberry and Phillip Goggin

1. Introduction

> In many ways, the environmental crisis is a design crisis. It is a conse-
> quence of how things are made ... constructed ... and used (Van der Ryn
> and Cowan 1996:9).

Design is about conception and planning, the intentional shaping of ideas into everyday objects, systems and settings. As such, it occupies the space between people and their surroundings. A space that both influences, and is influenced by, wants and needs, material choices and actions. It is this unique position of design as the interface between consumers and the activities of consumption, which firmly establishes its potential to influence the environmental and social impact of products and services and hence, to contribute towards the goals of sustainable development.

This chapter explores the role that design activities play in promoting more sustainable patterns of consumption. We proceed by investigating particular strategies with reference to a specific context: clothes washing, or more specifically, the design, production and consumption of washing machines, new developments in textiles, washing and clothing services and the socially- and culturally-determined need to keep clean. The social and cultural phenomena that are the subject of this chapter are necessarily situation-specific, particular to the United Kingdom at the beginning of the twenty first century. Yet it is in gaining such specific knowledge about a narrowly defined area that we can begin to draw inferences about the broader industrial framework and the role that design might play in a new trans-disciplinary dialogue on consumption.

2. Design for Sustainability

We address the design dimension of the environmental and social crisis explicitly by using the concept of *design for sustainability*. Rather than an aesthetic, the ideas embodied in design for sustainability connect and form alliances between people and their surroundings and are not tied to any individual design profession. Their inclusion in design profoundly challenges the dominant market position and status quo. These ideas question the major role played by design activities in such things as product differentiation, branding and

Exploring Sustainable Consumption: Evironmental Policy and the Social Sciences, Volume 1, pages 213–224.
Copyright © 2001 by Elsevier Science Ltd.
All rights of reproduction in any form reserved.
ISBN: 0-08-043920-9

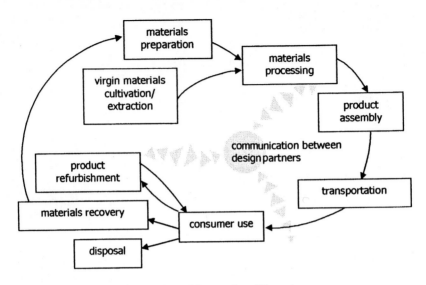

Figure 12.1: The product lifecycle.

advertising and in amplifying the consumption of material goods. They raise doubts about the reliance, in the conventional Western economic paradigm, on maximum consumption as a primary source of wealth creation and measure of happiness. They query unequal access to resources and exposure to risk between and within communities.

Proponents of design for sustainability typically express reservations about traditional views on who can design and what it involves (see, for example, Papanek 1995). Most fundamentally, they demand that an expanded view of design is taken, in which the implications of a design's entire *lifecycle* on both people and resource flows are considered. This involves connecting the design of a 'product' (an object, service or system) to the larger situation of materials extraction, production, use, reuse and disposal (refer to Figure 12.1). Focusing on the whole, rather than on fragments of systems, can reduce overall impact and prevent shifting resource consumption between different lifecycle stages. Lifecycle thinking necessitates a high level of design competence, intelligence and communication, supported by the involvement of new design partners such as community groups, the coming together of formal disciplines as diverse as anthropology and environmental science and bounded by the traditional, creative, organising skills embodied within design.

The importance of design as a force for sustainability has grown out of the realisation of its major role in determining the resources that are consumed. It is estimated that decisions made in design are responsible for 80 to 90 percent of a product's environmental and economic costs (Graedel *et al.,* 1995). Further recognition of its potential is found in environmental, economic and social policy documentation at national, regional and international levels (UK Foresight Programme 1998). This reflects the potential for design actions to be *preventative* actions. Preventing the conditions that lead to social and environmental problems is a key mechanism to achieve sustainability (as set out, for example, in Principle 8 of Agenda 21). Preventative measures reduce the need for remedial 'clean-up' activity as they look for solutions elsewhere in the industrial economy, namely in the areas of conceptualisation and design (Jackson 1996). The concept of prevention is a radical one and is difficult to implement because of its wide social and cultural remit. Unlike remedial approaches, which often defer responsibility for environmental problems to institutions and technology, preventative actions require widespread societal commitment and lifestyle change. They therefore impress on all aspects of society, making collective, preventative action *cultural change* (Hirschhorn *et al.,* 1993). It is this influence on people's ideas, values and actions — on culture — where design for sustainability ideally should be focused; on envisaging more sustainable patterns of consumption.

Design is a solutions-orientated discipline and, while much design-related activity is focused on commerce and profiteering through the proliferation of goods and services, a number of strategies addressing the need for sustainable consumption are beginning to emerge. These vary by degree of influence and timescale, and range, in the short term, from simple recycling, reuse and efficiency schemes, to more challenging and long-term ideas such as displacing products with systems of service delivery or emphasising local- or community-based solutions to human needs. In other words, design for sustainability comprises some strategies concerned with *redesigning* that which is consumed (consuming greener); others which *reorganise* the way consumption takes place (consuming differently); and others still which *rediscover* the nature of needs and associated satisfiers (consuming appropriately). These strategies attempt to influence both the quantity and quality of consumption and can be clustered in three broad categories, each with a different focus:

- Product focus — making existing products more resource efficient;
- Results focus — producing the same outcome in different ways; and
- Needs focus — questioning the need fulfilled by the object, service or system, and how it is achieved.

As illustrated in Figure 12.2, the potential environmental benefits associated with each of these three categories — although generalised — is predicted to vary between a factor of four for product focus strategies, to a factor of 20 for strategies which focus on needs (Brezet 1997; von Weizsacker *et al.,* 1997; Manzini 1994). The greatest factor improvements occur over a long period as they are perceived as difficult to implement and require some form of cultural change. Lower-level improvements, in contrast, can be realised more easily as they generally involve familiar product types and require little change to established behavioural patterns.

3. Product Focus

Design for sustainability strategies with a product focus attempt to influence the impact of consumption by making existing products more efficient. Most design for sustainability activity to date has been concerned with this focus and considerable research is being

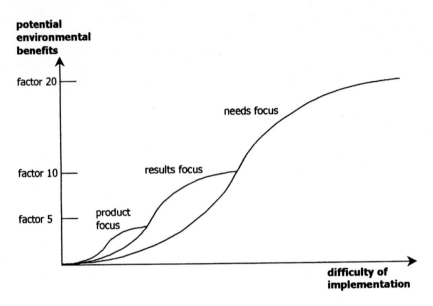

Figure 12.2: Approaches to design for sustainability.

undertaken on the development of methodologies (such as lifecycle assessment[1]) to further refine current products and processes. In the particular context explored here — clothes washing — improvements in the design of washing machines have been shown to have significant potential. For example, a Danish study found that energy consumption could be reduced by more than 70 percent if the most efficient washing machines replaced existing stock (von Weizsacker *et al.,* 1997).

For a typical washing machine, 95 percent of its total environmental impact arises out of the phase of the lifecycle when the machine is in use (refer to Figure 12.3). Although washing machine manufacturers have directed some attention to issues associated with energy, water and detergent use, partly because of the development of eco-labelling schemes (see for example, Roy 1996), there is little evidence to suggest that the environmental implications of the way people use washing machines have been fully considered. One of the UK's white-goods manufacturers has designed a washing machine that is able to mechanically wash clothes in cold water with comparable results to warm-water washing. Resulting from an innovation in detergent technology, it removes the need to wash in heated water, thus saving energy without requiring a change in behaviour. In addition, the simple detergent ball or tablet is not only more effective than the dispensing tray in delivering detergent to the laundry but it also reduces resource consumption because less detergent is required or wasted during the wash cycle. Such simple ideas remove the

---

[1]Lifecyle assessment (LCA) is a method by which key environmental burdens associated with a product, process or activity are recorded and assessed so that improvements can be identified.

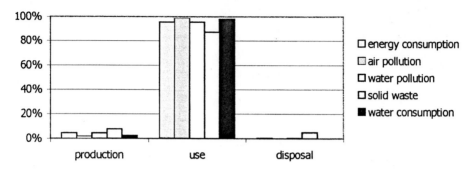

Figure 12.3: Contribution of lifecycle stages to total environmental impact for washing machines (PA Consulting Group, 1991).

need for complex water-heating and detergent-dosing mechanisms, as well as the sophisticated controls required to provide the range of wash programmes found in many machines.

Consumers' acceptance of product innovation is not straightforward. It can, for example, be inhibited by the sometimes-conflicting issues of product status, performance and cost. Features, such as cold-wash only, are seen by some companies as unacceptable platforms from which to launch and market new products. One UK firm, which conducted its own market research, convinced itself that inexpensive, simple, easy to use, reliable and long-lived washing machines would not sell because they were considered by potential customers as inferior and lacking status. This is a strong indicator of the enhanced image, choice and control (regardless of usefulness or environmental compatibility) that both companies and customers have come to expect of new products. A further factor limiting the acceptance of these technologies is the higher price frequently charged for environmentally superior machines, resulting in poorer households frequently being excluded from the potential benefits that these new technologies can bring. According to one study (Uitdenbogerd *et al.,* 1998) this is compounded further by poorer people not only using less efficient machines than those who are more well-off, but by them using these machines *more* frequently to do *more* laundry. It is suggested that this disparity may be because poorer households spend more time at home than their more affluent counterparts, and while at home textile maintenance is one of the jobs to be done, to take time over and/ or pride in.

In addressing consumption issues associated with clothes washing, efficiency improvements in machines can be complemented by designing clothes that are 'easier' to clean (that is, cause less impact as they are washed). Just as with environmental burdens associated with washing machines, those resulting from the clothing lifecycle are mainly a consequence of use (refer to Figure 12.4). It is worth noting however that the design of 'environmentally friendly' garments and 'environmentally friendly' systems of laundering those garments have developed in isolation (Fletcher 1999).

The environmental impact associated with clothes laundering, as influenced by clothing design, can be reduced in a number of ways, including washing less frequently, on lower temperatures and in fuller loads. Garments can be designed, for example, that are more

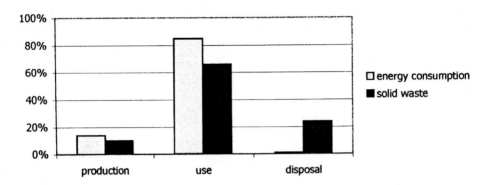

Figure 12.4: Contribution of lifecycle stages to total environmental impact for clothing
(Franklin Associates, 1993).

resistant to soiling and odour. Stain-blocking coatings form a barrier around the fibres
giving stain and soil repellency and deodorising fibres or layers act to control bacterial
growth on the fibre surface. Such developments reduce resource consumption if their
application translates into less frequent washing. However, without a change in current
laundering habits, in which it has been shown that consumers rarely wash clothes to
remove dirt (in Britain in 1993 there were on average only seven stains per load of
washing, approximately 4 kg of textiles), few benefits are likely to be gained. As it is only
when the removal of dirt is the principal motive for laundering that coatings begin to have
an effect on washing frequency and hence on resource consumption.

Where the potential environmental benefits from developments such as coatings are
determined by changes in behaviour, enquiries into current behaviour can also provide
scope for improvement. For example, surveys of consumer behaviour reveal that different
fibre types are laundered at different temperatures. Cotton items are commonly washed 'at
the boil' (70°C), whereas synthetics are washed at 40°C. This means that by substituting
'synthetic' fibres for 'cotton', there is considerable potential to reduce impact associated
with consumer care. Estimates suggest that making this switch can lead to up to 70 percent
of energy consumed in laundering being saved. Thus it seems that selecting fibres that
wash well on cool temperatures and dry quickly could bring major benefits. This is of
course dependent on consumers correctly differentiating between different material types
and washing them accordingly.

Evidence indicates, however, that this is not the case (Groot-Marcus and van Moll
1996). While there is approximately the same number of natural and synthetic textiles in
circulation, cotton or cotton blends make up the bulk (89 percent) of washing loads. This
perhaps indicates that cotton fabrics are laundered more frequently than synthetics (as well
as on higher temperatures) and consequently have a higher impact (and therefore should be
avoided). An alternative explanation could be that consumers are unsure of the fibre
content of textiles and unconsciously launder non-cotton articles as cotton. Further, when
studies of how people *sort* their laundry are taken into account, it is clear that in the
majority of cases, sorting is done on the basis of colour and not fibre type. These variously

sorted loads are then laundered at hotter temperatures if they are white or light coloured than if they are made up predominately of dark shades. This suggests that the effects of consumption could be reduced by changing garment colour. Yet while restrictive use of colour may lessen the environmental impact of consumption in laundering, it fails to take account of the wider cultural, psychological and spiritual significance of colour for society and indicates the importance of wide ranging expertise in developing theory and practice relating to sustainable consumption.

Design for sustainability therefore has a major requirement to understand consumer actions in their many modes of operation. As exemplified above, more sustainable patterns of consumption are restricted — not by innovation, technology or the products themselves — but by people's behaviour, something not central to the product focus of design for sustainability to date. Thus in addition to consuming redesigned, 'greener' versions of existing products, more effective solutions may be sought by consuming in different ways.

4. Results Focus

Design for sustainability strategies also investigate the way existing products and combinations of resources are distributed, organised and used. Under this banner, some significant attention has been paid to the development of products — and systems of products — which are compatible with, and advance, product sharing. Shared products meet the same needs with fewer units by intensified product use. Many examples of product sharing exist, such as laundry facilities in densely populated urban areas, which make use of community or local authority-run machines. Such schemes it is popularly argued are successful and are held up as examples of 'good', efficient design (see for example, von Weizsaecker *et al.,* 1997). The centralised, community laundry reduces the number of machines in use, so lessening materials and processing costs; it reuses warmth and water by washing continuously rather than in inefficient batches; its single location allows the easy introduction of more sophisticated, efficient machines; and, its local site means that polluting transportation is reduced to a minimum. Further benefits of community- and locally-based laundering schemes can promote other, more sustainable practices. They may, for example, promote conviviality and encourage communication within and across communities and stimulate a range of other services such as childcare facilities.

However, while the technology and product infrastructure to support resource efficient community laundries is already in place, the necessary accompanying social infrastructure, of environmentally appropriate consumer behaviour and cultural acceptance, is less well developed. Thus it can be argued that it is the 'people' element of a community laundry that limits environmental improvement. Consumers are free to continue bad laundry practice such as the incorrect dosing of detergents; unnecessarily high washing temperatures; and semi-full loads. What is more, without changes in consumer behaviour, there are no major environmental benefits to be gained from using fewer washing machines more intensively. While a product-sharing scheme employs *production* resources more efficiently (one machine meets many people's needs), it does not address resource efficiency in *use* (clothes are still washed as frequently). And when the environmental cost of the use phase of the lifecycle is significant, as with this case, intensified use does not address areas of major impact. Thus the actual number of washing machines in service makes little difference to the overall environmental impact of laundering. Rather, it is how the machines are used — consumer behaviour — which is most significant. A product-sharing scheme, such as a community laundry, therefore will bring few benefits if no change is made to consumer behaviour at the product interface. Further, these benefits will be dependent on cultural acceptance of the new scheme. In this instance, the social acceptance of community laundering would have to overcome obstacles that include the perceived inconvenience of clothes washing outside the home and the social stigma of laundries that are linked in many minds with poverty.

Many of the barriers to achieving significant environmental benefits from product-sharing schemes are also likely to affect the success of services. Preparing for the switch from the consumption of products to the utilisation of services is regarded as a key strategy in design for sustainability. Its basic premise is one that sees products as mere instruments or means to produce the needed functions to consumers (Meijkamp 1997), and thus the material components of the product are *utilised* rather than *consumed* by the user through a service or lease arrangement. The environmental benefits of selling utility or results rather than products arise out of the different role played by materials in the two schemes' drive for profit. In selling products, profit is maximised by selling more materials. In selling services, profit is maximised by serving more people with fewer materials. As the financial success of a service relies on resource efficiency; energy and materials inputs and associated environmental impacts have the potential to be reduced to a minimum.

There are already well-established laundry services that clean a range of textile products, most commonly hotel and hospital linen. These services offer wide-ranging environmental benefits: efficient, centralised operations reuse warmth, water and detergent; automatic dosing and loading of machines overcomes inefficient consumer behaviour; no direct access to washing machines dissuades consumers from 'casual' laundering. Yet, as with the design of product sharing schemes, it is unclear whether the design of services will bring unconditional environmental improvements. As argued above, intensified use of a product that causes most environmental impact as it is used, does not address key environmental problems. What is more, the requisites for a laundry service: higher washing temperatures (to maintain hygiene standards); clothes drying; and, transportation mean that a laundry service consumes more energy than private laundering (van den Hoed 1997).

In addition to overcoming resource inefficiencies, successful services have to engage with social, cultural and psychological issues, such as those surrounding material ownership and the need for display of status by means of prestige goods. While many services are based on material or product combinations of some sort (in this case, washing machines), the materials are not owned by, and in some instances are not visible to, the consumer. Yet, as is especially evident in Western culture, material ownership is a key symbol of wealth and social differentiation; materials being a culturally accepted satisfier of psychological needs. Against such a context, the lack of material presence of services may be seen to afford them dubious prestige. It is the prestige and the high levels of cultural attractiveness of alternative scenarios, such as services, that are widely accepted as imperatives for a smooth transition to a more sustainable system of production and consumption (Manzini 1994). Further, there is some concern that the disassociation between object and source of satisfaction in service design may threaten moves towards sustainable consumption. Evidence to support this negative influence can be seen in services that use products as a mechanism to deliver results, but which place little value on the products themselves (such as mobile phones). The products, and the associated embodied materials and energy, are thus seen as expendable, and are frequently discarded or updated with changing technological or fashion trends.

Given that behaviour in laundering restricts the resource efficiency of garments, it would appear therefore that one possible solution would be to design clothes never to be washed. In that way, consumer behaviour in, and attitudes towards, clothes washing would be irrelevant. Hygienically and culturally, durable, no-wash clothes are currently unacceptable. Less contentious in conventional cultural terms, disposable clothes may offer a means to reduce environmental impact arising out of washing. The concept of disposability, however, undermines the culture of sustainability's traditional message of longevity; the implications of which could be far-reaching and impact upon how all garments — durable and disposable — are used, maintained and discarded. While disposable clothes prevent significant environmental impacts arising as a result of laundering, other impacts associated with the environmental cost of production: materials extraction, processing, distribution, reclamation and disposal have to be assessed. Disposability also has considerable implications for the perceived value of textile materials and textile aesthetics. Aesthetics in particular is likely to play a key role in making any alternative and more environmentally preferential system more attractive to consumers. Thus, the environmental compatibility of this system is still dependent on individuals. Without consumer acceptance and understanding of their role in the product lifecycle, the value of a highly organised and efficient system of producers, distributors and reclaimers would be reduced. This acknowledgement of the need for behavioural change in the success of design for sustainability strategies emphasises that a results focus, like the product focus described earlier, requires broader, more inclusive, more heterogeneous design priorities than those currently in operation.

5. Needs Focus

Heterogeneity necessitates that in addition to strategies that focus on products and results, design for sustainability explores fundamental human needs. Max-Neef (1992) identifies these specific, identifiable, underlying needs that are the same, regardless of nation, religion or culture as: subsistence, protection, affection, understanding, participation, creation, recreation, identity and freedom. The nine needs fall into two broad categories: physical (material) and psychological (non-material) needs. Crucially, while these needs stay the same, what changes with time and between individuals is how these needs are met or *satisfied*. Different satisfiers have different implications not only for those involved, but also for external factors such as the environment. This relationship between satisfiers and resource use, waste generation and pollution is particularly acute in the consumer society, where most satisfiers (for both categories of need) are materials-based and personal psychological well-being is equated with owning things and activities (Goodwin 1997).

Where satisfiers are manifest as products or services, they are the traditional — if unconscious — focus of design. In making needs (not satisfiers) the conscious centre of design activities, solutions can be approached in a non-conventional way. As each way of meeting needs has different social, material and environmental implications, new solutions, which are both more appropriate to people's needs and less resource-intensive, have the potential to be developed. Thus, in the context of this chapter, the shifting design emphasis can be plotted and shown to move from clothes washing (a product focus) through conceptions of clean clothes (a results focus). Finally it arrives at considerations of cleanliness and clothes use as a direct influence on the fundamental human need of subsistence (a needs focus). This is not just a semantic shift but describes a substantial conceptual leap for problem-solvers (designers and others associated with satisfying needs) and makes explicit a requirement to resolve traditional divisions between industrial or academic sectors, as needs are not sector specific.

In the laundering context, a needs focus questions the resource efficiency of wearing and laundering clothes — as without clothes there would be no clothes washing; and it also encourages designers to engage with societal and cultural perceptions of standards of cleanliness. Naturism, as a means to achieve more sustainable patterns of consumption, brings with it requirements for major attitudinal and infrastructural change. Assuming nakedness was acceptable, to protect the body and keep it warm (the ostensible function of clothing), resources would likely be consumed in other ways. If hirsute bodies with a high proportion of fat were promoted, there would be greater requirements for calorific foods. If body warmth were maintained by taking more exercise, from living and working in hotter climates, buildings or in closer physical proximity with people and/or animals, there would be concomitant resource implications.

Similarly, a modification in the collective definition of 'clean' has implications associated with changing washing behaviour. Cleanliness, while originally motivated by disease prevention, is now driven by social competition and is linked to cultural values such as success, acceptance and happiness (Hoy 1995). Thus, keeping clean, a practice legitimised and amplified by the marketing and product world built up around a culture of 'whiter than white', is used to satisfy not only the fundamental (and physical) need to prevent disease and so survive, but also as a means to meet other fundamental (but not physical) needs such as participation, affection and understanding. Likewise, clothes do not just meet the physical need for subsistence, but are also used as a means to satisfy other needs, which include identity, participation and creativity, among others. This makes the apparent function of both clothing and cleanliness of less importance than their symbolic function, that is as a sign of wealth, as a signal of belonging to a particular social group, of differentiation from that group, of self-esteem and so on.

Thus to avoid depriving people of their fundamental human needs, the conspicuous consumption of clothes and cleanliness cannot be dismissed without first promoting alternative ways of signalling who and what we are to others and advancing new parameters of social acceptance. In other words, the significance of products as complex satisfiers of human needs has to be understood before consumption of these same products can be reduced. The sociology of consumption and the semiotic value of goods and services thus become crucial to the development of design strategies that promote ideas of more sustainable consumption. To move towards the dual goals of meeting needs more effectively and reducing material throughput and associated environmental impact, the relationship between needs, satisfiers and design output has to be disentangled. Thus enabling designers to engage with 'material' problems (like resource and energy efficiency) while at the same time, being aware of other needs and devising appropriate non-material satisfiers.

6. Conclusions

This chapter has explored the role played by design in achieving more sustainable patterns of consumption and has examined in detail a variety of approaches associated with clothes washing. While specific, the discussion has obvious relevance for all designed surroundings and includes various levels of approach which can include a focus on products, results and needs and also issues associated with materials, technology, systems, economics and consumer behaviour.

  — We have argued that achieving optimal environmental improvement through design is contingent on people and on understanding the way in which people respond to their material surroundings. Yet the most common approaches to design for sustainability tend to focus on pollution reduction and resource efficiency rather than human choices and actions. In contrast to this, design for sustainability with a focus on people considers ways of satisfying fundamental human needs. Here lies the greatest potential benefit: different satisfiers have different implications not only for people but also for other factors such as the environment. A focus on needs and the ways that needs are satisfied does not exclude the design and production of products, services or systems. Conversely, a focus on the design of products, services and systems cannot promote sustainable consumption without consideration of people's needs. Implicit in this is a requirement for designers to engage with issues underlying consumer actions, to understand behaviour in many contexts, and to connect with people's aspirations and expectations.

There is a dyadic relationship between design and policy where design not only makes policy real through practical output, but policy is also informed and revisited in the light of design practice. Design has potential as an agent of change for influencing more sustainable consumption. The design process itself is reflective, informed by other disciplines and areas of expertise and makes connections between people, policy and practice. As such, an effective manifesto for sustainable consumption can also be seen as a manifesto for design.

References

Brezet, H. (1997), *Dynamics in Ecodesign Practice*. UNEP Industry and Environment January–June, 21–24.

Fletcher, K. (1999), Environmental Improvement by Design: An Investigation of the UK Textile Industry. PhD Thesis. London: Chelsea College of Art & Design, The London Institute.

Franklin Associates. (1993), *Resource and Environmental Profile Analysis of a Manufactured Apparel Product: Woman's Knit Polyester Blouse*. Washington DC: American Fiber Manufacturers Association.

Goodwin, N. (1997), Overview Essay. In N. R. Goodwin, F. Ackerman & D. Kiron (eds) *The Consumer Society* (pp. 1–10). Washington DC: Island Press.

Graedel, T., Reaves Comrie, P., & Sekutowski, J. (1995). "Green product design." *AT&T Technical Journal* November/December, 18–25.

Groot-Marcus, A., & van Moll, M. (1996), "Textile characteristics, laundering and the environment." *Journal of Consumer Studies and Home Economics 20*, 261–273.

Hirschhorn, J., Jackson, T., & Baas, L. (1993), "Towards prevention — The emerging environmental management paradigm." In T. Jackson (ed.) *Clean Production Strategies* (pp. 125–142). Boca Raton: Lewis Publishers.

Hoy, S. (1995), *Chasing Dirt: The American Pursuit of Cleanliness*. New York: Oxford University Press.

Jackson, T. (1996), *Material Concerns: Pollution, Profit and Quality of Life*. London: Routledge.

Manzini, E. (1994), "Design, environment and social quality: From 'existenzminimum' to 'quality maximum'." *Design Issues 10* (1), 37–43.

Max-Neef, M. (1992), "Development and human needs." In P. Ekins & M. Max-Neef (eds) *Real-Life Economics* (pp. 197–214). London: Routledge.

Meijkamp, R. (1997), *Changing Consumer Needs by Eco-efficient Services. Towards Sustainable Product Design*. Conference Proceedings (unpaginated). Farnham, UK: The Centre for Sustainable Design.

PA Consulting Group. (1991), *Environmental Labelling of Washing Machines: A Pilot Study for the DTI/DOE*. Royston, Hertfordshire: PA Consulting Group.

Papanek, V. (1995), *The Green Imperative: Ecology and Ethics in Design and Architecture*. London: Thames and Hudson.

Roy, R. (1996), "Designing a greener product: The Hoover 'New Wave' washing machine range." Co-design: *The Interdisciplinary Journal of Design and Contextual Studies* 5/6, 34–39.

Uitdenbogerd, D., Brouwer, N., & Groot-Marcus, J. (1998), *Domestic Energy Saving Potentials for Food and Textiles: An Empirical Study*. Wageningen, NL: Wageningen Agricultural University.

UK Foresight Programme. (1998), *Sustainable Technologies for a Cleaner World*. London: Office of Science and Technology.

van den Hoed, R. (1997), *Sustainable Washing of Clothes. Towards Sustainable Product Design Conference*. Proceedings (unpaginated). Farnham, UK: The Centre for Sustainable Design.

Van der Ryn, S., & Cowan, S. (1996), *Ecological Design*. Washington DC: Island Press.

von Weizsaecker, E., Lovins, A., & Lovins, H. (1997), *Factor Four: Doubling Wealth, Halving Resources*. London: Earthscan.

Chapter 13

Sustainable Consumption: Environmental Policy and the Social Sciences

Joseph Murphy and Maurie J. Cohen

1. Introduction

The modern environmental era dawned in 1972 with the United Nations Stockholm Conference on the Human Environment. Around this time governments throughout the developed world began to institutionalise environmental protection. In 1971, for example, eight of the world's richest countries created environmental ministries. Other actions common at this time were the establishment of national environmental authorities and agencies and the inclusion of commitments to environmental protection in national constitutions. Slightly later, from the mid-1970s onwards, national environmental reports emerged and for many countries these were followed by environmental framework legislation (see Jänicke 1992).

From the outset government actions to solve environmental problems were based on an easily identifiable approach (see Chapter 1). Policymakers placed their faith in science and technology and in their own ability to craft ameliorative solutions to environmental problems. They reinforced the dominant role of scientists and technologists because of their tendency to understand environmental problems as largely related to wasteful or dangerous production processes. On the whole they faced each new challenge with reasonable optimism, confident in their ability to find a rational solution once they had identified basic cause and effect relationships. Although apocalyptic publications like *Limits to Growth* (Meadows *et al.*, 1972) and *Blueprint for Survival* (Goldsmith *et al.*, 1972) suggested things might be more complicated, policymakers did not seriously entertain the idea that environmental problems raised basic questions about the structure of society.

More recently we have witnessed the emergence of environmental issues that have dented the confidence of governments. The costs associated with environmental protection have become a serious matter. In the 1980s and 1990s this resulted in greater effort to identify tolerable (or at least acceptable) levels of environmental and health risk in order to balance threats against the costs associated with dealing with them (Cohen 1999). In Europe, following various widely-publicised environmental and health disasters, a previously unknown scepticism about the virtues of science and technology has emerged. In the late 1990s the conflict between environmental protection and trade liberalisation coalesced

Exploring Sustainable Consumption: Evironmental Policy and the Social Sciences, Volume 1, pages 225–240.
Copyright © 2001 by Elsevier Science Ltd.
All rights of reproduction in any form reserved.
ISBN: 0-08-043920-9

and governments became locked in conflicts pitching multi-lateral environmental agreements against free-trade rules. These developments have been associated with an increasingly desperate attempt to argue that there is no necessary contradiction between economic growth and environmental protection. However, although the basic approach is under attack, policymakers continue to maintain that technical solutions, although elusive, are not completely out of reach.

Interestingly, this approach to environmental problems is fundamentally different to the approach that is taken to problems elsewhere. Whether we are, to name a few examples, speaking of alcohol and drug abuse, teenage pregnancy or eating disorders, policymakers and others have accepted that these are "social problems." Activists may bring these issues to the attention of the public and policymakers, but they grow out of and reveal basic contradictions and inconsistencies within society. Though there are advocates of scientific and technological "solutions" to many of them, few people honestly believe that, to take one example, we will make substantial inroads into the use of illegal drugs via technology. The point of departure for addressing social problems constructively and meaningfully is to recognise their inevitability given the existing structure of society and to engage with their social dimensions.

Contrasting environmental problems with commonly-accepted social problems in this way reveals that governments and others have been surprisingly reluctant to acknowledge the social dimensions of environmental dilemmas. This may go some way to explain the emergence of more and more intractable problems. A benign explanation for this is that the physical nature of environmental issues, in combination with some notable technological successes since the 1970s, has led to the belief that they are, in fact, technical problems. They are similar to any other puzzle that an engineer faces everyday and therefore there is no need to consider social dimensions. More likely, however, approaching environmental issues as technical problems is attractive because it means that decision-makers can avoid grappling with complex and politically-divisive issues. We have, therefore, sought to "manage" our environmental problems without taking on the challenging task of trying to understand — or even identify — the conflicting tendencies responsible for them.

The recent emergence of an environmental-policy debate in the area of sustainable consumption, however, may represent an attempt to overcome several decades of denial of the social dimensions of environmental problems. That said, given the legacy associated with that denial it is not surprising that we find this is a challenging task. Rather than thinking originally and developing new approaches the predisposition has been to apply existing bodies of knowledge regardless of their fitness for use (see Chapter 1). In this book we have sought to move the debate forward. We have examined the emerging interest in consumption as a focus for environmental policy in order to assess its efficacy and to contribute constructively to the discussion. In this final chapter we summarise the understanding of consumption that has emerged. We discuss how policymakers can link consumption to the environment and outline novel approaches. However, one of our main conclusions is that sustainable consumption is not only a policy issue. It also has profound political implications. The pursuit of more sustainable consumption may ultimately have to be driven at the political level. We therefore also discuss the likelihood of a new politics of sustainable consumption.

2. Consumption and the Influence of Society

This volume clearly establishes that it is not possible to understand consumption by examining only what individuals do as autonomous actors. In reality people's consumption practices are profoundly affected, and possibly determined, by a broad range of societal influences. For this reason Josiah Heyman asks us in Chapter 8 to "widen the relevant units of consumption beyond individuals or other isolated entities." These factors, which are aspects of society first of all, come in various forms, but three of the most influential ones are network, infrastructure and group influences.

First, the interconnectedness of people and their location within consumption networks is a key feature of the consumer society. In this volume contributors discuss networks of consumption at every spatial scale and describe how they create the complex geographies of an increasingly globalised consumer society. In the case of food, as described by David Goodman and Michael Goodman in Chapter 6, the networks varied in scale from local to global. In Chapter 7, Michael Redclift discusses eco-tourism in Mexico and a network linking local entrepreneurs and affluent eco-tourists from Europe and North America. These networks and others are not necessarily tied to political-administrative boundaries and in many cases the actors have no meaningful contact with each another. However, they do have profound implications for consumption.

Drawing on Chapter 6 and the food example it is useful to consider networks at a material and a cultural-political level. As David Goodman and Michael Goodman point out the movement of foods in networks around the world has profound environmental implications. Impacts include the appropriation of land in the developing world for export crops, as well as the use of energy for transport and refrigeration. However, at the same time, at a cultural-political level, food labels such as fair trade, attempt to establish a link between producers and consumers in different parts of the world that may be beneficial in many ways. Although the environmental affects of the transport may be questionable, the fact that consumers can use their purchasing power and their position in a global network to demand improvements in producers' environmental and social performance can be positive.

Eventually, and inevitably, discussion of these networks leads us in the direction of a global political economy of production and consumption. These networks are not just spatially extensive they are also very hierarchical. All producers and consumers in affluent countries, as well as many in poorer ones, are part of this political economy and any credible explanation of consumption must acknowledge it. However, we do not need to rely on abstract theoretical arguments to establish the impact and significance of these global networks. Instead, it will suffice to draw attention to a prominent example. It is the case, for instance, that decisions made by the World Trade Organisation to promote less restrictive international trade can determine the mix of available products across whole continents, irrespective of the desires or preferences of individual consumers. It is clear that any explanation of consumption that hopes to form a basis for policy must be cognisant of the features of these global production and consumption networks.

Second, we can usefully distinguish network influences on consumption from the role of infrastructures and technologies — road systems, mobile phones and so forth. These influences are particularly apparent in Part V. Considering the case of water consumers on the West Bank, Heather Chappells and her colleagues in Chapter 9 show how the consumption pattern of a whole society is determined by the physical infrastructure. At the same time the infrastructure is itself a reflection of the prevailing political situation. The infrastructure simply will not provide water to some settlements at times of low flow, while it does to others.

One of the most interesting aspects of this discussion of water technologies is that it demonstrates how infrastructure and technology can have profound cultural impacts. In the case of water consumption in the UK, and the impact of the mains water system, for example, Chappells *et al.* argue convincingly "this invisible, inaudible, almost incomprehensible system of provision has arguably de-politicised both water and the practice of its consumption." In contrast, water in the Middle East is highly visible and charged with unavoidable political meaning and consequences. As well as availability, it is technology and infrastructure that is having a cultural impact on consumers in this case. Significantly, however, the material nature of infrastructures and technologies can lead to the mistaken assumption that their impacts are only physical.

Finally, to explain consumption practices often at smaller spatial scales we can examine various group influences, such as those linked to family or friendship groups. It is clear from the contributions to this book that residing in groups are rules, norms and assumptions about consumption and a person may or may not be aware of the extent to which these limit and shape choices. These norms can change, and they can be ignored, but they do exert powerful control over what people do, in part because they are often intangible and taken for granted. Josiah Heyman, for example, describes how a family's decision to move from a traditional rural Mexican village to an industrial city places its members in new social settings — schools, factories, and community groups — and these impose different norms of cleanliness on the new arrivals. Although this is not the only reason why a family might purchase a washing machine, and then connect to a centralised electric utility, it is a significant, albeit intangible, influence. On reflection it is immediately obvious that everyone is subject to these kinds of influences.

3. Consumption and the Goals of Individuals

The relationship between society and the individual, as numerous others have established, is complicated. Although it is common for people to claim that they have to consume in a particular way in order to live a "normal" life, this fails to account for how the actions of individuals create and recreate the society that constrains them. It is more accurate, and indeed more useful, to observe that constraints in many cases are both the context *and* outcome of individual action. Individual consumption decisions will necessarily reproduce *or* change existing networks, group norms and infrastructures. Therefore, consumers as individuals are not innocent and powerless in a simple sense. It is also not possible to draw a clear line between society and the individual.[1] With this in mind, however, we can

---

[1] This type of argument can be derived from various bodies of work, particularly that of Anthony Giddens (structuration theory) and Roy Bhaskar (critical realism).

consider the material, social and psychological goals of the individual which help to shape consumption patterns.

It is important to state that consumption by individuals is linked to the objective of staying alive and maintaining health. People routinely consume food for this reason. Clearly, the importance of the material dimension of consumption is seen in especially bold relief in developing countries. However, with respect to the majority of people in the richest countries, consumption cannot be explained entirely in this way. In fact, it seems likely that as people become wealthier the material significance of consumption declines as it begins to be linked to a range of other projects associated with social and psychological goals. Stephen Zavestoski's discussion in Chapter 10 is particularly interesting in this area. His contribution examines consumers in affluent countries who have voluntarily made the decision to reduce their levels of consumption. However, it is clearly not their intention to consume less than is required for survival or even a "comfortable" lifestyle. Nonetheless, they have become aware that their desire to consume is connected to a range of non-material objectives and at the same time they have begun to question the extent to which consumption can actually help them to achieve these. This is highly relevant from a policy standpoint because the tendency to view consumption from the "basic needs" perspective is quite strong.

With respect to non-material objectives we can usefully consider the social objectives of individuals first because of the connection with group influences discussed above.[2] A starting point is the desire for group membership. As previously mentioned, it may be more important to accept that certain consumption norms reside in groups rather than individuals, but in making consumption decisions individuals are often motivated by a desire to demonstrate group membership. In contemporary society individual consumption activities are some of the most powerful ways of conveying messages to larger groups. This is especially the case where personal relationships are ephemeral and communities lack familiar markers of stability.

Related to the social objective of group membership are goals such as status seeking within groups and what might be called distancing — the attempt to show that one is not a member of a particular group. Jouni Paavola describes in his chapter a consumption game in which neighbours or colleagues use consumption to display wealth and power. To assist distancing ideas of "good taste" and "bad taste" have been widely used by members of different classes to establish social distance between themselves and others. Although the people involved commonly refer to what they are buying as "better made" or of "higher quality", this creates the illusion of absolute criteria underpinning consumption rather than more fluid (and inadmissible) class-related ones (see particularly Bourdieu 1999).

Although the boundary is blurred there is value in distinguishing between the social and psychological objectives of the individual. The latter involve a range of issues tied to identity, or what Zavestoski refers to in his chapter as the "self-concept". The tourists in Michael Redclift's contribution, attracted by the idea of eco-tourism, in some way understand themselves to be concerned environmental consumers. This is their identity and the

---

[2]The distinction between material and non-material objectives or needs is fairly common (for other examples see particularly Jackson and Marks 1999; Max-Neef 1991 and 1995; Frank 1999).

act of consuming — going to the eco-park — plays a role in confirming it to themselves. It also provides entrepreneurs with a way of attracting rich tourists from Europe and North America to new resorts on the "Mayan Riviera". A more mundane example of this phenomenon is the purchase of a newspaper known for a particular political perspective. Clearly, a newspaper contains news and may be valued on this basis, but its title and its content also help to reconfirm the consumer's understanding of herself. We think most readily of the investment banker who carries a copy of the *Financial Times* or the *Wall Street Journal* that may never be read, and the left-leaning progressive who subscribes daily to *The Guardian*, but finds she is recycling mint copies.

Here it is important to introduce Kersty Hobson's Chapter 11 discussion of the argumentative nature of human psychology with thought being a constantly constructive and destructive act. This moves the debate away from the idea that consumption is merely an expression of inner beliefs. Rather, people find it necessary to continually find ways to re-establish and reaffirm their identities. As Hobson argues:

> [H]uman thought is not reducible to isolated logic, but is instead a constantly constructutive and destructive act. By paying attention to the argumentative dimensions of social life, rather than lamenting them, we can move away from an approach that considers expressed attitudes as verbalisations of inner beliefs, to an understanding of justifications and criticisms as rhetorical stances, realised in the context of social controversy.

The act of consuming is easily brought into this view of psychology and Hobson's distinction between "practical consciousness" and "discursive consciousness" seems particularly useful. Routine and habitual consumption is likely to involve practical consciousness and is rarely questioned, although it may provide the service of continually confirming who one is. Change requires consumption to become an issue of discursive consciousness, but here adjustment may be resisted because of the threat to one's "ontological security".

4. Consumption and Properties of Objects

Our discussion so far has focused on consumers, either as parts of society or as individuals. Before moving on to link environmental concerns to consumption we also need to consider the properties of objects. These properties form an essential part of any explanation of consumption. We can focus on usefulness, interconnectedness and symbolism.

A standard way of understanding consumption is in terms of the usefulness of specific products. The assumption is that objects are valued to the extent that they do what they are supposed to do — fitness for use. From this perspective products are compared with other products in the same category — say electric cookers with gas cookers — because it is against similar products that consumers can make meaningful comparisons. The key assumption is that within a certain price bracket a consumer will attempt to maximise utility — ability to satisfy human wants. However, although this perspective is useful and powerful, it is incomplete. It tends to link consumption to pragmatic concerns about workmanship, durability and price. In practice, usefulness and related concerns comprise only part of the motivation of the consumer. Two other important properties of consumption goods that also influence consumers are interconnectedness and symbolism.

The interconnectedness of objects and services is easy to understand. It is clear that goods are not purchased in isolation based only on their usefulness and in direct comparison with other products in the same category. Instead, objects are consumed in association with a wide variety of other objects and services. This happens, for example, where the benefit of a particular item cannot be gained unless a particular service is also purchased. The house in the country cannot be purchased unless the family also has two cars. On a more mundane level, as Kate Fletcher and her colleagues describe, household appliances sustain particular lifestyles. The clothes dryer is, for all intents and purposes, a necessary and complementary object to the washing machine. In reality there are very few consumer goods that are not linked in similar ways.

Interconnectedness is perhaps easier to understand than symbolism, but the chapters in this volume also illustrate that the latter is a property of many consumer goods. Research in this area is closely associated with the work of French sociologist Jean Baudrillard (1998:27). In language typical of this particular school of social theory he explains

> Few objects today are offered *alone*, without a context of objects which "speaks" them. And this changes the consumer's relation to the object: he no longer relates to a particular object in its specific utility, but to a set of objects in its total signification. Washing machine, refrigerator and dishwasher taken together have a different meaning from the one each has individually as an appliance. The shop-window, the advertisement, the manufacturer and the *brand name*, which here plays a crucial role, impose a coherent, collective vision, as though they were an almost indissociable totality, a series. There is, then, no longer a sequence of mere objects, but a chain of *signifiers*, in so far as all of these signify one another reciprocally as part of a more complex super-object, drawing the consumer into a series of more complex motivations.

Stephen Zavestoski's chapter suggests that some consumers, namely those he describes as voluntary simplifiers, have become disenchanted with the "complex super-object", rather than any specific good or service. And clearly the level of symbolism is connected to group influences on society and the social and psychological objectives of individuals discussed above. Marketing experts often exploit this cultural dimension of consumption, but it rarely becomes the focus of public policy.

5. Consumption and Environment Relationships

In this chapter we have tried to develop a complex and multi-layered understanding of consumption. However, although we believe that such an understanding should inform policies aimed at achieving more sustainable consumption we have not so far attempted to link consumption to the goal of sustainability. As a first step in this process we can now explore the relationship between consumption and the environment at three levels: the physical, the cultural and the ethical.

It is the physical link between consumption and the environment that often motivates environmentalists. Issues such as the destruction of rainforests, climate change, hazardous-waste disposal and declining biodiversity are central to debates about the ecologically destructive impacts of consumption in rich countries. We have not included in this book a systematic assessment of the state-of-the-environment or the extent to which particular consumption practices are responsible for specific problems. This has been done else-where (see, for example, UNEP 1999 and the annual State of the World reports produced by the Worldwatch Institute). However, contributions contained in this volume have addressed many of those forms of consumption that are most problematic. For instance, Michael Redclift's chapter discusses the ecological implications of tourism. David Goodman and Michael Goodman focus on food consumption. Kersty Hobson considers the utilisation of energy and the management of household wastes. These and others are all areas where trends suggest that the environmental burden will grow in the future in an unsustainable way.

The physical relationship between consumption and the environment is important because, as Markku Oksanen argues in Chapter 4, in a liberal society interference by government into the lives of people must be clearly justified. Probably the most compel-ling justification in this area emerges when the actions of one group of consumers are judged to be imposing unacceptable harm on others and violating their rights at the phys-ical level. This involves violation of what Oksanen and other political theorists refer to as the "harm principle". However, in the context of a world divided into nation-states experiencing complex environmental problems efforts to link cause and effect are fraught with many difficulties. Furthermore, people tend to value residents of distant communities less than they do those who live in closer proximity. The geographic displacement of the ecological impact of consumption therefore poses profound dilemmas, especially given the fragile status of international institutions empowered to address environmental issues on a global scale. For these reasons and others there are various significant risks associated with focusing only on the physical relationship between consumption and the environment.

Considering the cultural aspects of consumption and the environment is one way of ensuring that the debate does not remain stalled at the physical level. An example is the discussion of the idea of nature in Redclift's contribution to this volume. Examination of the culturally determined qualities of the environment in Western civilisation tends to start with the ancient Greeks and moves forward assessing such issues as the changing understanding of nature (Glacken 1967). Academics often draw on the arts, writing and painting in particular, to analyse the relationship between people and the environment at various points in time (see, for example, Schama 1995). What is important here is that history helps to produce, at a cultural level, a particular type of relationship between envi-ronment and society and this has implications for consumption practices. Environmental history thus provides much that appeals to the marketing expert in her attempt to increase sales. For instance, it is easy to see the influence of nineteenth century Romanticism, especially its engagement with wild mountains, in the images used to sell cars. Arguably, without our collective memory of the Romantic period the open road winding through a mountain pass would make less sense and would be useless for the purpose of producing a readily accessible and understandable promotional message. This collective conscious-ness also provides a potential resource for public policy.

Less historically, it is also important to note that in advanced industrial countries "the environment" as something jeopardised by consumption is a highly contested social construction. People hear about the probable consequences of climate change on the tele-vision news and read about threats associated with genetically modified organisms in newspapers, but different stakeholders provide conflicting accounts. Consumers have no access to independent information about the extent to which their actions are actually contributing to environmental damage. What is clear though is that the public is now less likely to accept science or the government as authorities (for further elaboration see, for example, Irwin and Wynne 1996).

The third link between consumption and the environment is the ethical one, although it is certainly possible to argue that ethics is simply an aspect of culture. Jouni Paavola discusses the ethics of consumption in detail in Chapter 5. It is worth reiterating here the three value positions that he identifies and how they relate to consumption choices:

- Assessment of consumption choices based on their future consequences for individual welfare (egotistic) or the welfare of society (social) — a "utilitarian consequentialist". Here welfare is a narrowly defined term. Consumption that results in increased happi-ness for the individual in the future, such as the purchase of a new car, is consistent with the egotistic version of this position.
- Assessment of consumption choices based on their future consequences, but not in a way that makes individual welfare consequences the decisive issue — a "non-utilitarian consequentialist". This value position could involve other outcomes being treated as intrinsically valuable. For example, consuming in a particular way could be judged to be good if it successfully protects endangered species, if the preservation of species is considered intrinsically valuable.
- Assessment of consumption choices in a way that does not judge the goodness of the choice according to its consequences but instead attaches value to behaving in a certain manner or according to certain rules — a "deontological" value position. For example, if it is considered that genetic manipulation of nature is wrong, such a consumer may refuse to consume genetically modified crops and derived produce, regardless of welfare and other consequences, because it is the right thing to do.

This summary reveals how complex the ethical dimension of consumption-environment interactions can be. Moreover, Paavola correctly complexifies the picture further by reminding us that not only do different people hold different value positions, but any indi-vidual may simultaneously make consumption choices informed by any or all of the positions outlined above — inter- and intra-personal value pluralism. This is a more accu-rate description of values and consumption than the one offered by neo-classical economics where the only accepted motivation is egotistic welfare satisfaction.

6. Sustainable Consumption and Politics

Implicit throughout this volume is the claim that sustainable consumption is both a political and a policy issue. Many of the chapters raise questions about affluent societies that are beyond the remit of policymakers and fall more directly within the realm of politics. Indeed attempts to restrict the sustainable consumption debate to the policy level are not just flawed, they serve the interests of those stakeholders who may find their positions weakened if the agenda is ever embraced at a political level. In this section we consider three related dimensions of the politics of sustainable consumption, before moving onto more specific policy issues in the final section.

The assumption that increased consumption improves quality of life sits at the heart of politics in rich countries. It is largely for this reason that economic growth, which it is assumed gives more people more opportunities to consume, is seen as a worthy objective. Political parties on the so-called right of politics (Conservative in the UK and Republican in the US) in particular champion the individual as a consumer, but those on the left are also basically committed to the same argument. Furthermore, from a government perspective consumption is not simply a desirable goal because it enhances quality of life. Greater levels of consumption are also necessary to deliver economic growth. As a result, governments regularly use a wide variety of instruments to encourage people to consume more — tax reductions to put more money in every pocket, reduced interest rates on savings to encourage people to save less and spend more, relaxed credit laws that enable consumers to consume by borrowing against future earnings. The circularity of the argument in this area is immediately obvious.

It is clear that in many poor countries increased consumption is necessary and will improve quality of life for many people. However, in affluent countries, as various contributions to this book show, it is not as easy to draw this conclusion — more time to spend with friends and family may be better (see also Frank 1999). Perhaps the most important treatment of this issue is Stephen Zavestoski's discussion in Chapter 10. He focuses on small groups of people who have decided to voluntarily scale down their lives by consuming less. Zavestoski argues that this is not because these people are interested in saving the environment, although some of them are, but rather because they have begun to question the connection between increased consumption and enhanced quality of life. At a social and psychological level this issue is complex, but it may be linked to feelings of inauthenticity, placelessness and so forth. For proponents of more sustainable consumption this is highly significant.

Michael Jacobs (1997) provides one of the few discussions of the practical politics of sustainable consumption in advanced industrial countries. He argues that any programme of action by government must begin by challenging the position of private consumption in politics in a compelling way. Merely instructing people through policy interventions to consume less (or differently) is not convincing. The approach that Jacobs recommends is to focus on quality of life because this has more political potential. At the same time, he advises policymakers to draw attention to the concrete gains that people will achieve through alternative forms of consumption. Jacobs argues that the idea of quality of life challenges the politics of consumption side-on. It does not attempt to deny that

consumption contributes to well-being. Instead, the focus on qua
other goods also contribute and the goal of public policy shoulc
level. The political feasibility of a quality of life led argument in
consumption is important to remember, even if action is justified f

Second, this book also raises questions about collective action thr
individual action in the marketplace and the role for leadership and
for agreed collective action. The chapters by Markku Oksanen ¡ _ ...... ı aavoıa, ıor
instance, both examine the role of individuals expressing their preferences in markets and
compare this with the role of collective action implemented by governments. For different
reasons, both authors raise doubts about the current emphasis on individual action in markets
in the area of sustainable consumption. Paavola argues that even in a society comprised of
significant numbers of environmentally and socially aware people, who are prepared to act
on their beliefs in the market place, it may still be appropriate to emphasise collective action
for various reasons. Free-riding individuals may determine the outcome and cannot be
prevented from benefiting from the actions of those who bear the cost. Collective action also
has the advantage of enabling concerned individuals to avoid constant moral dilemmas associated with consumption. More practically, people may not be able to afford to act as they
would like, they may not know how to do so and there may be no viable alternatives.

These contributions suggest the current emphasis on market-based strategies to achieve
sustainable consumption needs to be reconsidered. However, they do not address the issue
of leadership and coercion. Beyond the collective action position is a position where
government effectively is no longer neutral but, in Oksanen's words, becomes "perfectionist" and actively promotes an alternative view of the good life. When faced with the
choice a public may not vote for such a programme, but it may be necessary nevertheless. It
is difficult to examine some parts of the sustainable consumption debate without coming to
the conclusion that political leadership is necessary and governments may have to ask
people to make lifestyle changes despite their unwillingness to do so. This is particularly
clear in the case of energy consumption and climate change. The use of fossil fuels is so
central to lifestyles in affluent countries, and the amount of change required over a relatively short time-scale is so great that it is difficult to imagine publics acting quickly enough
without leadership and coercion. Clearly such action, even if justified by the threat, will
expose any government to the accusation that it is violating the principle of the neutral state.

Third, in this book's opening chapter we pointed out that for various reasons the
tendency has been to reduce the sustainable consumption debate to a discussion about the
physical impacts of consumption and the energy and material flows through society. This
is easily explained. Amongst other influences the types of knowledge that dominate policy
networks encourage this kind of radical simplification. Such an interpretation, however,
fails to acknowledge the existence of issues that are widely accepted as part of sustainable

---

[3]Jacobs also emphasises the need to see the value of consumption as something separate from its material nature.
It is possible for the value of consumption to increase whilst its material impact falls. Potentially this overcomes
the obvious objections associated with changing consumption patterns. Jacobs' is also critical of ideas of voluntary downshifting. He argues this will be marginal because of the very social nature of consumption. Only the
very strong-willed or those with alternative social networks will be successful. The vast majority of people living
ordinary lives will not be successful in simply deciding to consume less.

ment and therefore must be part of sustainable consumption, particularly social
s and intergenerational justice.

Of the contributions in this volume David Goodman and Michael Goodman are particularly critical of the exclusion of the social dimension from debates about sustainable
consumption. As an example they describe how the growing international trade in organic
food promotes a relationship between wealthy consumers in affluent countries and the
environment in developing countries. Although often championed as an example of
sustainable consumption in practice the exclusion of issues like wages and the working
conditions of employees on organic farms raises doubts given that it is widely accepted
that sustainability in the world's poorest countries involves dealing with poverty and other
social issues. Michael Redclift's analysis of eco-tourism also questions the standard
approach to sustainable consumption. Travel promoters and resort developers appeal to an
absolute and real nature that we can apparently try to protect while we avoid complex
questions about the kind of nature we actually want. Sustainable consumption in this area
presumably involves some kind of eco-tourism, but the examples from the coast of Mexico
convincingly show that it is not easy to identify in any objective way a type of tourism that
is sustainable, particularly because of cultural issues. As these examples show the ambit of
sustainable consumption can be drawn narrowly or broadly and there is a tendency for
politics to simplify and to restrict what is in reality a large and complex debate.

7. Sustainable Consumption and Policy

Governments are not the only actors in society and their ability to influence consumption
is limited. However, they do have more tools at their disposal to encourage sustainable
consumption than any other actor. For this reason public policy is central to the sustainable
consumption debate. In this final section we outline six approaches to policy in the area of
sustainable consumption that have been raised in this book, although this does not represent a comprehensive account.

First, drawing particularly on Chapter 6 it is useful to link sustainable consumption to
the creation of new production-consumption networks. This is likely to mean networks
where non-market values to some extent cement network relationships. However, as David
Goodman and Michael Goodman point out, creating and sustaining such networks is likely
to be difficult. Their example is the organic food network in California. This network was
originally associated with a range of social and environmental values expressed in
commitments to local markets, family farms, on-farm inputs and so forth. However, with
its success the network increasingly became associated with intensive industrial growers
buying organic inputs globally and supplying global markets. While preserving the
organic nature of the enterprise in a strict sense the network values began to change and it
became associated with the use of immigrant labour and poor working conditions. In other
words success, growth and expansion of the network was associated with its "translation"
and the loss of many of its sustainable aspects.

We can imagine alternative and more sustainable production-consumption networks in
areas as diverse as clothing, transport and housing. Through consumption these networks

would allow people to give expression to values and concerns that they cannot express normally. Various policies aimed at encouraging and protecting such networks could prove fruitful. This may involve sponsoring start-up costs at the local level, as well as removing legal barriers at the national level that protect the embedded practices of existing production-consumption networks. It may also involve subsidies and public endorsement by political leaders and opinion formers. However, we should remember the lessons learnt in California. It is clear that public authorities must not act in a way that encourages the translation of nascent networks so that aspects of sustainability are lost. This means providing some protective cover and insulating them from harmful influences. In particular this involves recognising that processes of codifying and formalising, amongst other things, are opportunities for actors in larger networks to co-opt, constrain or destroy emerging ones. Accordingly, it may be more useful to aim to recreate small networks in new locations, rather than scaling up successful operations.

Second, as discussed above new infrastructures and technologies have massive implications for consumption because they create a large part of the context in which it occurs. Although in recent years some progress has been made in assessing the impacts of new infrastructures and technologies the focus is still on immediate environmental and health and safety issues. Impact assessments usually fail to examine the implications of millions of consumers acting through new infrastructures and technologies either at the physical, cultural or ethical levels. This suggests that sustainable consumption can be linked to a major programme of reform in the area of technology and infrastructure assessment. Government action and public policy is central to this because in many ways it would involve new institutions and procedures that democratise infrastructural and technological change. At the same time, the scope of assessment should expand beyond immediate environmental and health related concerns to more broadly consider cultural and ethical issues. New evaluation procedures and institutions should make it possible to ask important questions about consumption and new technologies and infrastructures. Do we want these infrastructures and technologies? Do we need them? Do they improve our quality of life? What are their cultural impacts? What do they mean for sustainable consumption? Such an approach entails the creation of institutions that offer meaningful participation where incommensurate perspectives can be discussed.

Third, we can consider group norms and assumptions and the pursuit of sustainable consumption. As discussed above these are relatively stable and endure over time, but they may be open to questioning and revision. In Chapter 8 Josiah Heyman provides an excellent example. He describes in detail the consumption implications of the "rigid time" that rural Mexican families encounter when they move to the city and family members begin working in factories and start attending schools:

> [A]ppliances and commoditised inputs facilitate the coping of Mexican households with profound transformations of time. These households had shifted from "freely" allocating among farming and household tasks the full set of adult males, females, and children of both sexes, toward a more rigid model in which adult males devoted a considerable amount of time to paid labour and children many hours to school.

In this example it is important to distinguish between the rigidity of time and the fact that household members are occupied elsewhere for more of their time. Differentiating between these makes it possible to identify consumption impacts associated simply with work norms about time. Similar impacts are seen every weekday morning and evening on roads throughout the developed world and elsewhere as people travel between home and their workplaces.

Even minor changes to group norms and assumptions in various areas could make a significant contribution to more sustainable consumption practices. A long list of unquestioned group assumptions with implications for consumption could easily be developed in a deliberate lifestyle review. With respect to policy it is useful to note that government action will, in many cases, reinforce existing practices. For example, road building to cope with peak time demand helps to perpetuate norms about appropriate hours of work. As one of the biggest employers in any country office dress codes are continually recreated in government buildings every day. Whilst trying to avoid such reinforcing actions using policy to promote the questioning of group standards is likely to involve people in countless individual locations — home, work, school and so forth. Drawing on the insightful lessons of Kersty Hobson's discussion in Chapter 11 policy would aim to stimulate discussion and debate rather than telling people how to be more sustainable.

A fourth approach to sustainable consumption emerges out of the focus on the material goals of individuals, the usefulness of objects and the physical relationship between consumption and the environment. For those interested in reducing the environmental impact of consumption this produces a range of proposals aimed at producing a good that does the same job more efficiently or a service that replaces the physical product and thus encourages dematerialisation — selling the output rather than the product. This material level of the consumption debate has received a lot of attention in recent years and involves what Kate Fletcher and colleagues refer to in the previous chapter as the "redesigning" and "reorganising" approach to consumption. There has been significant and tangible progress in policy debates in this area in recent years. At the centre of this discussion is the improvement of the "eco-efficiency" of production-consumption systems (see Schmidheiny 1992; De Simone and Popoff 1997; OECD 1998).

This is a valuable and constructive policy debate and instruments and approaches such as the life-cycle assessment of products have a significant contribution to make in enhancing the environmental performance of consumption. We can also point to important connections between these developments and the discussion of infrastructures and technologies above. However, the limits to eco-efficiency type approaches in the area of consumption are clear. Because they take particular consumption practices as given, and ask how they can be most effectively met, they provide no basis for examining, understanding and questioning consumption and lifestyles. For this reason eco-efficiency approaches are always likely to focus on product performance or the replacement of products with services.

One way to move beyond the eco-efficiency approach is to engage with consumers' non-material social and psychological objectives and to focus on how these are currently bound up with the consumption of material goods. This book makes it clear that consumers regularly use material goods to achieve non-material (social or psychological) objectives. The purchase of a car and goals such as respect, status and autonomy are obvious examples. It is clear that advertising and the media more generally, particularly film and television, are central to this process and this suggests that sustainable consumption may involve strategies focussed on the management of promotional information and media messages. Although controversial this already happens, particularly where health and welfare are involved. There are numerous pieces of legislation controlling advertising and the media more generally in areas like smoking, pornography, violence, racism and so on. It is unlikely that the negative social and environmental aspects of consumption can be treated in the same way, but these examples suggest how the media can be used to create ideas of appropriate behaviour. Such things as voluntary codes of media conduct, control of product placement in films and more advertising free public space are all in line this kind of thinking.

However, we must bear in mind though that excessive public control of advertising and the media is clearly impossible politically and undesirable socially. Therefore an alternative approach focussed on actively encouraging people to find less socially and environmentally damaging ways of achieving their social and psychological goals is also important. Here Kersty Hobson's insights into the effectiveness of information campaigns are important. Given people's genuine need to deliberate about their life choices, and to establish and to maintain their identities, we must discard the one-way model of information flow. We should strive to replace such clearly limited conceptions with policy interventions designed to engage people in dialogues about their consumption practices and their impacts. It should be remembered that any action that tries to limit the use of material objects but does not offer alternative ways of satisfying social and psychological objectives is likely to fail.

The sixth and final cluster of ideas emerges out of thinking about objects of consumption themselves in novel ways. It is clear that policymakers commonly focus on usefulness as the primary property of consumption goods. This approach leads to strategies designed to change purchasing practices within a given product category. The European eco-labelling scheme is a good example. However, such approaches do not acknowledge and exploit the fact that goods are also interconnected in various ways and that they have symbolic properties that are not the same as their properties of usefulness. This opens up the possibility for more creative lines of thinking. The symbolic characteristics of objects can be used as an example. As discussed above symbolism is to some extent a characteristic of the good itself and not the person or group that uses it. We can view the meaning attached to it as an intrinsic feature that is analogous to its colour, shape, and texture. With this in mind there may be opportunities for policymaking bodies to learn from the private sector and to think less about information provision on products and more about branding. The typical approach of labelling as a means of encouraging consumers to view goods differently stands in sharp contrast to the methods used by marketing experts to sell products, which involves very little practical information and plenty of images and symbolism.

In sum, it would appear that a more expansive understanding of consumption, in particular one that recognises the impact of context, the social and psychological objectives of people and the various characteristics of objects, offers considerable potential for creative policymaking. The suggestions we have advanced are intended to be more illustrative than exhaustive as our intention is to push the sustainable consumption debate into new areas rather than to set out a definitive blueprint.

References

Baudrillard, J. (1998), *The Consumer Society: Myths and Structures*. London: Sage.

Bourdieu, P. (1999), *Distinction: A Social Critique of the Judgement of Taste*. London: Routledge.

Cohen, M. (ed.). (2000), *Risk in the Modern Age: Social Theory, Science and Environmental Decisionmaking*. London: Macmillan.

De Simone, L., & Popoff, F. (1997), *Eco-Efficiency: The Business of Sustainable Development*. Cambridge, MA: MIT Press.

Frank, R. (1999), *Luxury Fever: Money and Happiness in an Era of Excess*. Princeton University Press: Princeton.

Goldsmith, E., Allen, R., Allaby, M., Davoll, J., & Lawrence, S. (eds). (1972), *Blueprint for Survival*. Harmondsworth: Penguin.

Glacken, C. (1967), *Traces on the Rhodian Shore: Nature and Culture in Western Thought From Ancient Times to the End of the Eighteenth Century*. Berkeley: University of California Press.

Irwin, A., & Wynne, B. (eds). (1996), *Misunderstanding Science? The Public Reconstruction of Science and Technology*. Cambridge: Cambridge University Press.

Jackson, T., & Marks, N. (1999), "Consumption, sustainable welfare and human needs — with reference to UK expenditure patterns between 1954 and 1994." *Ecological Economics 28*, 421–441.

Jacobs, M. (1997), "The quality of life: Social goods and the politics of consumption." In M. Jacobs (ed.) *Greening the Millennium: The New Politics of the Environment* (pp. 47–61). Oxford: Blackwell.

Jänicke, M. (1992), "Conditions for environmental policy success: an international comparison." In M. Jachtenfuchs & M. Strübel (eds) *Environmental Policy in Europe: Assessment, Challenges and Perspectives* (pp. 71–97). Baden-Baden: Nomos Verlagsgesellschaft.

Meadows, D., Meadows, D., Randers, J., & Behrens, W. (1972), *The Limits to Growth*. London: Pan.

Max-Neef, M. (1991), *Human-Scale Development — Conception, Application and Further Reflection*. London: Apex Press.

Max-Neef, M. (1995), "Economic growth and quality of life — a threshold hypothesis." *Ecological Economics 15*, 115–118.

OECD (Organisation for Economic Cooperation and Development). (1998), *Eco-Efficiency*. Paris: OECD.

Schama, S. (1995), *Landscape and Memory*. London: Harper Collins.

Schmidheiny, S. (1992), *Changing Course: A Global Business Perspective on Environment and Development*. Cambridge, MA: MIT Press.

UNEP (United Nations Environment Programme). (1999), *Global Environment Outlook 2000*. London: Earthscan.

Index